CAMRA's
Good Cider
Guide

CAMRA's Good Cider Guide
Editor: David Matthews

Cover design: McKie Associates
Cover photography: Tracey Sherwood
Maps: Perrott Cartographics

Managing Editor: Mark Webb

Printed by Albert Gait, UK

ISBN 1-85249-143-4

Published by CAMRA Books, Campaign for Real Ale Ltd, 230
Hatfield Road, St Albans AL1 4LW

© CAMRA Books 2000

Contents

Forward 5
Introduction 6
Cider and Perry 10
Potted History of Cider 14
Cider Houses 20
A Long Look at Perry 26
Making Cider in Gloucestershire ...30
Asturias – Cider Capital 36
Wassail 45
Small Scale Experience 48
Cider in the Pays d'Auge 54
Cooking with Cider 62
CAMRA and Cider 66
Old Orchards: Vintage Fruits and
Wildlife 70
Cider on the Net 72
A Short History of American Cider 78
Rough and Smooth 84
Cider Bars at Beer Festivals 88
Pacific North West Cider 92
Brothers in Cider Making 98
Third Barrel in from The Road ...102
Bedfordshire Outlets 105
Berkshire Producers 107
Berkshire Outlets 110
Buckinghamshire Outlets 111
Cambridgeshire 114
Cambridgeshire Outlets 116
Other Places of Cider Interest in
Cambridgeshire 117
Cheshire Producers 118
Cheshire Outlets 120
Cornwall Producers 123
Cornwall Outlets 128
Cumbria Outlets 131
Derbyshire Outlets 134
Devon Producers 137
Devon Outlets 153
Dorset Producers 158
Dorset Outlets 160
Other Places of Cider Interest in

Dorset 161
Durham Outlets 162
Essex Producers 164
Essex Outlets 166
Gloucestershire & Bristol Producers
... ...169
Gloucestershire & Bristol Outlets 179
Hampshire Producers 186
Hampshire Outlets 189
Herefordshire Producers 191
Herefordshire Outlets 208
Other Places of Cider Interest in
Herefordshire 216
Hertfordshire Outlets 220
Isle Of Wight Producers 223
Isle Of Wight Outlets 225
Kent Producers 226
Kent Outlets 234
Other Places of Cider Interest in Kent
... ...240
Lancashire Outlets 242
Leicestershire Outlets 244
Lincolnshire Outlets 247
Greater London Producers 251
Greater London Outlets 252
Greater Manchester Outlets 257
Merseyside Outlets 261
Norfolk Producers 263
Norfolk Outlets 268
Northamptonshire Producers ...273
Northamptonshire Outlets 274
Northumberland Outlets 277
Nottinghamshire Outlets 279
Oxfordshire Producers 281
Oxfordshire Outlets 282
Shropshire Producers 284
Shropshire Outlets 285
Somerset Producers 288
Somerset Outlets 308
Other Places of Cider Interest in
Somerset 317

Staffordshire Outlets 318
Suffolk Producers 320
Suffolk Outlets 324
Surrey Outlets 325
Sussex Producers 330
Sussex Outlets 335
Tyne & Wear Outlets 338
Warwickshire Producers 341
Warwickshire Outlets 342
West Midlands Producers 344
West Midlands Outlets 345
Wiltshire Producers 348
Wiltshire Outlets 349
Worcestershire Producers 351
Worcestershire Outlets 355
Other Places of Cider Interest in
Worcestershire 358
Yorkshire (East) Outlets 360
Yorkshire (North) Producers 361
Yorkshire (North) Outlets 362
Yorkshire (South) Outlets 365
Yorkshire (West) Producers 367
Yorkshire (West) Outlets 368
Glamorgan Outlets 372
Gwent Producers 375
Gwent Outlets 376
Mid Wales Producers 380
Mid Wales Outlets 382
North-East Wales Outlets 384
North-West Wales Outlets 386
West Wales Outlets 387
Dumfries & Galloway Outlets ...389
Grampian Outlets 389
Lothian Outlets 390
Strathclyde Outlets 391
Tayside Producer 393
Channel Islands Outlets 394
Producer Index 395
Appendices 396
CAMRA Membership Form 399

Acknowledgements

It has been my great privilege and pleasure to edit this Cider Guide. I would like to thank the following vast numbers of people who have worked so hard to put it all together:

The publisher, CAMRA Books, and especially Mark Webb, the Managing Editor.

The staff at CAMRA HQ.

The APPLE committee, particularly outgoing Chair Paula Waters and incoming Chair Marc Holmes. The APPLE reps for all their help.

The CAMRA members who did most of the ground work of surveying the pubs – unpaid volunteers all. Thanks to all of the Regional Directors, Branch Officials and ordinary members.

The other non-CAMRA volunteers who helped with the survey work.

All those writers and cider makers who contributed articles, often free of charge.

Those who gave or lent me photographic material – especially George Thomas of Bulmers, and Kevin Minchew of Minchews Real Cyder & Perry.

David Matthews, September 2000.

Foreword

It's funny how things come around, I became involved in CAMRA the Campaign for Real Ale through drinking cider and perry at beer festivals held in my student days, soon I was drinking beer as well and helping at my local festivals. Next thing I know I'm organising the biggest beer festival in the country and have been elected onto CAMRA's National Executive with the brief to Chair APPLE (the group who promote traditional cider and perry). Then came the idea of a new cider guide, it seemed obvious that I should volunteer to be on the book publishing committee, and before I knew it I was chairing that as well!

So this book is very important to me on many levels, I hope it will serve many people in many ways. For the drinker of traditional cider and perry, it will tell you where to go in order to get your favourite tipple, be it pub, off licence or direct from the producer. For licensees it should provide a stock list of ciders and perries with which to delight your customers. For cider bar managers at CAMRA festivals an invaluable reference book to assist in selecting and ordering an exciting range of cider and perries.

It can be very difficult to find a pint of decent cider and even harder to find perry, I hope this book eases that search and makes the reader more adventurous in seeking out new luscious varieties.

Cheers
Paula Waters

Introduction

Welcome to CAMRA's Good Cider Guide, the fourth edition of the series, and the first to be published since 1996.

Farmhouse ciders and perries are some of the world's greatest drinks. To some they may be an acquired taste, but the effort needed to become familiar with their rich and varied flavours is repaid time and time again. The aim of this guide is to help you to find Britain's finest ciders and perries, so that you too can enjoy my favourite style of beverage.

THE GUIDE

The guide is organised into counties, with each county section containing a map, listings of all cider makers, a selection of cider outlets, and information about any other places of cider interest.

Photo: Sign outside The Appletree, Bedminster, Bristol. Photo: Dave Matthews.

Producers

I have tried to list each and every commercial cider maker, no matter how large or small, that produces 'Good Cider'. Cider makers seem to be far more accessible than brewers, and I can heartily recommend visiting them to taste and buy their cider, but please telephone ahead first.

Outlets

The pubs, off-licences and other cider outlets listed in this guide have been selected and surveyed by unpaid volunteers from CAMRA (the CAMpaign for Real Ale) and APPLE (CAMRA's cider and perry organisation). Of course, some of the outlets will have shut/stopped selling cider/started selling other ciders before you read this, but I'm afraid that this is unavoidable. Please also remember that a quality, seasonal, craft product such as farmhouse cider is often only made in small quantities, and so some outlets may only stock it between spring and autumn. Here is a sample entry:

Town ➡	**OADBY**
Pub name ➡	**Cow & Plough**
Address and directions ➡	Stoughton Farm Park, Gartree Road
Telephone number ➡	☎ 0116 2720852
Opening hours ➡	*5pm-9pm Mon- Sun*
Cider available ➡	⏝**Saxon Platinum Blond; Westons Old Rosie**
Description ➡	Converted barn on the Farmworld Leisure Park, crammed with breweriana, and much loved by locals and cider/beer lovers alike. Interesting range of Real Ales. Family room, snug and no-smoking areas. Disabled access.

Key to Symbols

⊄	Lunchtime meals available, substantial fare.
▶	Evening meals available.
~~REAL ALE~~	No real ale
☆	Rare and unspoilt pub interior of outstanding historic interest.

Cider Houses

I have decided to highlight our 'Cider Houses', a handful of National Treasures, pubs that sell draught cider but no draught beer; and 'Cider Pubs', pubs that stock draught beer, but which sell a greater volume of cider. (See also the feature article on page 16.) Pubs that qualify under either of these criteria will be flagged up as follows:

 CIDER HOUSE

national treasure – sells draught cider but no draught beer

and

 CIDER PUB

sells more cider than beer!

GOOD CIDER

What is 'Good Cider'? There is no one simple answer, but for the purposes of this guide, the APPLE committee and I decided that 'Good Cider' is either of the following two types:

CAMRA campaigns for real cider through a dedicated committee called APPLE.

1. Any draught or bottled cider that contains live yeast. 'Real Cider'.

2. Any filtered cider, draught or bottled, that conforms to the following exacting criteria:

- Is not pasteurised
- Is not artificially carbonated
- Is made from 100% juice
- Is not made from concentrate

Of course, I'm not saying that there's anything wrong with ciders that match neither 1 nor 2 above, but surely you don't need a guidebook to help you find a pint of Dry Blackthorn or a bottle of Diamond White? Cider makers that *only* produce Industrial Cider have not received a listing in this guide, but makers of Good Cider who also produce other types of cider have had these other ciders listed in brackets as: (also available:...). The factory-produced brands such as Strongbow are skilfully marketed and help to give cider a strong national profile, but typically are made by adding sugar and water to apple juice, and then pasteurising and carbonating the fermented product. I feel that this produces a drink with less flavour and character than a farmhouse cider, which is typically made from 100% fresh apple juice, with nothing added and nothing taken away. As we move into the 21st Century demand is set to increase for flavoursome natural products that are free from additives – so be part of this movement and drink Good Cider!

David Matthews
September 2000

Photo: Running well at Minchew's Cyder and Perry.

Your editor

David Matthews, 91 Black Oak Road, Cardiff, CF23 6QW, UK.
Email:
1Bethan@talk21.com

Cider and Perry

Geoff Morris, proprietor of Leominster's specialist off-licence Orchard, Hive & Vine, *introduces two of his favourite drinks.*

Cider

Cider is made by fermenting the juice of apples. In principle any apple could be used but different areas have different traditions. In the West Country, and Herefordshire, Worcestershire and Gloucestershire, special cider apples are used. These have higher levels of tannin than eaters or cookers. The tannin helps to lengthen the taste, without making the cider too bitter. In East Anglia and the South-East a blend of cooking and eating apples is used. For many cider drinkers the Eastern ciders have something missing, whilst for others the tannin in West Country ciders is an unpleasant taste which they are quite happy to be without.

Cider-apple varieties are divided up into four categories: the Sweets are high in fermentable sugar, whereas in Bitter-Sweets the sugar is complemented by high tannin levels. Sharps are acidic varieties and Bitter-Sharps contain high levels of both acid and tannin. Most West Country and West Midlands ciders are made by blending these four different types. Of some of the better-known varieties, Kingston Black and Stoke Red are Bitter-Sharps, Foxwhelp is a Sharp variety while Yarlington Mill and Michelin are Bitter-Sweets. Each cider-maker has his or her own blend of the hundreds of varieties and the composition of the blend is usually a closely guarded secret. The National Collection of Cider apples is at Brogdale in Kent.

There are a few single variety ciders available. They are not just curiosities because each variety has its own character. In the 17th and 18th centuries ciders based on Foxwhelp were held in the greatest esteem, but these are far too acidic for the modern palate. Nowadays Kingston Black seems to be the favourite for single variety cider. It is also a Bitter-Sharp but not so searingly acidic as Foxwhelp. There are often two fermentations in cider, one performed by yeast to convert sugar to alcohol (usually in the autumn) followed in the spring by a malo-lactic fermentation which converts the sharp-tasting malic acid into the more gently acidic lactic acid. The mellow fruitiness of Kingston Black ciders is largely thanks to the Malo-lactic bacteria which

bring about this transformation. A side effect of the Malo-lactic fermentation, is a substance, biacetyl, which has a buttery or sometimes butterscotch taste. (Lovers of New World Chardonnay will also know this taste but may be surprised that it can also be found in cider.)

Yarlington Mill Cider Apples. Photo: Dave Matthews

Traditional ciders are served still, and are often cloudy. Apples contain pectin, which is better known to jam-makers as a setting agent. It also contributes to the cloudiness in ciders and perries. Cider which has been left to mature in the tank will, in time, throw a deposit of pectin, leaving the cider clear.

Perry

Perry can be made from any pear but the best drinks are made from perry pears. They are usually small, hard and tannic, and are of no use for anything else. They grow on large trees which do not reliably take to grafting onto dwarfing root-stocks. They are becoming rare even in their heartland of Herefordshire, Worcestershire and Gloucestershire. Perry pear varieties revel in names such as Merrylegs, Painted Lady, and Gin. In a good year the variety Thorn can make perry of over 11% abv, well over the Customs & Excise limit of 8.5%. Kevin Minchew has recently discovered a single tree of what he thought was Late Treacle. However it is not Late Treacle but nobody knows what variety it is.

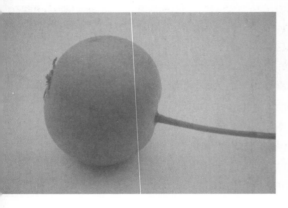

*Longstalk perry pear.
Photo: Kevin
Minchew.*

Peter Mitchell, of the Pershore Group of Colleges, has tried to track down Tettenhall Dick but this turns out to be, fortunately, not a medical condition, but the Black Country name for any perry pear, or sometimes even crab-apple, and is not a single variety.

Perry is like cider's more sophisticated cousin and a well-made perry is a wonderful drink. It can be a drink of real quality. Please check it out. Bottle-fermented perry is amazing (none available commercially at present, but watch this space). One leading Worcestershire Hotel used to give a complimentary bottle of champagne to its VIP guests, but people they really liked were given perry. There are reliable stories of bottle-fermented perries being passed off as champagne in hotels and restau-

Hugh Vincent and Larry Pope, of Green Valley Cyder, levelling apple pulp during cheese building.
Photo: Nigel Albright

rants. In another leading hotel, allegedly, it was their best-selling champagne and very popular.

Perry is more difficult to make than ciders. The tannins are more complex, and the juice is often left exposed to the air to reduce the level of tannin. However, the juice is more prone to oxidation, and the acids in the juice are more difficult to balance. The rarity of the fruit, and the difficulties in balancing fruit flavour, sweetness, tannin and alcohol mean that most perries are a blend of several varieties but some superb single varietal examples are available, notably from Minchew and Gwatkin.

Cooking with Perry

Dry perry can be used in cooking instead of white wine, often to the improvement of the dish. Moules marinieres in dry perry is wonderful. Chicken in perry with rosemary, onions and garlic is delicious, and finally try plaice, or other flat fish, poached in dry perry, and served on a bed of green lentils. It is wonderful.

Potted History of Cider

Stephen Fisher traces the history of cider in Great Britain from its earliest records.

We cannot say anything with certainty about cider in this country until 1204, when we have our first written record of a manorial tithe paid in two mues of cider at Runham in Norfolk. As a finally adopted Norfolkman, I have just done my 25 years, I am very pleased about that. However, I come from Devon and I suspect it is the West Country that has the older claim.

It is more than likely that the Celts made some sort of cider, but with just the juice from native crab apples, it would have been pretty rough stuff. Cider making would have continued and improved considerably under the Romans, who had such regard for the apple, that the Goddess Pomona was created to look

after them. Certainly, the Romans had the equipment for crushing the fruit and sophisticated presses for the extraction of the juice; not so different to the presses used up until the 19th Century and a few of us still use today. Pliny, writing in his Natural History in the 1st Century AD, mentions over twenty varieties of apple, and along with their apple trees, the Romans brought an elementary understanding of soils and the arts of pruning and grafting.

The original Redstreak cider apple. From the Herefordshire Pomona.

Then came the Anglo Saxon invasions and occupation. These were, generally speaking, beer drinking races, who pushed the beleaguered Romano Celts into the West Country; where no doubt some form of cider-making continued. As for cider in the East, notably Norfolk, Suffolk, Kent and Sussex with their use of culinary and dessert apples, I suggest that, following 1066, the Normans and attendant Bretons reintroduced cider here. It is interesting to note that the other bastion of cidermaking is found amongst the Basques – a Celtic race.

During the Dark Ages the monks did much to preserve the classical knowledge, and by 1230 the Bishop of Bath is ordering cider presses for his monasteries. Henry VIII must have added stimulus to the cider industry, when he sent the Royal Fruiterer Robert Harris to Normandy in 1533. He returned with new varieties, namely Pippin apples, and laid the foundation for Kent to become the fruit basket of England. Within a hundred years, cider had become a highly regarded drink and a favourite of the richer classes. With the invention of stronger glass bottles by Sir Kenelm Digby, it was found that a superior cider of champagne quality could be achieved by bottling just before fermentation had ceased (in the manner of Normandy and Brittany cider today). Dr Beale, in his treatise on cider, mentions that the late King Charles I and the gentry of Worcestershire – brought to Herefordshire as prisoners – preferred cider to the best wines available.

The gentry of the day spent long hours arguing the benefits of one variety against another, though it was generally agreed that the Redstreak was the best.

A cider glass dating from around 1750. Part of the Bulmer collection. Photo: HP Bulmer Ltd.

Recommended Reading

The Woodlanders –
Thomas Hardy

Chief amongst this group was Lord Scudamore, said to have first raised the Redstreak from an apple pip, who spent a lifetime planting apple trees, studying their virtues under different soil conditions and experimenting with cider. Two other gentlemen of the period must be mentioned: Sir John Evelyn, whose book Pomona (published 1664), contains detailed essays by leading ciderists of the day, often with conflicting views. The other, John Worlidge of Sussex, wrote Vinetum Britannicum (published 1676), a book covering all aspects of cider. He was also the inventor of the Ingenio apple mill, which he based on a Cuban sugar cane mill. This machine of two interlocking cogs turned by a handled flywheel provided a great boost to the industry, as it was considerably cheaper than its forerunner, the circular stone trough, around which a nag trudged, pulling an upright millstone along the chase. What a boon to a county like Norfolk, that has no stone. Its relative cheapness and portability must have soon halted the construction of any further stone mills. There was also a general improvement in the quality of the cider. It had been found that if the pomace was ground up for too long in the chase, the apple pips became crushed and these imparted a bitterness into the cider.

Viscount Scudamore, who developed the Redstreak apple. Photo: HP Bulmer Ltd.

Cider presses, however, have retained significant regional differences. Generally, the West Country press consists of a hewn out stone trough, with two screws, one either side, that wind down a considerable oak beam from above. These presses are open sided and the juice pours out from the cheese, to be caught in the stone trough one is pressing into, and then channelled off into a pail.

Regrettably, the spout from the channel was often of lead and, unknowingly up until the 1790s, resulted in such serious cases of lead poisoning that its medical name was Devon Cholic. A great advantage of these presses was being able to press the pomace between straw or cloths. Straw was by far the cheapest to use and the press was easily emptied. In areas where stone was not available, notably Norfolk, Suffolk and parts of Sussex, the press is much smaller, capable of taking up to one third of a ton of apples. The press is completely made from English oak and is best described as a box on legs, standing up to eight feet tall. The cheese is stacked up in the box and rising above the top lip using layer upon layer of woven horse hair cloths, each filled with about 50lbs of pomace, a single screw exerts pressure from the beam above. The box and sides of the press have thin batons of oak nailed to them to allow the juice to run down these channels, and out through a drilled hole in the centre of the wooden base. Most presses extant today have iron screws, but those made prior to the industrial revolution were of carved wood, often pear or apple wood.

By the 18th Century cider was the established drink of all classes living in cider producing counties. The very best could fetch high prices at two shillings a gallon, whilst from the press the juice averaged twopence a gallon. Cider made up an important part of the agricultural workers' wages, as it was not until the 1887 Trucks Act that payment in kind became outlawed. It was a foolish farmer who did not take care with the quality of his cider; come the annual hiring for servants and labourers he would find himself at a disadvantage in getting the more fit and able to work for him. The farmer and his employees drank cider from a second pressing. The pomace was removed from the press and placed into an open wooden trough, where it was just covered with water and left overnight. The reduced pomace acted like a sponge, soaking up the water and could then be repressed the following day. The resulting liquor would have an alcoholic content of just 2 to 3%. The agricultural labourer's usual allowance was half a gallon for breakfast and half a gallon for lunch and he carried a half gallon wooden costrel and his horn beaker, that would not

An Ingenio *cider mill (left) and a Norfolk box cider press (right) in use at the Norfolk Cider Company. Photo: Steven Fisher, Norfolk Cider Company.*

break if knocked against the stones in the fields. The cider from the first pressing, with a natural alcohol level of between $6^1/_2$ to $8^1/_2\%$ was sold and formed an extra source of income for the farmer. The orchard, once established, gave grazing for pigs, sheep and poultry, who benefited from overlooked fruit. This premium cider went to local hostelries or, more often, was bought by brokers who distributed it to centres of urbanisation. Delays in sale and lack of care meant that the cider rarely reached the towns in prime condition. To give some uniformity to the product, towards the end of the 19th Century, cider factories began to appear. The Ingenio became obsolete, the pressing cloths of woven horse hair were replaced by manilla and cocoa fibre, the new carbonisation was added, together with colouring, water and preservatives such as sulphur dioxide. Cider was never to be the same again and today most of it is made from imported concentrate and not always apple, but pear as well.

But fear not, in the lanes and byways of rural England, Wales and recently Scotland, a few individuals still make cider as it used to be made. It is 100% pure fresh apple juice, with nothing added and nothing taken away. Natural yeasts and time do the rest.

Recommended Reading

*The Book of Apples –
J.Morgan &
A.Richards.
Edbury Press*

Stephen Fisher is from the Norfolk Cider Company.

Cider Houses

David Matthews introduces the handful of fully licensed premises that sell draught cider but no draught beer.

National Treasures, no less, is the best description of our four remaining Cider Houses. "Cider houses are different," cider wholesaler Jon Hallam told me, "there's a different feeling, a unique atmosphere, you know you're not in a normal pub." He's right, and it's not just down to the lack of beer. In the way that a bar (a licensed shop) feels different to a pub (a licensed house), then for me the intrinsically rural Cider House has the atmosphere of a licensed farm.

YE OLDE CIDER BAR in NEWTON ABBOT, DEVON, has perhaps the most urban setting of our Magnificent Four, but this belies its rural origins. It was once a farm, and the main bar area was formerly a cobbled yard entrance, where cider was once consumed with only scant protection from the elements. Prior to 1962, hogsheads of cider were stillaged on the floor amongst the customers. The landlord kept the glasses in the kitchen, and customers requested a refill from him by chinking their glasses. Today the Cider Bar is welcoming and traditional, having an interior with stone and wood, a real fire, and with the barrels of cider stillaged behind the bar. Be-whiskered licensee Richard Knibbs is a rare example of the Old School landlord – no bad language is tolerated, and he was once even taken to court for refusing to serve a pint to a lady.

Fittingly for a Devon cider house, Richard's two best-selling ciders are from a Devon cider maker – Sam's Dry and Sam's Medium – and others on offer include Weston's Traditional Scrumpy, Weston's Perry, Thatcher's Farmer's Tipple (Dry and Sweet), and

Thatcher's Cheddar Valley Dry (affectionately known as 'Diesel'). There are 18 fruit wines to choose from, but beer has never been sold from the premises. Food is limited to genuinely jumbo-sized pies and pasties.

Every Sunday lunchtime the Cork Club meets at the Cider Bar, with the aim of raising funds for an annual members' outing. Each of its 30-40 Cider Bar regulars carries a cork bound in a brass cylinder, upon which is stamped their initials and a number. Failure to produce their cork

Licensee Richard Knibbs at Ye Olde Cider Bar, Newton Abbot. Photo: Dave Matthews.

on demand results in a fine, much laughter, and more funds for the summer trip.

The CIDER HOUSE at WOOTTON GREEN, SHROP-SHIRE, is the busiest of the four. "We can sell 10-13 tons of cider a week in the summer," licensee Brian Jarvis told me, "including one hundred-plus 11-gallon kegs of Bulmers Special Cellar alone." The Cider House stands isolated in the Shropshire countryside, but customers pour into its large car parks, and it is particularly popular with Asians. "The Moslem faith prohibits the drinking of alcohol," explains Brian, "but to them cider is not alcohol, it's apple juice!" Bulmers Special Cellar, a keg 7.2% sweet cider (only available at a handful of outlets) is the Asian favourite and overall best-seller, but there's a full range of 13 different

Cider Site

Ye Olde Cider Bar, 99 East Street, Newton Abbot, Devon. Telephone: 01626 54221.

Cider Site

The Cider House, Wootton Green, Bridgnorth, Shropshire, WV15 6EB. Telephone: 01746 780285.

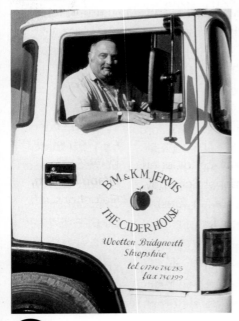

Licensee Brian Jervis at the wheel of one of his mobile cider bars. Photo: Dave Matthews.

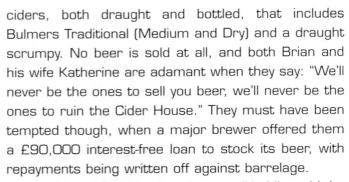

ciders, both draught and bottled, that includes Bulmers Traditional (Medium and Dry) and a draught scrumpy. No beer is sold at all, and both Brian and his wife Katherine are adamant when they say: "We'll never be the ones to sell you beer, we'll never be the ones to ruin the Cider House." They must have been tempted though, when a major brewer offered them a £90,000 interest-free loan to stock its beer, with repayments being written off against barrelage.

The Cider House was originally a small-holding with its own orchards, making and selling cider on the premises. More recently, Brian and Katherine ran it for Bulmers from 1983, buying it for themselves in May 1986. Today's customers can play Evesham Quoits in the Bar (a traditional pub game played throughout the Welsh borders, always the sign of a good pub!), can squeeze into the Snug (once the old ladies' parlour), or can relax in the Orchard Room with its wood-burning stove, quarry tiled floor, leather bench seating and brick/oak bar. From May onwards the double servery is opened to the outdoor drinking area, and barbecues are held on summer weekends.

Another string to the Cider House's bow are its four mobile cider bars that Brian and his team take to many of the major agricultural shows, steam rallies and race meetings.

Bought from Scrumpy Jack, they offer show-goers the Cider House's complete cider range.

The CIDER CENTRE at BRANDY WHARF, LINCOLNSHIRE, is the youngest member of our four famous cider houses. Originally it was the Anchor Inn, a run-of-the-mill Bass-Charrington waterside pub. Its transformation began in 1981, when it was bought by current licensees Ian and Gill Horsley. They had visited a successful waterside cider house in the West Midlands (the Blue Bell at Hockley Heath), and so started emphasising cider in their own pub. The bold step of removing beer completely was taken at Christmas 1986. Nowadays the Cider Centre offers what is probably the largest range of ciders found in a fully-licensed premises anywhere in the world. Approximately 60 different ciders are available, 15 on draught and 45 bottled, including cask-conditioned ciders from Westons (Old Rosie, Traditional Scrumpy, Bounds Brand Dry and Vintage), from Saxon (Easter to October), and occasional guest cask ciders, all dispensed by gravity.

The Cider Centre has a riverside bar, the 'Apple Foundry', and a lounge, the 'Cider Boutique', in which locals and water-borne tourists alike can seek advice

The Brandy Wharf Cider Centre. Photo: Brandy Wharf Cider Centre.

Cider Site

The Cider Centre, Brandy Wharf, Waddingham, Gainsborough, Lincolnshire, DN21 4RU. Telephone: 01652 678364.

Cider Site

The Cider House (The 'Monkey House'), Woodmancote, Defford, Worcestershire. (On the A4104.)

The Monkey House. *Photo: Dave Matthews.*

from staff when choosing which cider to sample. There is a museum exhibiting over 2000 different empty cider bottles, and the orchard whose 180 trees now surround the Cider Centre was re-established in 1978. The orchard is the venue for some of the events on the Cider Centre's calendar – a Wassailing ceremony with 300 guests in January, Apple Day in October, and a Tree Dressing Day in December.

The 'MONKEY HOUSE' at DEFFORD, WORCESTERSHIRE is the most picturesque of the cider houses, with its thatched roof, hanging baskets, wooden barrels, and air of unspoilt charm. More properly known as the Cider House, history does not record how it became known as the 'Monkey House', but licensee Graham Collins recounts a likely theory: "It's said that many years ago a cattle-driver left the cider house a little the worse for wear, and fell in some brambles, scratching his face. When asked how his face had been scratched, he replied 'A monkey scratched me!'." Originally the 'Monkey House' made its own cider from an adjacent orchard, and in 1850 there is a record of Master Baker John Hayward baking bread and selling cider from the premises. The family line has remained unbroken with Graham's wife, Gill, herself a Hayward. Around 1960, the orchard was grubbed up and cider production stopped. In order to replicate the brew, one of the Bulmer family took a sample back to Hereford and produced Bulmer's Woodmancote (6% abv), still made today, and exclusive to the 'Monkey House'. It's a fully traditional cask cider, hazy gold, dry, with a beautiful balance of fruit and sharpness; or just "nectar", according to the regulars.

Inside the Old Bakehouse at the Monkey House. Photo: Dave Matthews.

Up until a few years ago Bulmer's Woodmancote was supplied in 40 gallon wooden casks, but modernisation of Bulmer's cider mill means that 18 gallon metal casks are now used. Now as before, Graham dispenses his cider by gravity into a jug, before pouring it into the customer's (often ceramic) mug. He also sells a smaller amount of Bulmers Traditional Medium.

As you walk up the path towards the 'Monkey House', past the pony, you'll be greeted first by Tapper the white terrier. After buying a pint from Graham's hatch under the thatched roof, you can choose to sit on a bench in the garden, or to venture into the tiny old bakehouse, with its open fire. Either way, you'll be drawn into conversation with the other customers in no time at all. What a lovely place.

"Cider houses are different," "there's a different feeling, a unique atmosphere, you know you're not in a normal pub."

The 'Monkey House' is hard to find, there's no sign, and opening hours are limited (lunchtimes Friday to Monday, evenings Wednesday to Sunday). But nevertheless you must go there. It won't be around in its present form forever.

A Long Look at Perry

Jean Nowell reminisces about the drink that has brought her so much success.

Steep grassy banks ran down to the brook at Glewstone, planted with rows of daffodils and a higgledy-piggledy orchard of cider apples and perry pears. In my first childhood I used to look forward to the time of year when one particular perry tree dropped its fruit and the grass was carpeted with deliciously sweet tiny round yellow pears. I wonder what they were? But as for perry, the end product, that was not for children. We were restricted to cider from the barrel in the cellar. We were free to help ourselves ad lib and spent much of our time down there drinking cider, sitting on the coke under the low roof, where the draught would whistle up through the gaps between the boards above our heads and lift the sitting room carpet till it floated several inches above the floor. (It was a strange feeling on a windy day to tread the sitting room carpet down as you walked across the room to the security of the furniture. Even the lino in the hall used to rise a little.)

Jean Nowell drinks a toast from her Big Apple trophy. Photo: Dave Matthews.

My first memory of the perry itself is seeing a big wet stain on the dining room ceiling the morning after my father had proudly opened a bottle of his champagne perry for our neighbours the Jacksons. "Bunty" had apparently also received a full frontal delivery in one extravagant display of what, I have no doubt, was wonderful sparkling perry. The memory of the exquisite fragrance that lingered in that room remains with me to this day.

That unforgettable fragrance, associations with childhood, a sense of being part of a tradition, and the hope of achieving some sort of elusive imagined perfection. That's what makes perry special for me.

Fortunately, in my second childhood I have been able to make perry for myself and that gives me a lot of satisfaction. Fermentation is ticking away quietly in my 1999 pressing in 180 gallon stainless steel tanks. I was lucky enough to obtain these tanks from Lyn Ballard, who also helped me and taught me some of the basics when I first started in 1984. The Ballard family are well known not only for perry but as achievers and inventors in many fields. Lyn's uncle was famous for using a one-wheel electric motorbike to turn his old mill.

A trailer-full of Dumbleton Huffcap perry pears, from Dumbleton, Worcs. Photo: Kevin Minchew.

Lyn's first lesson was fruit.

All the fruit that goes in my scratter has to be hand-picked, clean and fully ripe. Lyn taught me that over-ripe is better than under-ripe so I always delay my milling until the very last moment, even if I run the risk of some of the pears looking a bit over the top. If I fall behind badly and the fruit really "wants doing" as they euphemistically say, I keep that pressing separate, and sulphite it, and don't try to keep it for too long. But to be truthful I am constantly surprised by how good a perry can result from what looks rather like rotten fruit. It needs to be drunk in moderation, true, but nobody ever made good perry out of unripe fruit. I don't like throwing perry away. Or pears!

I prefer making perry from a mixture of varieties. I find that as it matures the different characters seem to blend together into a balanced and complex drink, but that won't please the purists and of course you learn a lot more if you make interesting single varieties. I feel that if I can produce a good quality blend I am doing as much as can be expected of me! I don't blend perry once it has been made for fear of causing it to go irredeemably cloudy or of contaminating one perry by adding another which may be incubating a sickness that I have not been able to diagnose.

Perry pear tree in blossom at Ashchurch, Glos. Photo: Kevin Minchew.

In between my two childhoods part of my life was spent in the damp flatlands of Hatherley, near Cheltenham. I recall a typical family farm there with a wonderful ancient perry orchard that kept the farmer's press going with a succession of varieties from September to January. How much skill and knowledge of perry making would have been built up on that farm over the generations? Such a fund of knowledge would be rare indeed these days but my fear for perry making is that when the two-hundred and three-hundred year old trees that provide our pears have died, it will be lack of fruit not lack of skill which ends the perry making. Meanwhile we Wassail the old trees while we have the chance and keep planting a few Moorcrofts and Butts in the somewhat doubtful hope that they will survive for another three-hundred years.

I must say I feel myself very privileged to be involved with a drink which may one day be the stuff of legend.

Jean Nowell is a record five times winner of CAMRA's Perry of the Year Award.

Making Cider in Gloucestershire

Award-winning cider and perry maker Kevin Minchew describes the cider culture of his home county.

The county of Gloucestershire could be subdivided into three distinct areas. There are the world famous Cotswold Hills, whose coombes and valleys offer sanctuary for apples and pears, the higher land being more suitable for cereals and sheep grazing.

To the west of this area lies the Severn Valley, bounded by the counties of Herefordshire, Worcestershire and the Malvern Hills. This area is comparatively rich in orchards today, but was once home to thousands of acres of fruit trees, fragments of which survive and provide me with my raw materials.

In the south west of Gloucestershire lies the Royal Forest of Dean, home of the Foxwhelp apple and the

Blakeney Red perry pear. Freeminers excavate coal from the shallow deposits under an ancient Royal charter and this area provided many of the press beds and runner and chase mills, hewn from local

Foxwhelp cider apples at Minchews orchard, Aston Cross, Glos. Photo: Kevin Minchew.

quarries of sedimentary stone. These stones made it possible to mass produce pressing equipment and many are found many miles distant from their point of origin.

Across the Severn, to the east, lies the village of Slimbridge where the Workman factory revolutionised the rate of juice extracted with a wide range of very efficient mechanical mills and presses, many of which survive in service to this day. I know of one which is still operated in Southern Ireland.

I was born on a small-holding, in the parish of Ashchurch, near Tewkesbury, and for as long as I can remember there was always a barrel of cider and perry in the stable, for home consumption and for any visitors who wished to partake.

Cider was commonplace but perry has always been revered and kept for special occasions.

Although my father made his own cider and perry I took no real interest and, as a child, considered picking up fruit in the autumn a bit of a chore. But the smell of perry pears, in hessian sacks, never really left my nostrils and even today that autumnal scent floods me with memories of the pear orchards whose immense trunks and canopies brought about an almost religious awe, similar to the feeling one gets when amongst the columns of our churches, abbeys and cathedrals.

Perry pear orchards predominated over our apple orchards, although some were mixed, but this won-

Kevin Minchew taking delivery of his stone press bed. Photo: Kevin Minchew.

derful scene changed in the early mid-sixties when many orchards were felled and the roots grubbed out. Consequently perry became rarer and even more revered.

Factory cider became the norm as many farms lost their labourers and fruit was sold to merchants who delivered it to large-scale makers.

It was around this time, having progressed from sharing the gallon of cider at the Friday night youth club disco, that I started to travel further afield and became aware of cider-houses dotted around Bredon Hill. Cider had always been cheaper than beer and as a poor apprentice it was my first choice. Each of these cider houses had its own unique brew and it was possible to visit the Yew Tree in Conderton for Lanchbury's, the Plough at Elmley Castle for their home-brew, and the Monkey House at Defford for a final half or even a pint of Bulmers Woodmancote, before wending one's way home, very merry but with change in one's pocket.

Customers drinking outside the Plough at Elmley Castle, circa 1991 – the last year of the Plough's operation. Photo: Kevin Minchew.

These cider houses were like magnets to the hard core and attracted many 'characters'. I remember Harry Banbury telling me "to watch out because cider drinking would kill you – it killed my father. It took 85 years though!!".

I recall Barry and Tilley heading up the hill in the black of night when the cry went up "Barry, I've lost my shoe!...Never mind, we'll find it tomorrow". A few minutes later "Barry, I've dropped the cider...Standfast!"

Then there was the 'Junkers Club', in Gloucester, where any member caught drinking anything other than cider was 'tried' by his contemporaries, who wore judges' wigs whilst passing sentence.

A friend of mine once cycled from Stourbridge to Elmley, only to find it shut when he got there and no amount of begging and pleading would induce the landlady to bend the rules.

He now lives in Ireland but still brings a brace of demi-johns to a little village hall, in Putley, Herefordshire, for the annual cider competition, making it not only an international event (as far as I'm concerned) but proving beyond any doubt the devotion of the true cider drinker.

I shall always be grateful to another character, Dave `the cheese` (so called because he always drank his cider with a lump of cheese) who was a government farm inspector. He informed me of a new cider-making course being held at Hindlip Agricultural College, run in the evenings by a trained micro-biologist. I duly attended and learnt all about the use of chemicals and phenolics but I was most influenced by the emphasis on hygiene. The next season I proceeded to implement my new-found knowledge by painstakingly examining each individual piece of fruit and, although it took much longer, the resulting cider and perry was much improved.

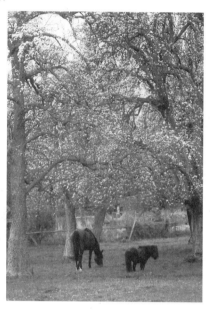

Huffcap perry pear trees at Walton Cardiff, Tewkesbury, Glos. Photo: Kevin Minchew.

It was also around this time that some like-minded drinking companions informed me of a cider competition in a little village hall, yes – you've guessed it, the aforementioned Putley, where you could taste all the entries, for a pound, which in those days amounted to quite a few! So, although my intentions were not entirely honourable at this stage, when I got there I found to my complete amazement a veritable cornucopia of colours, smells and tastes and I became aware that I could even distinguish the different acids, tannins and faults.

A wooden barrel originating from Severn Valley cider. Photo: Kevin Minchew.

I feel I ought to say, at this point, that these competitions brought together many different cider and perry makers and this resulted in the formation of the Three Counties Cider and Perry Makers Association.

The following year, having carefully sourced only dedicated varieties of cider fruit, I entered the result into the competition and to my utter astonishment I won and proudly carried the crown back to Gloucestershire. As my winning entry was one hundred per cent pure juice with no chemicals or artificial additives of any kind, this confirmed, to me, that my method of production was the way to go and it set the standards for my cider and perry which I still apply to this day.

I began making as many single variety ciders and perries as I could find and as demand for my products
grew I was encouraged to go into commercial production and progressed from draught, into P.E.T., and
finally into corked wine bottles.

When I first started searching for vintage quality fruit,
the youngest pear trees were about
twenty-five years old. Now I see new
trees being inter-planted in old
orchards and, even more encourag-
ing, new orchards of apple and perry
pears springing up again.

I, for one, am most heartened with
what appears to be a rekindled interest because cider, and especially
perry, are entrenched in this country's lore and I am extremely proud
to carry on with this ancient art, into
the New Millennium. Wassail!

*The label on an old
(circa 1964) bottle
from the Tewkesbury
Cider Co. Photo:
Kevin Minchew.*

Asturias – Cider Capital

There's a little bit of Green Spain that has the strongest cider culture around. Dave Matthews reports back.

Looking out of your hotel window you can see a cider bar just down the street. A further 20 cider bars lie within easy walking distance. There are half a dozen cider makers within the town limits, and a further dozen in the surrounding countryside. Have you died and gone to Heaven? No, you're in Villaviciosa, the little town known to the Spanish as 'the Apple Capital of Spain', which can be found nestling amongst the hills on the northern coast of the province of Asturias. There's a big cider factory on the town's outskirts, El Gaitero, that churns out industrial fizz for export to the four corners of the globe. But of far more interest is the great-tasting natural cider (sidra natural). It's drunk in all of the cider bars (sidrerias) and is unfiltered, unpasteurised, still, and sold in unlabelled green bottles with the maker's name stamped upon the cork.

Let's go for a stroll around some of Villaviciosa's sidrerias, and we'll start near the old town at Sidreria El Cañu (Carmen, 4). Bright and colourful, it's a real advert for Asturian cider, with an old press in one corner, two display cabinets full of a cider glass and cork collections, and a row of back-lit cider bottles above the bar counter. The house cider is the fruity (and the therefore aptly-named) Sidra Frutos. You order it by the bottle, and have it poured for you a shot at a time by the barman. And what a pouring ceremony: the barman holds the bottle above his head, and the glass down by his waist. Looking into the far distance he pours, and invariably catches, the cider in the glass. The glass is wide-brimmed and made of very fine glass that resonates as the cider hits it – the result is a glass of cider that looks whitish-gold due to thousands of tiny swirling bub-

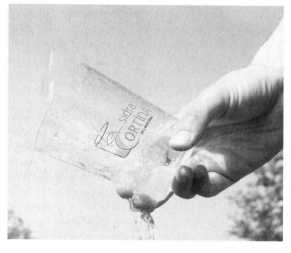

bles. Etiquette dictates that you drink each shot (or culín) in one go before the bubbles subside, without rushing it, and whilst appreciating the sight, aroma and flavour of your cider. Traditionally the dregs of each culín are poured onto the floor as a Celtic offering to Mother Earth. In effect you can only drink when the barman has a spare moment, and this takes a bit of getting used to. You could pour your own, but in practice this is not done, and on a busy evening the bar staff work extremely hard pouring cider almost non-stop. It is worth the effort, for the foaming cider is fresher and more lively, tastier and more rewarding.

We'll head towards the town hall square, stopping first beside the old market hall. On market day (Wednesday) the farmers' wives sit stoically on benches selling a few vegetables and jars of black honey from the mountains, whilst their husbands drink cider

Sidra Cortina is one of many traditional ciders made in Villaviciosa. Photo: Steve Wynne-Owen.

Opposite: Secundino Cardin Riera pouring cider in Sidreria El Cañu, Villaviciosa. Photo: Dave Matthews.

in Sidreria Bedriñana (Maliayo, 1). It has certain features in common with every other sidreria in town – wooden tables and chairs, a tiled floor, hams hanging up behind the bar, bottles of cider cooling in a sink of water, and the television in the corner is always on but no-one ever watches it. Unless the football's on, and today the owner, Señor Bedriñana, is getting excited because Real Madrid are winning. The house cider is one of a rotating range made locally, with the flavoursome Sidra Coro being the favourite of Francisco the friendly English-speaking barman. He removes the corks with a wall-mounted chigre, a sort of lever-operated corkscrew. Asturians have adopted the word chigre as affectionate slang for any sidreria.

There are plenty of good sidrerias to choose from at the town hall square. It's time for something to eat so let's go into Sidreria-Restaurant El Congreso de Benjamin (Generalisimo, 25). All of Villaviciosa's sidrerias offer some sort of seafood, but here there's a particularly good selection. There's a tank containing live crabs and lobsters, allowing you to point to your dinner, plus an extensive menu. There's also six different ciders to choose from, including the fruity and award-winning Sidra Roza from Nava. The walls are covered with cider posters and cider oil paintings – they really are so proud of their cider here

Nothing but cider bottles at Sidreria El Furacu, Villaviciosa. Photo: Dave Matthews.

in Asturias. Good grief, the two blokes drinking cider at the next table have just been served an enormous plateful of steaming sea urchins, spines and all.

Just a couple of doors away is Sidreria Furacu (Generalisimo), reputed to sell more cider than any other sidreria in Villaviciosa. It's a no-frills establishment, with strip lighting and a stainless steel bar top, but clean and welcoming with a good proportion of female customers. Without exception, everybody is drinking the cider (Sidra Trabanco for the record) and in the absence of any background music there's a lively hum of conversation.

Celestino Cortina Villar pouring a sample at Sidra Cortina. Photo: Dave Matthews.

Let's head back across the town, and find a backstreet locals' sidreria. Sidreria La Ballera (General Campomanes) is up at the southern end of town. There's sawdust on the floor, lots of dark wood and high shuttered windows. It serves the gently sharp and refreshing Sidra Cortina, made just around the corner. Cortina's cider mill (llagar) is typical of the region, although its output is one of the largest – two million litres of nothing but natural cider per year. Much of this is fermented and matured in 30 massive chestnut barrels (toneles), each having a capacity of up to 36,000 litres. Celestino Cortina and his father Eloy sample each tonel every week, and this allows them to determine which one to empty when a bottling run is needed.

OK, it's time to bribe or blackmail someone to drive us around some of the other excellent sidrerias that Asturias has to offer. A 15km drive south from Villaviciosa will take us through lush green countryside dotted with small traditional orchards, to the 'Cider Capital of Spain' - the town of Nava. Here you should visit the excellent Museo de la Sidra (Plaza Principe de Asturias). It's one of those modern 'hands on' museums, and as you go in they hand you an apple, which you insert into a glass-fronted machine. By pulling various levers you cause your apple to be washed, milled and pressed to give juice, all in front of your very own eyes.

There are many llagars (cider mills) in and around the town, and of course plenty of classic sidrerias. You could try Sidreria La Figar (La Riega, 15), or see Susana Ovín (winner of the 1999 Cider Pourers Championship, and the first woman ever to hold the title) pour at Sidreria La Barraca (La Barraca).

One of Nava's most famous sidrerias lies just outside town in the village of Quintana. Sidra Estrada supplies its

Sidreria Estrada.
Photo: Dave
Matthews.

own 'brewery tap' (Sidreria Estrada) and the two share the same building. The late owner had two great passions – cider and hunting – and his hunting trophies adorn the high walls of the sidreria. On being told that he only had six months to live he exclaimed: "I must have a bear!" A plane to Romania was duly chartered, a bear shot, and now the poor stuffed creature stands high atop a barrel behind the bar, dominating the sidreria. If you ask politely at a quiet time, you may be shown around the adjoining llagar. Inside the cool cellar you will be given a sample from a tiny tap bored into one of the chestnut barrels. The cider shoots out horizontally some four or five feet, before being expertly caught in a glass by your host. It tastes beautiful, so refreshing, even better (or so it seems) than from a bottle.

Driving on, we'll head to Oviedo, the capital city of Asturias, where all the best sidrerias are convenient-ly packed into one street – Calle Gascona. We won't stop for long because the vibrant sea port of Gijón is where we can find the sidreria reputed to be the best in Asturias: Sidreria El Cartero (Cienfuegos, 30). It's very much a blue-collar sort of establishment in a blue-collar part of town. On entering you pass a win-dow display of glassy-eyed fish and have to push past a heavy leather curtain. The clientele are 90% male and the cider pourers (escanciadors) are unerringly accurate. Today there's some free tapas on the steel bar counter – salted fish – that are giving us an even greater thirst for the fresh and appley Sidra La Mangada. The cider is stored in a temperature-con-

Getting there

By air:
Heathrow to Oviedo via Madrid, Iberian Airlines.

By sea:
Plymouth to Santander, Brittany Ferries. Portsmouth to Bilbao, P&O Ferries.

Accommodation

You could do no better than to stay with the amiable Vicente Alonso at his Hotel Avenida, Carmen 10, Villaviciosa. Tel: 98 589 1509. Web site: www.hotel-avenida.com

Asturian cider corks.
Photo: Dave
Matthews.

trolled stockroom, so there's no need for the usual bottles-in-the-sink routine. A classic indeed.

The Picos de Europa mountains in the east of the province are a popular tourist destination. There's not much cider made in the area, but there's somewhere on the way that we must visit. Take the road from Cangas de Onis towards Cabrales, and keep an eye out for a Llagar/Sidreria sign on your left. Turn off and let the signs lead you along increasingly narrow and twisting lanes until you arrive at the village of Sirviella and its Sidreria El Pareon. This is a true country cider house that makes and sells its own cider, in the tradition of our own, much-missed, Plough at Elmley Castle. The sidreria is a tiny single room with friendly locals, and the llagar is in the basement of the building opposite. They only make an annual 20,000 litres of their characterful Sidra Sirviella. Incredibly, the bottle store is at the far end of a cave, that drops into the bedrock from between the two tiny traditional box presses. Above the cider cellar are two tiers of

roofed but open-sided drinking areas. The upper of the two is under an ancient and beautiful granary. It's a lovely bright day so we'll stop up here a while, enjoying the view across the valley to the snow-capped Picos, savouring the tasty cider, and listening to the soothing peal of cow bells from the distant pastures. It's not easy to leave, but we have one last important stop.

A barman in Villaviciosa had told us that we must visit Sidreria Campanona in Amandi, a village just a couple of kilometres south of the town. "Es tipico, tipico, tipico." he had told us, and typical it turns out to be. It's a tiny gem of a place with room only for three tables, and is reminiscent of some of the better Brown Cafés in Amsterdam. It has a green tiled exterior, only one shuttered window, groceries fight for space with glasses on the wooden shelving behind the bar, it has lots of cider posters/models/photos/trophies, and it's packed with cider-drinking locals. There's a bottle of Sidra Trabanco to be drunk. We'll tip the last few drops onto the floor as an offering to Asturias. Long may she prosper, and soon may we return!

Cider information

A full list of Asturian cider makers can be found on www.sidra.com/

The Cider District of Northern Spain

ASTURIAS

COSTA VERDE

GIJÓN

N632

A8

VILLAVICIOSA

A66

THE CIDER DISTRICT

N634

OVIEDO

NAVA

SPAIN

Wassail!

Wassailing is so ancient that putting an actual date on when it began has been marred by time. Royal records show that it took place in the Royal household on 12th Night during the reign of Henry 7th (15th Century). Wassailing has fertilely given birth to customs as varied as first footing, carol singing, and wishing others good health when supping. The word wassail is derived from wes hál, which is an Anglo-Saxon phrase meaning "be whole" or "be of good health". By the 18th Century the word wassail conjured up images of drinking lots of ale and having a riotous time in the company of others.

The main purpose of wassailing is to perform a ceremony to protect the trees from evil and to make them bear a plentiful fruit crop in the coming season. Wassailing may have possible links with tree worship. The ceremony, however, is undoubtedly fun involving cider, songs, the firing of guns or thrashing of trees, horn blowing, and a community coming together on a cold Twelfth Night.

Gillian Williams describes a cider-orchard ceremony whose roots are lost in the mists of time...

(NB While Twelfth Night and Old Twelfth Night both exist, the older one is on the 17th of January as the calendar was shifted by 12 days in 1752.)

The ceremony took place in the orchard where the wassailers had previously chosen one tree to represent the whole orchard. As it grew dark the wassailers would gather around the chosen tree, carrying a pail of cider which would be used to toast the tree. A piece of toast, or a cake, soaked in cider would be laid

Leominster Morris Men lead the torch-lit procession to the orchard. Wassail at Lyne Down Farm, Herefordshire. Photo: Dave Matthews.

Cider Citations

The Dictionary of British Folk Customs – C Hole, 1978.

The Stations of the Sun – R Hutton, 1996.

Customs and Traditions of England – G Hogg, 1971.

The Folklore of Cornwell – T Deane, 1975.

in the tree fork or hung from the branches (for the robins who represented the future good spirits of the tree). In some orchards the wassailers mimed the tree bearing a good harvest by bowing down to the ground before it three times and rising slowly as if they were carrying a heavy sack of apples. Then a traditional song was sung to the tree. One version of the song runs:

"Here's to thee, old apple tree,
Whence thou mays't bud and whence thou Mays't blow
And whence thou mays't bear apples enow.
Hats full, caps full, bushel, bushel sacks full,
And my pockets full too!
Hurrah!"

When the formal toast and singing was over shotguns were (in modern times) fired through the topmost boughs (stones having been used more traditionally) while everyone shouted and blew horns. The overall aim was to drive away evil spirits and awaken the sleeping trees. In Sussex and Surrey the wassailers rapped the tree with sticks rather than using shotguns. This acted as an early form of organic pest control as any small bugs that may have climbed below loose bark and nested up for the winter were knocked off the tree and froze to death.

Wassailing has declined over the centuries but over the last forty years is now being actively revived again. It is well documented that by the 19th Century the custom was already in a fairly steady decline. This was mainly due to the draw of towns and employment removing people from the country and the subsequent engulfment of the country by the ever-growing towns. Orchards were seen as ideal spaces for a number of houses, as if the trees had served no other purpose but to protect the view for those who would live on top of them.

Gillian Williams is Secretary of APPLE. APPLE is a committee of the Campaign for Real Ale dedicated to promoting real cider.

The whole act of wassailing has changed with the decline in the number of orchards and our farming industry. An example of this decline is seen in the tradition of The Truro Wassailers. The Truro Wassailers are not chosen but rather each member retains their right to carry the wassail bowl in their family until the last member of the family has died. The honour then passes onto another family. Rather then carry out a ceremony in an orchard, they sing around houses and pubs carrying a "wassail bowl". It can be seen how the short step from a wassail bowl to vessel-cup can be taken. A vessel cup is carried around at Christmas, while carols are sung, to collect the money. It is sometimes accompanied with an icon type image and roasted apples.

Wassailing was a ceremony not just for apples, it was used as a charm or protection for the good health of farm animals and beehives, even field crops and humans benefit from the wassail toast. Contact you local APPLE Rep. to see where wassailing goes on in your area. Get out there and get involved in what is unquestionably an act of history and fun. Wassail.

Wassail at Honey Combe Farm, Filton, Bristol. Photo: Dave Matthews.

The Small-scale Experience

Andrew Lea was a flavour chemist in the Cider Section at the world-famous Long Ashton Research Station near Bristol until its closure in 1985. Now he lives in South Oxfordshire where he is a small-scale hobby cidermaker. This is how he does it.

Fruit

Of course it's possible to make good cider from any sound apples, but by general agreement some of the finest cider is made from the bittersweet and bittersharp apples which have been selected for centuries in South West England and North West France. So when I set up my own small cider orchard of thirty-three trees on about one-fifth of an acre, I chose some of those 'vintage' cultivars which would cross-pollinate each other and, when fermented and blended together, would give the balanced cider I was looking for. See Table below. I ordered virus-tested trees from a specialist nursery, and they were grafted for me on MM106 rootstock. This is semi-dwarf but fairly tolerant of adverse conditions, and since I wanted to grow my trees organically under low nitrogen input I needed something fairly robust. After four years growth and training, my first real crop arrived. Now, ten years on, I get the equivalent of 3-6 tons of fruit per acre – a pretty respectable organic yield.

Harvesting and juicing

In October the fruit starts to fall from the tree and by the time half of it is on the floor we start to gather the rest. It's all stored outdoors in 15 kg slatted plastic crates. Early fruit like Foxwhelp and Frederick are processed within a week or two. But the main crop bittersweets, like Dabinett and Yarlington Mill, are allowed to mature for a month or maybe more before they're milled and pressed. This is traditional practice which allows all the starch to convert to sugar and the fruit to become fully ripe. For a hobby cidermaker like me, who only has the weekends to play with, it also gives the chance of spreading the work to suit the time available – though in 1999 there was so much fruit that we were still pressing on New Years Day 2000! Just before milling, I wash every boxfull free of mud and bird droppings, rejecting all the mouldy fruit – traditional doesn't mean tainted!

Milling is difficult on a small scale. When I first started, I used an old German grape crusher which I'd picked up at auction when a local winery closed down. In truth

Andrew Lea with one of his Dabinett trees. Photo: Roy Bailey.

though it wasn't well suited to apples, and it made for many a cold and tedious autumn afternoon as we milled and re-milled the fruit to get it small enough! Recently I bought a purpose-designed Italian apple mill which works like a dream and reduces a 15 kg box to pulp in just a few minutes. The pulp is stored in plastic boxes (sometimes overnight) before pressing out on my home-made press. This is based on a North American design and is formed by a stout timber frame, in my case six-inch square ash timbers which came from trees felled when I had a house extension built. This gives space for six 16-inch square 'cheeses' of pulp to be built up in woven press cloths separated by wooden slats stacked on a marine-ply juice tray. Pressure is applied by means of an eight ton hydraulic bottle jack and the juice flows out to a plastic drum. The press takes about 60 kg of pulp from which we get about 40 litres of juice over an hour or so, before stripping down and starting the process again.

Fermentation

What happens next rather depends on the type of cider I'm going to make, but I always like to measure the sugar with a hydrometer or a refractometer and the pH with a meter or a narrow range test strip.

Andrew Lea's home-made press. Photo: Roy Bailey.

These numbers help me to decide where to go next. In my early years as a home cidermaker I pretty much followed what I'd learnt at Long Ashton in the 1970s – using sulphite to knock out the wild yeasts, adding a cultured wine yeast and then fermenting to dryness. I then bottled or cask conditioned with small amounts of added sugar to produce a natural carbonation through secondary fermentation.

After a while I wanted to make something a bit more distinctive and challenging, so I stepped back to the traditional pre-1960 Long Ashton ways of slow natural fermentation with a succession of wild yeasts, followed by bottle conditioning of the cider with its own residual sugar. This is difficult to do unless the nitrogen levels are low and under the cidermaker's own control, as they once were in the traditional farm orchards of the West Country and as they are under my own organic system. Nitrogen management is critical because if the levels are too high the fermentation goes too fast and then it's impossible to slow it sufficiently to get 'condition' without going all the way to dryness. I use the old technique of 'keeving' to help with this prior to fermentation. This means leaving the cold juice for a few days to trap the nitrogenous nutrients into a slowly formed pectin 'head', from which the juice is then racked before the main fermentation. I may also need to rack or filter again during fermentation to slow the system down. I don't use sulphite so much for these fermentations, unless the pH is above 3.8 when I need to be careful to avoid bacterial infection. It takes maybe from October to April until this sort of traditional cider is ready for bottling, and another six months before it's at its best – quite the reverse of modern factory cidermaking where speed is paramount! Few of the ciders listed in this guide will be made exactly like this, but many of them will be in some way similar. Like vintage wines, no two traditional ciders are ever the same – but that's all part of the fascination!

Further information about small-scale cidermaking in general, and more about how Andrew does his own, can be found on his web site at www.cider.org.uk

Table of Cultivars

CULTIVAR	TYPE	COMMENTS
Broxwood Foxwhelp	Bittersharp	Matures three weeks before the others and makes a big tree. Fruit does not store well but contributes plenty of acid and aroma to the blend.
Kingston Black	Bittersharp	Shy cropper. Somewhat affected by brown rot, hence not storing well. A useful aromatic contributor to the blend.
Stoke Red	Bittersharp	Very twiggy growth, pale green leaves and very biennial habit. Red fruits are small, but excellent and aromatic for the blend.
Frederick	Sharp	Very untidy reflexed growth and suffers badly with brown rot. Fruits are russeted dark red with a sharp and aromatic character.
Crimson King	Sharp	Large tree and large fruits, almost Bramley sized. Contributes acidity and bulk but more flavoursome than Bramley.

CULTIVAR	TYPE	COMMENTS
Harry Masters Jersey	Bittersweet	Small tree with high tannin dusty-red fruits providing bittersweet character to the blend.
Yarlington Mill	Bittersweet	A mild bittersweet, storing well till late in the season
Dabinett	Bittersweet	Compact and reliable. Small tree, giving soft tannin to the blend.
Medaille d'Or	Bittersweet	Brittle wood and very late flowering. Small and highly distinctive russeted fruit with exceptionally high tannin.
Sweet Coppin	Sweet	Large yellow fruits contribute slow fermenting bulk for blending with the bittersweets.
Sweet Alford	Sweet	Red fruits contribute quality bulk, but suffers from magnesium deficiency on my soil so needs help from Epsom salts.

Cider in the Pays d'Auge

Dave Matthews takes us on a tour of one of the world's most important cider-producing regions.

The Pays d'Auge in Normandy is one of France's most picturesque regions. Rural and unspoilt, its quiet roads lead you through a landscape dominated by orchards and ancient timber-framed farm buildings. Its people are warm and welcoming, and boast a gastronomy whose richness is derived from Pay d'Auge's fertile soils and temperate climate. Cows grazing in its orchards produce the milk for famous cheeses such as Camembert, Livarot and Pont l'Évêque. The orchards themselves provide the fruit for some of the world's greatest ciders.

The AOC label (Appellation d'Origine Contrôlée) is the French government's guarantee of quality and origin, currently enjoyed by a number of French wines and cheeses but so far awarded to only two ciders. Cidre

Appellation Pays d'Auge Contrôlée is one, and such cider must be produced from within certain designated areas within the Pays d'Auge and must use particular local apple varieties. Cidre Appellation Pays d'Auge Contrôlée must also meet strict production criteria: only 100% juice will do, no added water or sugar, no use of apple juice concentrate, and fermentation must be with natural yeasts. Thus the AOC label is also a mark of quality, and so its drinkers enjoy a tasty, full-flavoured cider.

Even big cider factories can produce stunningly good Appellation Pays d'Auge Contrôlée ciders. The Cidrerie de Pont l'Évêque churns out eight million litres of cider a year (most of which is distilled into Calvados), but alongside the huge 1200 hectolitre fermentation tanks are much smaller fermentation vessels reserved for the AOC product. Factory Director François Gilles told me that "For the AOC cider we try to source hand-picked apples, remove the rotten fruit by hand and use a smaller press. The whole process is more artisanal." Cambremer is a charming market town in the heart of the Pays d'Auge, and the countryside around it is a hotbed of craft cider making. Back in 1961, a group

Follow the apple sign on the Route du Cidre. Photo: Dave Matthews.

of local farm cider makers formed the 'Cru de Cambremer', and were amongst the first in France to bottle-ferment their cider, a practice now ubiquitous. To encourage visitors to their cellars they set up the Route du Cidre, a circular tour of cider farms in the Cambremer region. Route du Cidre leaflets can be picked up from the Tourist Information Office in Cambremer.

Let's go on a tour of the Cambremer region, visiting a representative sample of its many cider producers. We'll approach from the ferry ports to the north, and our first stop will be at Douville-en-Auge, South East of Cabourg. Eric Maertens is a cider dynamo, dashing about, promoting his excellent cider with gusto and enthusiasm. His 39 hectares of standard-tree orchards provide grazing for both his cattle and 'Chipie', the donkey who makes an appearance on all

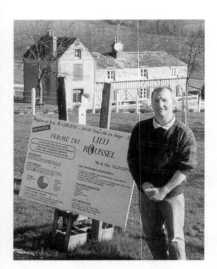

Eric Maertens, cider maker, Douville en Auge.

of Eric's labels. Eric will show you his Cider Cellar, with its apple mill and double-bed pneumatic press. Apples are matured for 2-3 weeks upstairs in the granary – a process, unique to the Pays d'Auge, that serves to concentrate the flavour as the apples respire and lose water. Eric uses a blend of 12 cider apple varieties, and his best batches may be lucky enough to achieve AOC status, leaving the remainder to be sold as Cidre Fermier (Farm Cider). Eric will pour you a sample to try. Orange-gold and with a gentle fizz, his AOC Cidre Lieu Roussel (4.5% abv) has a faintly smokey aroma with a tannic, apply flavour and a softly creamy mouth-feel. Excellent.

Continue south towards Cambremer, and you will find Dominique Denis' farm at St. Aubin-Lebizay. You'll see plenty of perry pear trees as you drive around the Pays d'Auge, but Dominique is one of the few that bottles perry (poiré) alongside his cider. His Poiré Fermier (4% abv) is a pale, gentle perry with a pronounced aroma of pears. In contrast, Dominique's Cidre Fermier (4% abv) is pale amber, full bodied and flavoursome – a good, honest, tannic farm cider. The first thing to strike you as you enter his cellar is the multitude of trophies on display – Dominique has had much success at the annual AOC competition held in Cambremer each May. You also can't miss his 18th century circular stone mill, that last saw active apple-crushing service in 1960.

Let's meander clockwise around Cambremer, and drop in to see father and son partners François and Stéphane Grandval at their beautiful manor farm in the sleepy hamlet of Grandouet. You can start your tour with an eight-minute video on 'Cider in the Pays d'Auge', with a choice of French or English commentary. Then wander into the cool and ancient cellar, with its beautiful 8,000 litre oak barrels (tonnes), one of which bears the carved legend '1792'. The feeling of timelessness is a little spoilt by a visit to the yard around the back, where steel fermentation vats and a gleaming cylindrical press ensure that the annual production of 100,000 litres is both efficient and profitable. This melding of tradition and technology produces a lovely cider – the AOC Cidre de Cambremer (4% abv) is light, fruity and medium-dry. Prices in the farm shop are typical for the region – 18 Francs for a bottle of AOC Cider, 16 Francs for the Cidre Fermier and only 15 Francs for a bottle of lemony-sharp Poiré. Ridiculously cheap compared to the UK, where grossly unfair levels of duty push the price up to the equivalent of 50 Francs.

Our next stop is with Luc Bignon at Saint Laurent du Mont, to the West of Cambremer. On the day of our visit we found him on his tractor in the orchard, repairing damage caused by the great storm (of December 26th 1999) that toppled 15-20% of all fruit trees in the Pays d'Auge. Luc is compact and amiable – the lady in our party wanted to take him home with her – and he will readily give you a tour of his ancient and atmospheric cellar. In common with

Web sites

www.info-cidre.com (French cider in general)

www.pays-auge.cci.fr/html/liste-produits.md (Pays d'Auge cider makers)

Tourist Information

Cambremer Tourist Office, Maison du Canton de Cambremer, rue Pasteur, 14340 Cambremer. Tel: 02.31.63.08.87 www.pays-auge.cci.fr/html/touri.htm

Cider Makers

Eric MAERTENS, Cour Roussel, 14430 Douville en Auge. Tel: 02.31.23.71.15

Dominique DENIS, Saint Aubin Lebizay. Tel: 02.31.65.13.39

François & Stéphane GRANDVAL, Le Manoir, 14340 Grandouet. Tel 02.31.63.08.73

other Pays d'Auge cider makers Luc offers his cider as either Dry (Brut or Sec), Medium (Demi-sec) or Sweet (Douce). Adding sugar is prohibited, so Luc slows the fermentation right down by racking off until the cider contains hardly any yeast. He bottles his Sweet cider when the specific gravity is 1029 to give a cider of 2% abv, his Medium at 1018 to give 3.5% abv and his Dry at 1014 to give 4 to 4.5% abv. Bottling cider with both the fruit's sugar and living yeast could lead to exploding bottles, but Luc is careful to let just the right amount of yeast through the filter – more into the Dry than into the Sweet – and judges the whole process with a practised eye. His ciders have a fruitiness that is most prominent in his Sweet, and a unique bitter flavour that is most pronounced in his Dry. For an appealing balance of the two flavours, try Luc's Demi-sec (Medium) cider.

If you're looking for Bed & Breakfast (Chambre d'Hôte) in the area, I can heartily recommend staying with the welcoming Madame Camus just a couple of miles outside Cambremer. Watch the Roe Deer from the shuttered bedroom window or stroll around the farm garden on a kind of cider-artefact treasure hunt. However, if the idea of sleeping with a cider press turns you on, then head straight for Madame Huet's Chambre d'Hôte at Saint Laurent du Mont. There's an ancient and massive oak beam press (with a beautifully carved wooden screw thread) at the foot of the stairs, and an old circular stone mill just outside the front door.

Madame Huet's Brother-in-Law, Pierre Huet, is one of

the most respected calvados (a type of cider brandy) producers in the area. Most cider makers produce a little calvados as a sideline – the whole village turns out when the travelling still arrives at Eric Maertens farm; and a more stationary still can be found at the far end of François Grandval's farm shop – but to Pierre it is the mainstay of his business. You'll find Pierre's manor farm on the outskirts of Cambremer itself, and it is here that he produces his cider, most of which he distils to produce a fine calvados. Most calvados is the result of a single distillation, but Calvados Appellation

A glass of cider in the Pomme D'Or (Golden Apple) at Pont L'Évêque. Photo: Dave Matthews.

Pays d'Auge Contrôlée undergoes a double distillation to produce an especially sought after spirit. Pierre is rightly proud of his manor farm, and one of his tours is highly recommended. His two calvados cellars are absolutely breathtaking – rows of huge oak barrels (fouders) that contain either ten or fifteen thousand litres of maturing calvados. The eight-year old Calvados (40% abv) is orange-gold and has a full, earthy-apples flavour. There's a little fire, but this fades to leave a long and mellow finish. The 18-year old Calvados (40% abv) also has the earthy-apples house character, but the extra ten years in the fouders has mellowed the fire, darkened the spirit to a pale amber, and allowed a greater complexity to develop. The oldest vintage on sale is a 50-year old, but

Cider Makers

Luc BIGNON, L'Eglise, 14340 Saint Lauren du Mont. Tel: 02.31.62.27.24

Pierre HUET, Avenue des Tilleuls, 14340 Cambremer. Tel: 02.31.63.01.09

Bed & Breakfast

Madame Camus, Le Mesnil, 14340 Cambremer. Tel: 02.31.63.00.28

Madame Huet, "La Vignerie", 14340 Saint Laurent du Mont. Tel: 02.31.63.08.65

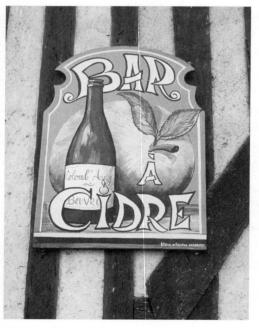

Sign outside the Colomb'Auge cider bar, Beuvron en Auge. Photo: Dave Matthews.

the Huet family can enjoy even older calvados from their own private cellar, with the most ancient vintage dated 1865. This was the year that François Huet founded the business, and three further generations (alternating with the names of Pierre and François) have continued the tradition. Pierre's son (François, of course) is a guarantee of its future.

The Cheval Blanc restaurant at Crèvecoeur-en-Auge is a lovely place to enjoy Pierre Huet's products as an accompaniment to fine food. As an aperitif you could try his Pommeau (18% abv), an outstanding example of the style (a blend of apple juice and calvados). Dark gold with an appealing, perfumey aroma, it is smooth, fruity, complex and characterful. The menu at the Cheval Blanc offers you a beautiful selection of traditional Norman cuisine – various meats cooked in cream and cider or calvados, unpasteurised local cheeses – and a wine glass or two of Pierre's cider complements it perfectly. Drinking calvados during your meal has been proven to aid digestion, yet calvados is famous as an after-dinner digestif, so when you've finished eating sit back and savour a glass of one of Pierre's best vintages.

La Route du Cidre

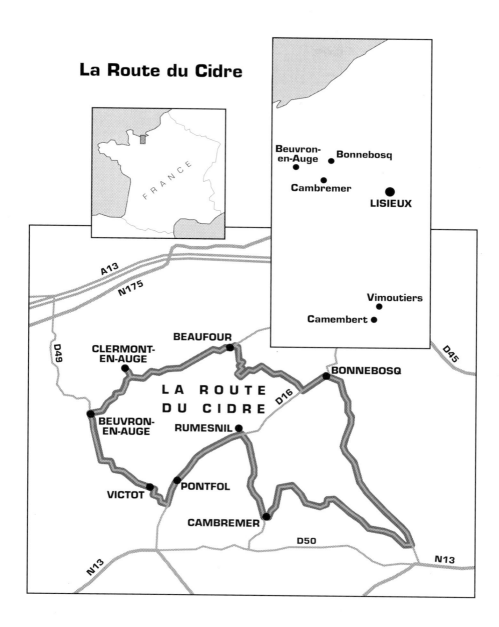

Cooking with Cider

Susie Dunkerton shares her thoughts and recipes.

The tradition of regional cooking seems to have been more lasting on the continent, hence no surprise at crepes being served with a bottle of local cider in Normandy; and when there we expect to enjoy creamy cider and apple dishes using pork, pheasant or fish. Real cider adds real flavour to almost any dish, although in England recipes using French wine have tended to dominate the kitchen. We don't need to be at war with France to turn to cider as an alternative. Reach for it anyway, and experiment in sauces, cakes, casseroles and marinades.

Now that cider drinkers are demanding more apple flavours in the glass, it is time to use cider as another dimension in our cooking. But beware – if you are

as interested in real food as you are in real cider, it is of little point to pick up an industrial supermarket cider to enhance your dishes: the higher the quality of your ingredients the tastier your food. Find if you can, using this book, a drier traditional cider. You can always sweeten the dish, but you cannot remove the sugar.

Susie Dunkerton in her Cider House Restaurant. Photo: Dunkertons Cider.

However, if the cider has considerable tannin, use a little less in the particular recipes to start with, as often the tannins concentrate to bitterness if cooked for a long time.

The main thing is to enjoy the adventure. As a guide, try substituting a quarter of any cooking liquid for cider, and don't drink the rest of the bottle straight away whilst at the stove – in case your tastebuds indicate that another drop in the pan would be a good idea. Here are three recipes to tempt you.

Leek and Apple Soup

1 medium onion	1 tsp. honey
2 leeks	150ml ($^1/_4$ pt) cider
2 firm eating apples	450ml ($^3/_4$ pt) stock (chicken or vegetable)
2 cloves garlic	1 bayleaf / 2 sprigs thyme / 2 sage leaves /
25g-50g (1oz-2oz) butter	small bunch of parsley /sprig of rosemary

1. Thinly slice onions, leeks and garlic. Cut apples into 1cm cubes.

2. Melt 25g (1oz) butter. Add onions, leeks and garlic and cook gently for 5 minutes stirring occasionally.

3. Add apple. Cook 5 minutes.

4. Bring to boil stock, cider, honey and any or all of the herbs in separate pan and simmer 10 minutes.

5. Pour through strainer onto vegetables and simmer 10 minutes more.

6. Adjust seasoning and sweetness, and serve.

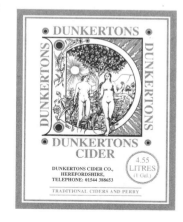

P.S. for a heartier first course, serve with croutons of toasted cheese, or add some cooked haricot beans before the final simmer.

Fillet of White Fish in Mustard and Tarragon Cream (for 4)

1¹/₂lb white fish fillets: cod, hake, pollock, halibut or haddock.

25g-50g (1oz-2oz) butter

25g (1oz) flour

1 small onion chopped fine

300ml milk

150ml cider

2 tsp. mustard (prepared)

2 cloves garlic chopped fine

1 tsp. dried tarragon or

3 tsp. fresh tarragon

1 stick celery, chopped fine

25g (1oz) butter

25g (1oz) olive oil

Dunkertons Cider House Restaurant. Photo: Dunkertons Cider.

1. Melt butter in saucepan, stir in onion and garlic and cook gently till soft. Add celery and a little more butter if necessary. Cover with lid and stir occasionally till soft.

2. Add flour off heat, cook gently 1-2 mins.

3. Bring to boil the milk in a separate pan and whisk into other saucepan off the heat. Whisk in mustard and cider.

4. Return to heat, bring to a simmer stirring.

5. Add herbs and leave to simmer gently for 10-15 minutes.

6. Slice fish into 4-inch pieces.

7. Melt butter in the oil in a frying pan and fry fish

gently till golden about 5 minutes each side – immediately before serving.

8. Check sauce for seasoning, intensity of flavour, consistency (add a little cream if too thin) and pour over fish to serve.

Apple and Raisin Cider Cake
(A recipe from our cidermaker Robert West)

50g (2oz) raisins
137ml (1/4 pint) medium sweet cider
150g (6oz) apples – peeled, cored and coarsely grated
2 large free range eggs
100g (4oz) raw brown sugar
75ml (3 fl.oz) sunflower oil
100g (4oz) self-raising flour
1/4 teaspoon ground ginger
50g (2oz) walnut pieces

1. Put raisins in bowl and cover with cider. Soak for at least 2 hours, preferably overnight.
2. Grease and line 500g (1lb) loaf tin.
3. Preheat oven to 190C/375F/Gas 5.
4. Whisk sugar and eggs together until mixture is thick and creamy.
5. Whisk in very slowly oil, then add flour – blend for 1 minute.
6. Fold in ginger, apples, drained raisins and walnut pieces, mix until evenly combined.
7. Spoon into prepared tin and level surface.
8. Bake in preheated oven for 30-45 mins.

Susie Dunkerton is Chef at the Cider House Restaurant, Dunkertons Cider, Pembridge, Herefordshire.

CAMRA and Cider

CAMRA promotes real cider. Mick Lewis explains how.

In 2001 CAMRA celebrates its 30th birthday, and I find it amazing that after all this time most people still think that it is a beer-only organisation. But let me assure you, this is certainly not the case.

CAMRA has officially supported cider since 1977 and continues to do so. Unfortunately, until the late 1980s, it was done in a very haphazard way. Most beer festivals, for example, sold cider, but it was often dotted about amongst the beers, with no real promotion. There were also a number of cider experts within CAMRA, all collecting their own information and doing very little with it. But in 1988 all this changed. This is when the Apple and Pear Produce Liaison Executive – APPLE – was set up within CAMRA, specifically to promote, campaign, advise and collect information on all aspects of cider and perry. (The alternative Always Paralytically P*ss*d Late in the Evening was no reflection on the original members of course!) This committee has always included a mixture of both experts and enthusiasts, and often includes members with technical expertise as well. There are also regional

Most festivals have a separate cider bar.

APPLE contacts, now covering most of the country.

So what does CAMRA actually do with cider and perry? Well, for most people, their first port of call will be a beer festival. Most of these now have a separate cider bar, usually staffed by someone with some knowledge of the product and often this is the first time that drinkers get the chance to sample a real cider or perry. In fact, it is only at CAMRA beer festivals that most people have the chance to drink perry at all. So the first step down the line is to let people try real cider and let them see the variety and range of flavours that are available.

It is also important to explain to the public just what goes into their cider when they purchase a fizzy orange liquid in their local pub. And this is one of the main problems with cider today. Most keg cider is made using apple concentrate, which can come from almost anywhere in the world and has a hefty dose of water as well as juice. Ask most people what cider is made from and they'll say apples. Unfortunately, there are only enough cider apples grown in this country to produce a small percentage of the cider that is actually made. So when you drink keg cider, you have no idea what is actually in it. This couldn't be one of the reasons why the larger producers have very little interest in seeing ingredient labelling introduced for alcoholic drinks, could it?

One of the biggest problems with getting more real ciders into our pubs is that the Big Two – Bulmers and Matthew Clark – control over 90% of the UK cider industry, leaving hundreds of producers fighting for the little bit that is left. This is the type of uphill battle that we are facing.

Another problem with the Big Two is their apparent apathy to promoting their own real ciders. Here we are at CAMRA telling everybody about cider, while the two biggest companies would rather invest their capital in only advertising their keg brands, and then inventing new, exciting products which usually disappear in a couple of years. As the two major companies with proper national distribution, it is a travesty that so little of their real cider is available in pubs. And here we hit another problem – breweries and pub chains. Very few of them have a policy of stocking real cider. Even the more enlightened breweries would rather you drank a keg cider in their pubs, even though you might find a phenomenal range of real ales.

Even worse is the modern practise of conning the customer. Over the last ten years, we have seen a number of ciders being sold using fake handpumps as the method of dispense. Mostly, these are keg ciders served in what looks like a traditional manner, using what appears to be a handpump. Even lager drinkers would associate a handpump with something real, and many drinkers have been surprised when they're given a fizzy drink. In the case of Addlestones – a real cider – it was served using a gas system through what looked like a real handpump, though thankfully this practise is ceasing. CAMRA will always campaign rigorously against any misleading forms of dispense.

CAMRA also puts on several cider-only festivals. In the past we have had four National Cider and Perry Exhibitions in London, and several cider festivals still take place at local level each year. Some of these bars are incorporated into Apple Day, every October, and CAMRA ran a cider bar at the very first one, which took place in Covent Garden, even if my main memory is the wind, where we had to Bluetack the beer mats to the bar!

We have, for many years now, a Cider and Perry of the Year award. These days a judging panel tastes all of the finalists and comes up with a winner. Currently this takes place at the Stockport Beer and Cider Festival at the end of May.

For cider lovers who have never seen cider being made, most years a trip for members takes place in the autumn, usually visiting several producers, where you can watch the cider being pressed and be given a talk by the maker, as well as sampling the products. And jolly little affairs they are too!

So you can see, in a small way CAMRA is helping to promote real cider and perry against all the odds and I shall give just one example of our success. In the 1990 edition of CAMRA's Good Cider

Ciders & Perries of the Year		
Year	Cider	Perry
1989	Wilkins	Lyne Down
1990	Billings	Dunkertons
1991	Theobalds	Lyne Down
1992	Theobalds	Lyne Down
1993	Biddendens	Lyne Down
1994	not held	not held
1995	Gwatkin	Lyne Down
1996	Janets Jungle Juice (West Croft Cider)	Weston's Perry
1997	not awarded	Summers
1998	New Forest Cider	Dunkertons
1999	Weston's Old Rosie	Weston's Perry
2000	Weston's Old Rosie	Dunkertons

Guide, I wrote "...at the bigger festivals you may expect to find up to 20 different ciders, and perhaps two or three perries." These days, even medium-sized festivals often have 15, while the larger festivals are now up to the 50-60 level. At the Great British Beer Festival one year, we even had 20 perries. Now that's success.

Old Orchards: Vintage Fruits and Wildlife

"Who sets an apple tree may live to see it end ... Who sets a pear tree may set it for a friend" or as they say in Herefordshire "Plant pears for your heirs".

Old orchards are special places. With their mistletoe-laden, knotty boughs spreading above permanent grassland, they represent a close relationship with nature passed down through generations of growers sensitive to the limitations of local soils, weather and traditional fruit varieties. These cultural landscapes, rich in biodiversity, enhance local distinctiveness and epitomise a more gentle, sustainable approach to rural living.

Traditional apple and pear orchards were established by grafting the chosen cropping cultivar onto a seedling rootstock. Because of the replanting that has gone on over many years, infilling gaps and replacing blocks of trees, old orchards that survive today contain a great mixture of trees of different varieties and considerable age. Traditional varieties still found include perry pears with names like Clipper Dick, Bloody Bastard, Blakeney Red otherwise known as Lightning Pear 'goes straight through' or Circus Pear 'once round and out', Merrylegs, Startle Cock and Stinking Bishop, reflecting local provenance. Old orchards with such varieties are often attached to smallholdings, like my own property at Gregg's Pit which dates from at least 1785, where the orchard contains the Gregg's Pit perry pear, whose trees are only found in and around Much Marcle, Herefordshire.

As the trees themselves grow older (it is not unusual to find perry pears 100-150 years old and cider apple and cherry trees more than 60 years old) they develop standing dead and decaying wood, heart rot, hollows, holes and sap runs rich in sugar. These are all niche habitats for a range of threatened insects, common and less common birds (including woodpeckers, owls, spotted flycatcher, treecreeper and tree sparrow) and bats. Old orchards can also support a vibrant mix of plants including wild daffodils, cowslips and orchids, as well as fungi and lichens. And let's not forget the wild yeasts which leave their 'taste print' on each artisanal producer's craft cider and perry.

In contrast to modern commercial orchards, the mixture of fruit species and of early and late flowering varieties in old orchards gives good protection against pests and diseases. Chemical sprays are rarely used and the natural predators of pest species, including ladybirds, hoverflies, earwigs, tits and finches, can reach high enough numbers to balance any potential pest problem.

Commercial demand for such organically produced fruit is growing, and this together with the altogether more ancient, but still constant demand for the deliciously distinctive ciders and perries pressed and fermented from them, means that the future for our old orchards has at last a rosy glow again.

Perry Pear trees at Gregg's Pit, Much Marcle. Photo: James Marsden.

Taken from a paper written by **James Marsden** *'Apples don't have maggots – an overview of orchards and wildlife' given at the 'Orchards and Wildlife' conference organised by Common Ground with English Nature in September 1999. For a copy of the conference proceedings, please contact Common Ground, PO Box 25309, London NW5 1ZA.*

Cider on the Net

Dave Matthews slips into his surfing gear...

There's a whole world wide web of cider sites on the internet. Search engines such as **www.google.com** will find many for you, but in the meantime here's a random selection for you to try.

Cider Makers

I've published web site addresses, where they exist, with each cider maker in the main body of this guide. But here's a few of interest:

Bulmers Cider
www.bulmer.com

Below: A fruity web site from Burrow Hill Cider.

❥ Links to Bulmers' subsidiaries across the world.
❥ Visit a virtual reality pub, the Cider Surfers Arms.

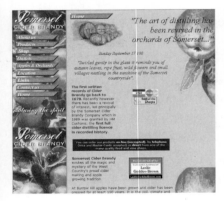

Burrow Hill Cider
www.ciderbrandy.co.uk

❥ Information on products, outlets and how to order online (secured).
❥ Links to other food and drink sites.
❥ Offers a 360° panoramic view of the distilling area.

Lambourn Valley Cider
www.westberks.demon.co.uk/lvcider/

❥ Links, information on the products.
❥ Articles by the company owner, cider writer Roy Bailey. His piece on the late Ray Hartland can be found at:

www.westberks.demon.co.uk/rhb/hartland.htm

Westons Cider

www.westons-cider.co.uk/

❥ Information about the company, its products, its tours, etc.

❥ You can download some Westons wallpaper for your desktop!

Cider Outlets

Orchard, Hive & Vine

www.orchard-hive-and-vine.co.uk/index.html

❥ An excellent website from the online cider sales specialist.

❥ Secure on-line shopping, with bottles from over a dozen craft cider makers on offer.

❥ Photographs and details of each bottle of cider or perry.

❥ Also available: bottle-conditioned beers, meads, UK wines.

English Farm Cider Centre

www.farm-shop.co.uk/cidershop.html

❥ Web site under reconstruction at the time of writing.

Cider Information

Wittenham Hill Cider Page
http://ourworld.compuserve.com/homepages/andrew_lea/homepage.htm

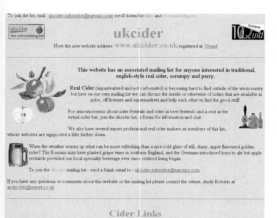

➤ Web site run by Dr Andrew Lea, ex Long Ashton Cider Research Station.

➤ In-depth, scientific advice on small-scale cider making.

ukcider www.ukcider.co.uk

➤ Andy Roberts' website for cider-drinking enthusiasts.

➤ Lots of cider links, lists of cider websites, ideas on where to find good cider and cider pubs, links to buying cider on-line.

Above: front page of ukcider, on the world wide web

The Scrumpy User Guide
www.scrumpyandwestern.co.uk/scrumpy.html

➤ Paul Gunningham's practical guide for real cider enthusiasts, part of the "Scrumpy & Western" music site.

➤ Where to find scrumpy, how to store it, books and links, etc., plus details of recommended scrumpy makers.

breWorld
www.brewworld.com/homebrew/ciderperry/index.html

➤ breWorld's cider and perry site, run by Gillian Grafton.

➤ Lots of useful information, including pages on cider books, plans for constructing presses and mills, selling home-brewed cider and perry, cider recipes, links, etc.

CAMRA's APPLE
www.camra.org.uk/apple/apple.html

➤ CAMRA's cider page that details what its cider organisation, APPLE, is all about. Information on Good Cider and how to serve it.

CAMRA's Apple page is a good place to start your browsing.

Core Food & Drink
www.corefoodanddrink.co.uk/

➤ A division of the Pershore Group of Colleges, and the Centre of Excellence for the Cider, Food and Drink Industries.

Pershore Group of Colleges knows its net design and its apples.

➤ The website provides information on their lab services, cider training courses, cider processing and packaging services, cider consultancy, and their cider research and development projects.

➤ Information, too, on their products – Hindlip Ciders and Perries.

Electronic Cider Forums

There's a couple of excellent email cider newsgroups which are free to subscribe to:

ukcider

subscriptions: **ukcider-subscribe@egroups.com**

Andy Roberts' British cider forum.

Discussions typically centre on where to find Real Cider, but also include wider cider issues.

In order to join in (it's free) send an email to the address above, or visit **www.egroups.com/subscribe/ukcider**

Cider Digest

subscriptions: **cider-request@talisman.com**

The Digest Janitor is Dick Dunn, of Boulder, Colorado. Submissions typically centre on the additive-obsessed US cider home-brew scene, but there's plenty of other news and contributions from around the globe.

Cider Around the World

Foreign language web sites can easily and quickly be translated using the web site at:

http://translator.go.com

Spain

www.sidra.com/

❥ The official web site for Asturian cider.

❥ Includes full information on each and every cider maker in the region.

❥ Cider merchandise (baseball caps, lighters, t-shirts) available.

Canada

www.countycider.com/

❥ The web site of Ontario's County Cider Company.

❥ Products, links, cider recipes, etc.

France

www.pays-auge.cci.fr/html/liste-produits.md

❥ Part of the Pays d'Auge tourist information site.

❥ Lists producers of cider, poiré, pommeau, calvados and cheeses. Product range and prices given for each producer.

USA

www.ciderspace.com/

❥ Site under reconstruction at the time of writing.

Minchew's

TEL: 01452-538683
   or mobile O797-4034331
FAX: 01452-538682
E-MAIL: KevinorNikki
@minchewscyderandperry.
freeserve.co.uk

MINCHEW'S AWARD-WINNING REAL CYDER & PERRY

We produce the World's largest range of single variety cyders and perries. Hand-crafted from orchard to table, using dedicated varieties, without the use of chemicals, additives or artificial assistance.

Most of our cyders and all of our perries are of organic quality.

A Short History of American Cider

Bob Capshew gives us the low-down on apple cider and pear cider, from the early settlers to the modern revival.

Apples and cider have been a part of American history since the earliest settlers arrived in the New World. Apple tree seedlings were among the items the English colonists brought to Massachusetts shortly after the Pilgrims settled Plymouth in 1620. The first British governor of Massachusetts planted apple trees in an orchard near what is now Boston harbour. John Josseln remarked upon them in 1639 and again in 1671, when he noted that apple trees were "prospering abundantly" in New England.

From the trees brought to the New World, new varieties were selected from seedlings as early as the 1630s. William Blaston, a clergyman, moved from his farm on Beacon Hill in Boston to Rhode Island in 1635 and eventually produced the Sweet Rhode Island Greening, probably the first truly American apple variety.

Peter Stuyvesant, the last Dutch governor of Nieuw Amsterdam, boasted that he grafted the first truly American tree on his farm in what is now lower Manhattan in 1647. He used wild American rootstock, which were mainly small, extremely bitter crabapples. That historic tree, still bearing fruit, was knocked down by a derailed train in 1866.

The climate of the colonies, with hot summers and cold winters, seemed especially suited for apples. The widespread adaptability of apples as well as their ease of growth quickly made them the favourite fruit of the New World settlers.

The ability to grow fruit in New England was noted by Thomas Budd in 1685, "Orchards of Apples, Pears,

Quinces, Peaches, Aprecocks, Plums, Charies and other sorts of the usual Fruits of England may be soon raised to advantage, the Trees growing faster than in England, whereof great quantities of Sider may be made."

For the early American settlers, apples were eaten much as today: fresh or dried, cooked or baked into desserts, especially pies. According to tradition, students at Yale University (founded in 1701) were served apple pie at supper every evening for 100 years. It was cider, however, that gave apples such a prominent role in New World life.

Pre-prohibition US cider glasses. Photo: Maggie Oster.

Few colonists drank milk for fear of sickness. Tea and coffee were too expensive for the average person. Beer was a popular beverage, but it was locally produced cider, including pear cider ("perry") and peach cider ("peachy") that was the drink of choice.

No other drink had such simple requirements. No

malting or boiling was needed as in beer, no distillation as required in brandy or whisky. Simple equipment was required to make cider - a maul, a hollowed log with holes and a barrel. Cider was cheap (about 3 shillings a barrel) and plentiful. There are records as early as 1671 that one orchard alone grew enough apples to make 500 hogsheads of cider. A community of forty families in the 1720s made 3,000 barrels of cider.

The role of cider in everyday colonial life was underscored by Benjamin Franklin in Poor Richard's Almanac March 1736, "Never praise your Cyder, Horse, or Bedfellow."

Among the folklore of apples in American life, none is more prominent than that of Johnny Appleseed. John Chapman (born 1774), was an eccentric who helped spread apples trees westward to the new territories. For forty years he travelled through Ohio, Indiana, Illinois, and as far west as Iowa. He obtained seeds from apple cider mills, then gave them to settlers or planted them in what he considered likely spots.

Although the best apples are produced by grafting superior scions onto rootstock, most apples were spread by seed as the frontier became more and more populated. With so many seedling trees, a great many were selected as superior and became named varieties.

Politics

Cider played a noticeable role in American politics from its earliest days as well. George Washington, who later became the first American president, supplied the voters of Frederick Virginia with cider and other spirits despite a statute that prohibited treating voters with alcohol at elections.

In 1840, William Henry Harrison from the frontier state of Ohio, defeated Martin Van Buren for the presidency with a campaign based on the symbols of cider and the log cabin. A Baltimore, Maryland newspaper ridiculed Harrison by saying, "Give him a barrel of hard cider, and settle a pension of two thousand a year on him, and my word for it he will sit the remainder of his days in his log cabin..."

The public responded with sympathy for Harrison, a war hero fallen on hard times. It probably did not hurt that hard cider was freely distributed at Harrison rallies. Harrison also supposedly decreed that wine be outlawed from his table and cider served at mealtimes instead.

One of Harrison's campaign songs had the following verses:

Let Van from his cooler of silver drink wine
And lounge on his cushioned settee;
Our man on his buckeye bench can recline
Content with hard cider is he!

Decline

Several factors combined to bring a severe decline to American cider. The United States was primarily a rural country in 1790, with 96 percent of the population living on farms. By 1900, migration to the cities resulted in an urban population of 56 percent. City dwellers were less inclined to own apple trees or to continue the rural cider traditions.

One invention that had a profound effect on alcoholic beverages was the invention of the crown cap for bottles in 1892 by William Painter. The crown cap provided a standard for bottling that is still used today. Bottled beverages such as beer and carbonated soft drinks could now be effectively and economically sealed. The crown cap also led to more efficient mass production which gave urban beer factories an economic advantage over small-scale cider producers.

Prohibition

The excesses of nineteenth-century drinking drew the continuing ire of the temperance movement. Temperance groups broadened their campaigns until the total prohibition of alcohol sales became a political reality. By 1912 nine states had outlawed the sale of alcohol. Prohibition then became the national law in January 1919.

American Prohibition, which lasted until 1933, not only destroyed the cider and beer industries, but also resulted in a uniquely American cider term. In 1905, Trowbridge in his The Cider Makers' Hand Book, defined cider as "the vinous liquor produced by fermentation of the juice of apples." In the ensuing years, the term "sweet cider" became known as unfermented apple juice while "hard cider" means fermented apple juice. This oxymoron was probably devised by Prohibitionists to popularise the unfermented drink.

Revival

American apple growers have concentrated on sales of fresh apples and apple juice. The industry was challenged in 1996 by outbreaks of e-coli infection from windfall apples. Apple juice (sweet cider) producers are now required to pasteurise apple juice or put warning labels on their products due to public health reasons. Ironically, fermentation destroys e-coli contamination. Despite the shortage of true cider apples, a resurgence of American cider has recently occurred. Most of the new American cider makers are small-sized producers who seek quality rather than quantity much as the parallel movement in American craft beers. The cider industry has exploded from 271,000 gallons in 1990 to over 5 million gallons in 1996. Plantings of "antique" English, French and American cider trees have also been established. At last, the American cider industry has renewed hope for quality cider although the quantity will never rival the frontier days.

Left: Gast, Crofts & Co., Louisville, Kentucky (circa 1902-1919.) Right: Clarksville Cider Co., St.Louis, Missourii (circa 1867-1905). Photo: Maggie Oster.

Rough and Smooth

Mark Foot is the author of Cider's Story – Rough and Smooth. Here he describes how he wrote his excellent book, and introduces some of the characters he met along the way.

I have always contended that the best place to drink cider is next to the barrel. The taste, the smell and the company provide the perfect mix. From my childhood, there was something wonderfully timeless and reassuring about the cider barrel.

When I set out to write my book on the history of the drink and the long line of genuine characters that it produced over the generations, I was determined to spend time chatting to the cider-makers. I wanted above all the human story. Others could be safely left to catalogue more technical matters.

I make no excuse for being an incorrigible romantic. My forebears were all country people. I took my first tentative sips of cider under watchful, smiling eyes of my grandparents who came from deepest Somerset. I served a willing apprenticeship, drinking sensibly – not excessively – and always appreciatively. Research for my book was a joy. I didn't visit too many factories but strolled

Marcus Govier, Glastonbury. Photo: Mark Foot.

down dozens of winding lanes to isolated farmhouses. Small cider makers generously gave me their time, their personal memories and countless stories that they had plucked from rural folklore – and which had often been embroidered a little in the telling. But not in every case, I suspect. The gargantuan thirst of some cider drinkers, at times the farm labourers who toiled in the field at harvest time and were given cider in lieu of wages (a practice appallingly abused), was truly remarkable.

I stretched beyond the West Country, Herefordshire and East Anglia as I gathered my material. Kent had its own tradition, of course. And that reminds me of the late Bob Luck, a John Bull-like figure from the Weald.

As was the custom in that county, Bob added sugar to the cider and then left it three years to mature. The result, he used to claim, was that his 'apple juice' was the strongest in the country. He was selling it at £4.50 a gallon back in 1975. What was more, he used to say it was better than any fertility drug.

"There's a baby in every bottle," he'd joke. Yet maybe it wasn't entirely a joke. "On several occasions, young couples trying in vain to start a family, were known to click after knocking back some of Bob's potent stuff." And that wasn't all. His other good-natured boast was that he could get the sex of the child right, too. Explanation? "I don't know how it works. Perhaps it just makes people relax!"

Today there are still some marvellous characters around. In Somerset, I think at once of Harold and Frank Naish, bachelor brothers from West Pennard, and Marcus Govier, from Glastonbury...the list is limitless. Or if you want excellent cider, strong and wise opinions and a jolly history lesson on the drink and farming in general, what about Roger Wilkins, from near Wedmore?

For most of this century, the cider market has been dominated by firms like Bulmers, Coates, Whiteways, Gaymers, Taunton Cider and Henleys. Many have been bought out or merged with others in a rational commercial bid to kill off the competition. Bulmers and Matthew Clark these days overshadow the market.

Well known firms such as Westons, Thatchers and Merrydown are a long way behind in terms of production size. Then come the smaller makers, in some cases doing it as a hobby to satisfy their own thirst or that of a few friends.

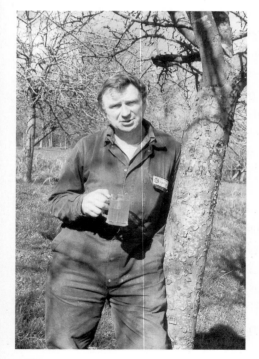

Roger Wilkins.
Photo: Mark Foot.

Have you noticed in recent years that a number of vineyards have followed the Merrydown example of producing not only wine but cider? This falls neatly into the seasonal nature of production. These vineyards tend to be in the lower regions – Biddenden in Kent, Somerset, Devon and the Isle of Wight.

Cider drinking is all part of a fiercely competitive drinks market. Some makers, like Sheppys and Perrys have deftly taken advantage of the West Country tourist trade. Even back in the 50s, Creedy Valley, of Crediton, Devon claimed they were the first to supply stoneware jars for the tourist market.

Julian Temperley, of Kingsbury Episcopi, Somerset, an intrepid individualist and passionate champion for cider, has looked for markets as diverse as the Glastonbury Festival and top London stores. He has also promoted his cider brandy. Like others, among them James Lane, Alex Hill and Nigel Stewart, he produces bottle fermented cider. They are proud of it, even though the tax imposed for this is crippling.

There has been a genuine crusade by Temperley, Barry Top, Kevin Minchew and others to promote quality natural ciders. The fact that the word 'traditional' appears to be used at will these days makes the task of the authentic producers all the harder.

It's a tough old fight, made no easier by the wayward image that has been needlessly attached to our beloved cider. One reason I wrote my book was to make a modest attempt to put on record some of the cherished names, customs and exploits before they were lost for ever.

Names like West Country farmers Dunkerton, Staples, Wear, Adams and the incredible Burnett Champeney...Lovely stories like that of Compton Dundon man Bob Burt who made the request that his funeral cortege should stop at his local on the way to church. As his son said: "He told us when it was time to bury him, his friends should stop for a drop of cider, because he wouldn't be with them on the way back."

Cider's Story – Rough and Smooth (forward by Acker Bilk) is available from Mark Foot, 8 Kingston Drive, Nailsea, North Somerset, BS48 4RB, at £9.99 plus £1.00 postage.

Cider Bars at Beer Festivals

APPLE committee man Mick Lewis introduces some of the best places to drink real cider and perry.

OK, so what's so different about cider bars? After all, they're just another bit of a beer festival. But are they? I think not.

You can almost guarantee that anyone who's not quite normal coming into a beer festival will head straight for the cider bar, and I'm including the staff here as well. There's just something about the drink that attracts a different type of person.

They don't just arrive at the bar, ask for a drink and go again. They want to know about the ciders, how they're made, what varieties of apple are used, which village the producer is in, but basically, they want to chat. By comparison, the beer bars are just serving hatches. At the cider bar, it is far less formal, and more akin to a pub bar.

The Cider & Perry Bar, Great British Beer Festival, Olympia, August 1999. Photo: Dave Matthews.

Part of this deliberate chatting to the customers is, of course, primarily designed to encourage them to come back. This is vital for drinkers who have never tasted real cider before, and to this end, we have a policy of giving tasters to the customers so we find something that they like.

Another strange thing is the number of animals that manifest themselves behind the cider bar. Fox glove puppets seem to be the most popular, but others such as pigs and racoons have also appeared. And that leads us on to the bar decoration.

For many years at the Great British Beer Festival, the bar would be covered with foliage and a snail placed somewhere in it. The first customer each session to spot the snail would get a free pint. This worked very well until one year when the snail deliberately hid for a week and only sprang to life on the last day. There was also one year in August when the festival was held in Brighton, during one of the hottest weeks of the year, when the bar was done up in Christmas decorations, complete with two trees. Don't ask me why, it just was. But don't think that it's all hard work - it isn't, but there is one gruelling ritual which takes place every year at the Great British Beer Festival. All the cider and perries are graded 1-12, from dry to sweet. So the day before we open, all 50 have to be tasted. It's such an arduous task that we have to go round the hall with a shotgun to force staff to participate. It's probably a reflection on the cider bar staff that not only can they survive this torture, but have recovered enough to work there for the rest of the week. We sure are a dedicated bunch.

As with beer, there are now a small number of cider tickers doing the rounds, with their little books, writing down everything that they drink. The most bizarre that I've come across was a woman who wanted a four-pint carry-out. She pointed to four different ciders and explained that she wanted a pint of each in the one container. Having asked her for an explanation, she informed me that they were the four ciders that she hadn't tried! When she turned up several months later at another festival, she refused to be

"The most bizarre that I've come across was a woman who wanted a four-pint carry-out. She pointed to four different ciders and explained that she wanted a pint of each in the one container."

served by me on the grounds that the last time I'd laughed at her. Me? Never.

And then there was the year of the "foodies" at the Great British Beer Festival. This couple drank every cider we had, whilst making copious notes on what food would best go with each one. Now I'm into food as much as anyone, but...! When asked if they'd tried the perries, they looked horrified, said that they would never mix the two, and would be back the next day for perry. They never did come back. Probably too busy deciding whether organic or ordinary celeriac could be better with a Lyne Down Kingston Black.

So you see what I mean. We've had cider barrel dancing, women stripping on top of the bar counter to make sure they get served first, umpteen outbreaks of "Have you got anything that tastes less of apples" (funny thing, these real ciders, made with real apples, you know), thousands of stories of "When I was in the Army/Air Force/Afghan Freedom Fighters stationed in Devon/Somerset/Kew Gardens I used to drink 27 pints for breakfast, and then I used to fall over", and many other strange goings-on that couldn't possibly be mentioned in a family publication. But the strangest of all was the customer who came up to the cider bar and said, "Can I have a pint of cider, mainly to take away?" I rest my case.

Pacific North West Cider

Alcoholic cider, known to Americans as "hard cider", was once a common drink in North America.

But today it occupies a tiny portion of the market. For most Americans, "cider" is the sweet fresh apple juice sold in gallon jugs at roadside stands and served at children's parties.

A handful of American cidermakers are trying to change that image. In the Pacific Northwest, as in New York State, in California, and in other locations, a growing number of local and regional brands are available in pubs, restaurants, grocery stores and bottle shops. Unfortunately, many of the most widely-distributed ciders are also among the least interesting. Because the larger cider producers are trying to sell their products into the American beer and wine

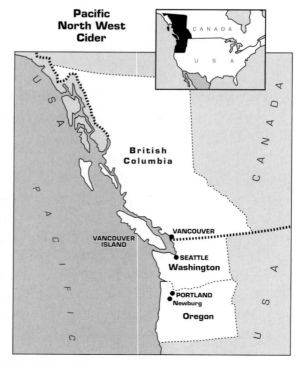

cooler markets, they want a product that remains consistent from one year to the next. To accomplish this, these producers make their cider from concentrated juice rather than fresh fruit.

The biggest regional cider producers in the Northwest, including Spire Mountain and Spanish Peaks in Washington, and Grower's in British Columbia, all offer both apple and pear ciders (the term "perry" is entirely unknown here). Their ciders contain blends of sweet table fruit, such as Red Delicious, Granny Smith, and Macintosh apples, and Bartlett pears that lack the complexity (and the tannin) of traditional English and French cider varieties. All of these brands are relatively easy to find - they're in many Washington and Oregon supermarkets and B.C. Provincial liquor stores. On both sides of the border, you can expect to find at least one brand of cider in most pubs, taverns and restaurants that offer microbrewery beers.

Spanish Peaks is one of the big brands which is widely available in supermarkets and pubs in the American Northwest.

Fortunately, there are a few islands of quality in this sea of bland cider. Several smaller cider makers in the Pacific Northwest offer other, more interesting products. In the states of Oregon and Washington, and in the nearby Canadian province of British Columbia, a handful of orchards are growing traditional cider apples. Some of these growers make their own cider, while others sell their fruit to independent commercial and hobby cidermakers. In Mount Vernon, north of Seattle, Washington State

University's Skagit Valley Research Station has been working for more than a decade toward identifying the best cider apple varieties for the local growing conditions. The produce from the WSU experimental cider orchards, and the periodic "cider seminars" sponsored by the Research Station have played an important role in the development of an emerging regional cider style and the growth of a cider enthusiasts' community in the Northwest.

Irvine's Vintage Cider is made by Ron Irvine on Vashon Island near Seattle, and available in two places at Seattle's Pike Place Market: in bottles at the Pike and Western Wine Company, and by the glass at the nearby restaurant Matt's in the Market (upstairs in the Corner Market Building). The fruit that goes into Irvine's Ciders come from several orchards in western Washington. As the name implies, Irvine's Vintage Ciders are supplied in vintage-dated 750ml wine bottles. Each year's production may include several different "varietal" ciders made from a single apple variety, most recently Kingston Blacks and Cox's Orange Pippins.

The Merridale Cider Works is British Columbia's only "estate cidery". Located in the Cowichan Valley town of Cobble Hill on Vancouver Island, Merridale is owned and operated by Al Piggott, whose orchard contains

Below: Ron Irvine's eponymous vintages from Seattle.

Merridale Cider, from Canada, uses a wide variety of apples.

a huge assortment of English, French and German cider apples. Along with his Merridale Cider, which has been rated the "best English-style cider in Canada", he also makes Merridale Farmhouse Scrumpy, a traditional Somerset-style rough cider, and a dry, Normandy-style cider. The Scrumpy and Normandy cider are generally available only at the cidery; the flagship Merridale Cider is also sold in a handful of restaurants, pubs and large liquor stores in Vancouver and Victoria, including the Railway Club (579 Dunsmuir Street) and The Fish House (8901 Stanley Park Drive) in Vancouver, and Spinnakers Brewpub (308 Catherine Street) in Victoria.

Alan Foster's White Oak Cider also resembles a typical English farm-house cider. Foster's orchard near Newberg, in the heart of the Oregon wine country, contains more than 80 varieties of English and French cider apples, and about 60 heirloom dessert apples. White Oak offers several vintage-dated, aged-in-oak ciders, including a blend of apple types, and a vari-etal Kingston Black cider. White Oak Cider is available at Matt's in the Market in Seattle, and several places in Portland, including

Above: Merridale Normandy-style.

Below: The Kingston Black apple made the journey from old to new world cider.

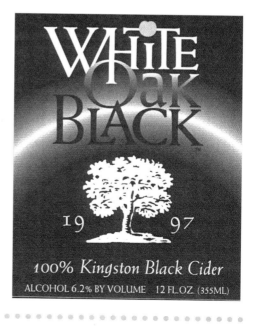

Belmont Station (4250 S.E. Belmont Street), the Burlingame Grocery (8502 S.W. Terwilliger Blvd.), Elephants Delicatessen (13 N.W. 23rd Place), and Higgins Restaurant & Bar (1239 S.W. Broadway).

In addition to the dedicated cider producers, several Oregon and Washington microbreweries have added hard ciders to their lines of handcrafted beers. Some of these ciders are sold only at the brewpub, while others have some limited retail distribution. Almost all of these ciders are made from dessert fruit (most often from concentrate) rather than traditional cider varieties. For example, Portland's Widmer Brothers offers Wildwood Hard Apple Cider on draft and in bottles. Wildwood is made from a blend of local apples, with a German-style altbier yeast. Like other Widmer products, Wildwood Cider is distributed throughout the western United States, and in New York, New Jersey, and Washington, D.C.

The McMenamin brothers operate an ever-growing chain of brewpubs and restaurants in both Oregon and Washington that offer a hard cider made from concentrate at their Edgefield Winery, located in Troutdale, Oregon, south of Portland. The Edgefield property also includes a small pear orchard; they plan to introduce a pear cider within the next couple of years.

Cider is still a novelty in most of North America, but it's out there for those who search for it.

John Ross is a freelance writer and home cidermaker based in Seattle.

American Northwest Cider Contacts

Spire Mountain Draft Ciders

Silver Lake Winery

17721 132nd Avenue NE

Woodinville, Washington 98072

+1 425 486 1900

www.washingtonwine.com/catalog/ciders.

Spanish Peaks Apple Cider

Spanish Peaks Brewing Company

120 N. 19th Avenue

P.O. Box 3644

Bozeman, Montana 59772

+1 800 790 CHUG

www.spanishpeaks.com/cider.html

Irvine's Vintage Cider

P.O. Box 833

Vashon, Washington 98070

+1 206 463 5538

Note: Ron is moving the winery/cider mill this spring - please check with John Ross for a newer address before publication.

Merridale Cider Works

1230 Merridale Road

RR3 Cobble Hill, British

Columbia VOR 1LO

+1 250 743 4293

White Oak Cider

18450 N.E. Ribbon Ridge Road

Newberg, Oregon 97132

+1 503 538 0349

www.crockettdesign.com/whiteoakcider

Wildwood Hard Apple Cider

Widmer Brothers Brewing Company

929 North Russell

Portland, Oregon 97227

+1 503 281 BIER

www.widmer.com/biers/wildwood.htm

Edgefield Hard Cider

McMenamins Edgefield Winery

2126 SW Halsey Street

Troutdale, Oregon 97060

+1 503 669 8610

Washington State University Mount Vernon Research and Extension Unit

1468 Memorial Highway (mail: 16650 State Route 536)

Mount Vernon, Wash. 98273

+1 360 848 6131

Brothers in Cider Making

*Steve Bradley
of Heron Valley
Cider muses on
the lot of small
cider makers in
Devon.*

Some time ago I was at Chris Coles' Green Valley Cider Shop in Exeter, enjoying a glass of Rum Tiddly Tum and musing on a fine piece of furniture I had seen and admired earlier in the day. This was a handsome refectory table, beautifully made from hand-crafted oak, and large enough to sit a good number of friends around for a convivial supper. The table carried a small plaque, discreetly attached to one end, which bore the legend Cap of Liberty.

In case you are wondering what is the connection, let me tell you that Cap of Liberty is the name of one of the large oak vats (many cider makers used to use them and they ranged in capacity from 1,000 gallons to as much as 25,000 gallons) sold off from Inch's Cider premises in North Devon in 1998.

The giant company which bought Inch's moved the entire operation, which was the last remaining of its size in the county, up country to merge with its existing enterprise, which initially seemed a great shame, or was it?

What remains in Devon today – if you judge professional cider makers by the yardstick of production of more than 1,500 gallons; that is the amount which obliges you to register with, and invite the keen attention of, the Customs and Excise authorities – are just eleven stout souls who run their smallish operations with great dedication and enthusiasm, and who succeed in making a decent drink out of our local apples. Cap of Liberty was just one of the huge oaken vats bought by furniture makers and transformed by them into works of art of a different kind. There were just not enough cidermakers left in the area to find a use for these vats, and large commercial cidermakers tend to favour stainless steel and fibreglass in which to concoct their drinks. Among the band of eleven brothers (cidermakers tend to be male I'm afraid) are Chris Coles, aforementioned; the writer of this article; and David Bridgeman of the Winkleigh Cider Company, who, in partnership with his wife Jackie (oh! there are lady cidermakers after all), his brother Graham and his wife Margaret, are making cider at the very premises once owned by Inch's and closed down by Bulmers when the operation they bought was moved to Hereford a few years ago.

David Bridgeman worked at Inch's for 30 years and he and his partner's love of cider has kept Winkleigh associated with the trade and has ensured the replacement of a large factory type cidery with a small 'hand made' marque. Thus the Bridgemans have strong links with all of us who are in their own way trying to produce a top quality product which refuses to give up its strong historical roots. The merging of large national companies has left a vacuum which is being filled to some extent by a group of thriving, smaller, 'real' cidermakers who are catering for an expanding discerning public.

In South Devon, we are blessed with a busy tourist trade and an abundance of country pubs whose licensees actively encourage locally made produce – and they know there is an increasing market for it. This niche area leads to a kind of cross fertilisation of tastes which enables the interested customer to order a glass of local cider, or beer, to wash down his oysters from the River Avon, Exe and Teign, or his Devon Blue Cheese or Sharpham Brie (the latter company also makes one of the very best English wines on the market).

So, far from being the tragedy for local cider that the closure of Inch's threatened to be, it has provided space for the starting up and growth of several family run businesses, my own included.

Working in conjunction with other quality food producers in the area, we are actually stimulating an increasing desire for tasty local products from an area where we can still find the time to seek out treats not normally available at the supermarket. Many of us ferment our cider naturally, which is to say that the yeasts present on the outside of the apples eat the sugars within, giving the by-product (and what a by-product!) alcohol.

Obviously it would be impossible to maintain the individuality of this organic process if thousands upon thousands of gallons were made at one time. Thus we have the advantage of offering you a rich and differing experience every time you try individual Devon ciders where every barrel sampled can be deliciously different.

There are further spin-offs from this exciting interest in local food and drink products. In our area we have Orchard Link, a body which seeks to promote and maintain local apple orchards by acting as a non profit making broker, putting owners of small orchards, or even a few garden trees, in touch with cidermakers and jam and chutney producers.

Finally as for Rum Tiddly Tum. Barrels used in the traditional cider industry normally follow a progression from Sherry or Port cask to Highland Whisky or Rum barrels before finding their way via the second-hand market to us cidermakers. If you put made cider into recently bought rum casks (whisky doesn't seem to work well, though port is a fine thing) you produce a deliciously mellow, alcoholic, aromatic and intoxicating brew which is a true assault on the taste buds – Rum Tiddly Tum; and you'll have to wait a long time before you find a bottle of that on your local supermarket shelf!

Orchard Link

Contact: Trudy Turrell, South Hampshire District Council. Tel: 01803 861234.

Third Barrel in from the Road

John Perry, of Perry's Farmhouse Cider, on Somerset Cider

We come up from Somerset where the cider apples grow. Ask anybody in the United Kingdom where cider comes from and they will say Somerset.

The tradition of cider making in the county of Somerset stretches back to Norman times. The climate and soil combine to provide ideal growing conditions for the apple tree. There are over 158 varieties of apple trees which are thought to come from Somerset. These include varieties which are still being planted in modern orchards and include Dabinett, Chisel Jersey, Somerset Redstreak, Yarlington Mill, Tremletts Bitter and the famous Kingston Black. Sadly, Slack Me Girdle, Tom Putt, Fill Barrel and many other old varieties are no longer common.

With cider no longer being needed to sustain the farm workforce, there has been a steady decline in the number of orchards. In 1894 there were 24,000 acres of orchards in Somerset but in 1973 there were only 2,500 acres. The traditional cider apple tree is sadly no longer part of the countryside scene but there have been considerable plantings of the more productive bush orchards in recent years. Whereas cider was made on nearly every farm up until just over 40 years ago, there are only a few farms now keeping the tradition alive. Cider was once part of the farm worker's wage and it was common practice for them to drink up to 12 pints a day to see them through their labours.

The smaller producers continue to thrive despite high duty costs, the decline in draught pub cider sales and competition from cheap smuggled foreign beers. They continue to make first class draught traditional ciders and some have also introduced interesting new single variety ciders. Some, such as Perry's, have found new markets by opening up their Cider Mills (with its added rural life museum) to both the local and tourist trade. The large commercial cider makers have come and gone. Taunton Cider grew big, was taken over, and no longer exists. Coates and Showerings have also come and gone and now we have the anonymous Matthew Clark, owned by a multinational, to represent our county. Thatchers however continue to thrive. Good luck to them.

Cider as a way of life is fast disappearing but the tradition lives on at Eli's famous Cider House at Huish Episcopi, where until recently the regulars used to serve themselves. Roger Wilkins` cider farm is another which should not be missed. Enjoy them while you can.

There is nothing like good Somerset cider. It has a character all of its own and should be enjoyed by all. What better epitaph can you have than from one of its yeoman farmers from the little village of Dowlish Wake. When Harold was on his deathbed he asked the doctor if he could have one last drink. The doctor said yes and Harold sent his son to the cider cellar to draw a glass from the third barrel in from the road – his very best barrel! When he drank the glass he smiled peacefully and passed away.

BEDFORDSHIRE

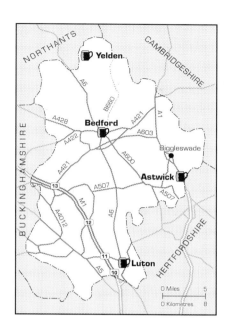

Bedfordshire Outlets

ASTWICK

Tudor Oaks

1 Taylors Road

☎ 01462 834133

11-11; 12-4, 7-10.30 Sun

⏺**Westons Country Perry, First Quality; Richs Farmhouse; Wilkins Medium**

Tudor pub and restaurant with lots of open fires, beams and up to 7

varying real ales. Westons Perry is always available, and 1 or 2 of the ciders are always on. Separate restaurant open at weekends, serving freshly prepared food. Has 13 letting rooms available.

⏺ ▶

BEDFORD

Wellington Arms

40-42 Wellington Street

☎ 01234 308033

12-11; 12-10.30 Sun

⏺**Addlestones**

Former Charles Wells pub now refurbished and leased by the B&T brewery. Sells up to 8 cask ales, both the B&T range and beers from other breweries (including micros). At the time of writing there are plans to offer full meals as soon as work on the kitchen is completed.

LUTON

Wheelwrights Arms

34 Guildford Street

☎ 01582 759321

10.30-11; 12-10.30 Sun

⌂Bulmers Traditional

Grade II listed building built around 1840. A friendly locals pub in the centre of town, and a good choice for Bed & Breakfast.

YIELDEN

Chequers

High Street

☎ 01933 356383

12-2.30 (Not Mon), 5.30-11; 12-11 Sat; 12-10.30 Sun

⌂Addlestones

Village pub with family/skittles room and restaurant. Large garden and good value food (food available Wednesday to Sunday). Yielden is on the Three Shires Way walkers route.

BERKSHIRE

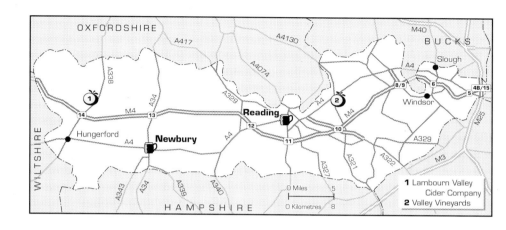

Berkshire Producers

LAMBOURN VALLEY CIDER COMPANY

The Malt House, Great Shefford, Hungerford, Berkshire, RG17 7ED.

☎ 01488 648441

Email
LVC@WESTBERKS.DEMON.CO.UK

Web site
WWW.WESTBERKS.DEMON.CO.U
K/LVCIDER/

THE LAMBOURN VALLEY CIDER COMPANY

The Malt House
Great Shefford
Hungerford RG17 7ED
Tel: 01488 648441

ROYAL COUNTY

Natural Berkshire Cider
Produced in 1998 from local apples
6·5 - 7% ABV

Roy Bailey is one of Britain's most talented cider writers, and running his very own cider company allows him to practice what he preaches. Roy formed Lambourn Valley Cider in 1995 to produce real Berkshire cider from local apples. Apples of all types are used – cookers, eaters, crab apples and even some cider apples from the grounds of Douai Abbey. All of his perry comes from the fruit of one huge old perry pear tree – almost certainly an Oldfield – growing happily in a Berkshire paddock.

All of Roy's ciders and perries are natural, unfiltered and completely organic. His web page – packed with items of use and interest – is well worth a look, and contains details of Roy's keeving experiments – a method of producing a naturally sweet cider without adding sugar.

Ciders

Royal County Cider, 6.5-7% abv.
Kings Ransom Cider, 6-6.5% abv.
Old Berkshire Perry, 5.5-6% abv.
(All available in 1 gallon polycontainers, $4^1/_2$ gallon polypins and 5 gallon polybarrels.)

(Due to fruit availability, Kings Ransom and Old Berkshire Perry are produced on alternate years, ie KR 1999, OBP 2000, etc)

Annual Production

900+ gallons.

Outlets

• The Swan, Lower Inkpen, Hungerford, Bucks.

• The Royal Oak, Newbury Street, Wantage, Oxon.

• The Bucks Goat Centre, Old Riseborough Road, Stoke Mandeville, Bucks.

• The Chiltern Brewery, Nash Lee Road, Terrick, Aylesbury, Bucks.

• Wholesaler: Jon Hallam (0117 966 0221).

Awards

Kings Ransom: Cider of the Festival, Milton Keynes & N.Bucks CAMRA, July 1998.

Royal County: Cider of the Festival, Milton Keynes & N.Bucks CAMRA, July 1999.

VALLEY VINEYARDS

Stanlake Park, Twyford, Reading,
RG10 OBN

☎ 0118 9340176

Email vvineyards@aol.com

As the company's name suggests, wine is the most prominent product at Stanlake Park. However, the wine-making equipment is put to good use to convert their apple crop into a filtered cider.

Cider

Percy's Old Garden Cider, 7% abv (750ml glass bottles)

Annual Production

1500 litres

Visitors

Welcome

Directions

The vineyard is on the B3018, 3/4 of a mile south of Twyford.

Sales

The vineyard shop is open 10-5, 11-5 Sat, 12-5 Sun.

Photographs

'The Guv'nor!', Lambourn Valley's Roy Bailey.

Photo: Roy Bailey

Lambourn Valley Cider Partners Roy and Alice Bailey being presented with their prize-winning certificate in August 1998.

Photo: Roy Bailey

Berkshire Outlets

NEWBURY

Hogshead

1-3 Wharf Street

☎ 01635 569895

12-11; 12-10.30 Sun

⏚**Biddenden; Westons Old Rosie**

Large converted auction rooms next to the Kennet & Avon canal. Vast range of real ales. Over 21s only.

Monument

57 Northbrook Street

☎ 01635 41964

11-11; 12-10.30 Sun

⏚**Westons Old Rosie**

A Tap & Spile town centre boozer, named after Newbury's 17th Century subscription to help the homeless after the Great Fire of London.

READING

Hobgoblin

2 Broad Street

☎ 0118 950 8119

11-11; 12-10.30 Sun

⏚**Bulmers Inch's Stonehouse**

Friendly, no-frills local pub in the centre of Reading, with the emphasis firmly on excellent beer. Very popular with CAMRA members.

Hogshead

76-78 Kings Road

☎ 0118 950 8119

11-11; 12-10.30 Sun

⏚**Bulmers Inch's Stonehouse**

A fairly typical member of the Hogshead chain. Built on two levels and overlooking the River Kennet.

Hope Tap

99-101 Friar Street

☎ 0118 958 2266

10-11; 12-10.30 Sun

⏚**Addlestones**

A town centre Wetherspoons pub that attracts a mixed clientele. Allegedly built on the site of a long-since deceased brewery.

BUCKINGHAMSHIRE

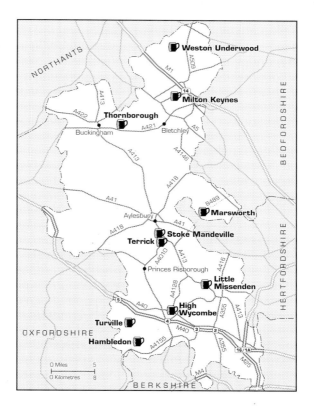

Buckinghamshire Outlets

HAMBLEDEN

Stag & Huntsman

1 mile N of A4155

☎ 01491 571227

11-2.30 (3 Sat), 6-11; 11-3, 7-10.30 Sun

⌂Thatchers

Three-bar pub in a National Trust village. The emphasis is on food and the beer is also excellent.

◖ ◗

HIGH WYCOMBE

Hogshead

120 Oxford Road

☎ 01494 528335

12-11; 12-10.30 Sun

⌂Westons Old Rosie

Huge open-plan bar on two stories, catering for a mainly young clientele.

Wycombe Wines

20 Crendon Street

☎ 01494 437228

10-10; 12-2, 7-10 Sun

⌀**Westons Old Rosie, bottled range**

Popular off-licence near the station offering several beers and a cider on draught (gravity dispense).

LITTLE MISSENDEN

Crown

Off A413

☎ 01494 862571

11-2.30, 6-11

⌀**Cider varies (summer only)**

A traditional pub with no juke-box, TV or fruit machine. Just lots of lively conversation and good things to drink.

◖

MARSWORTH

Red Lion

90 Vicarage Road

☎ 01296 668366

11-3, 6-11; 12-3, 7-10.30 Sun

⌀**Westons Bounds Brand**

Three-bar 17th century village pub

on the Grand Union Canal, not far from Bridge 130.

MILTON KEYNES

Wetherspoons

201 Midsummer Boulevard, Central Milton Keynes

☎ 01908 606074

11-11; 12-10.30 Sun

⌀**Addlestones**

About 5 minutes walk from Milton Keynes bus & railway station, this pub, at the time of writing, is the only purpose-built member of the Wetherspoon chain.

STOKE MANDEVILLE

Bucks Goat Centre

Layby Farm

☎ 01296 612983

10-5 Tues-Sun & Bank Holiday Mondays

⌀**Lambourne Valley**

Farm shop at a centre for rare breeds of goat. The shop sells various types of country produce, including the cider by gravity dispense.

TERRICK

Chiltern Brewery

Nash Lee Road

☎ 01296 613647

9-5 Mon-Sat; closed Sun

⌒**Westons Old Rosie**

Off-licence in a micro-brewery, selling Old Rosie from a 22 litre barrel on the counter, and in flagons and bottles. There's a large selection of bottles stocked, and of course their own beers are available on draught. Brewery tours are held most Saturdays at noon, and there's a small museum to see too.

THORNBOROUGH

Lone Tree

Bletchley Road

☎ 01280 812334

11.30-3, 6-11; 12-3, 6.30-10.30 Sun

⌒**Westons Traditional Scrumpy (can vary)**

Food-oriented roadside 17th Century inn, with an inglenook fireplace and exposed brickwork walls. The interesting beer range is changed on a regular basis. Worth a visit.

◖ ▶

TURVILLE

Bull & Butcher

OS 768911

☎ 01491 638283

11-3, 6(6.30 Sat)-11; 12-3, 7-10.30 Sun

⌒**Westons Bounds Brand**

First licensed in 1617, this pub is set in attractive countryside near the Chitty Chitty Bang Bang windmill. No food Mondays.

◖ ▶

WESTON UNDERWOOD

Cowpers Oak

High Street

☎ 01234 711382

12-3, 5.30-11; 12-3, 6.30-10.30 Sun (open all afternoon during the summer)

⌒**Thatchers Dry (can vary)**

An old village local. William Cowper spent some time in the area and his connections may go further than the pub's name. Northampton Skittles and Bar Billiards are played in one of the two bars. The large garden and paddocks house a mini farm. No food Sundays or Mondays.

 ◖ ▶

CAMBRIDGESHIRE

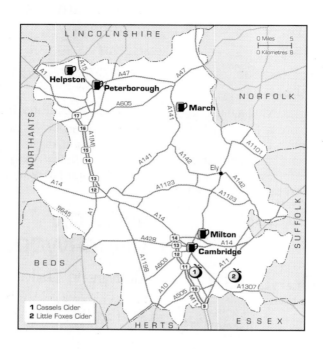

Cambridgeshire Producers

CASSELS CIDER

72 High Street, Great Shelford, Cambridge, CB2 5EH.
☎ 01223 842373

Jim and Lucy Cassels founded Cassels Cider in 1995. Jim is originally from "Devon farming stock!" and has planted a small orchard of West Country cider apples, which he blends with local Cambridgeshire apples to produce his prize-winning dry cider. Jim now has a legion of local admirers who follow his maxim: "Forget your hassles – have a Cassels!"

Cider

Cassels Natural Dry, 7% abv (25 litre poly barrels or 15 litre manu-cubes)

Annual Production

1500 gallons

Visitors

Welcome

Sales

Farm gate sales (all reasonable hours, please phone ahead)

Outlets

• Cambridge Blue, Gwydir Street, Cambridge

• Waggon & Horses, Milton, Cambridge

• Live & Let Live, Mawson Road, Cambridge

• Empress, Thoday Street, Cambridge

• Wrestlers, Newmarket Road, Cambridge

• Jug & Firkin, Mill Rd, Cambridge

• Queen's Head, Newton, Cambridge

• Bushel & Strike, Mill Street, Ashwell

• Pig & Abbot, High Street, Abington Pigotts

Awards

'Cider of the Festival' at many beer festivals around the country.

LITTLE FOXES CIDER

Little Foxes, Fox Road, Balsham, Cambridge, CB1 6EZ.

☎ 01223 894502

Email 106377.607@com-puserve.com

Mike West produces his unfiltered cider from a blend of cider apples and locally grown culinary fruit, and ferments and stores it in oak casks. He uses no additives, and has planted a small orchard of cider apples and perry pears for the future.

Cider

Tom, 5% abv

Dick, 5.5% abv

Harry, 6.5% abv

(Customers should provide their own containers, to be filled straight from the barrel)

Annual Production

250 gallons

Visitors

Please ring first.

Sales

Farm gate sales, please ring for availability. Also on sale: honey.

Cambridgeshire Outlets

CAMBRIDGE

Empress
72 Thoday Street
☎ 01223 247236

11-2.30, 6.30-11; 12-2.30, 7-10.30 Sun

⌁**Cassels Shelford; Crones Organic**
Thriving back-street pub.

Live and Let Live
40 Mawson Road
☎ 01223 460261

11.30-2.30, 5.30-11; 12-2.30, 7-10.30 Sun

⌁**Cassels Shelford**
Friendly back-street pub.
◖ ◗

HELPSTON

Blue Bell
10 Woodgate
☎ 01733 252394

11-12(3 Sat), 5(6 Sat)-11; 12-3, 7-10.30 Sun

⌁**Bulmers Traditional**
Stone-built village pub dating from the 17th Century with a traditional public bar and a quiet, comfortable lounge. The inn sign has a blue bell on one side and a bluebell flower on the other. No food other than Sunday lunches.

MARCH

Rose & Crown
41 St Peters Road
☎ 01354 652879

12-2.30(3 Sat), 7-11; 12-3, 7-10.30 Sun; closed Wed lunch

⌁**Thatchers or Rich's (can vary)**
150 year-old traditional pub with two rooms, one of which is non-smoking. Six cask ales offered at any one time, 825 different ales stocked to date. Food limited to bar snacks, Thursday to Saturday.
◖ ◗

MILTON

Waggon & Horses
39 High Street
☎ 01223 860313

12-2.30(4 Sat), 5(6 Sat)-11; 12-3, 7-10.30 Sun

⌁**Cassels**
1930s Mock Tudor village local. Extensive hat collection, large child-friendly garden.
◖ ◗

PETERBOROUGH

College Arms
40 Broadway

☎ 01733 319745

11-11; 12-10.30 Sun

🍎**Addlestones**

Large Wetherspoons pub housed in a modern building of some character. On the site of a former technical college.

◖ ▶

Hand and Heart

12 Highbury Street

☎ 01733 707040

11-11; 12-10.30 Sun

🍎**Cider varies**

Vibrant back-street 1930s local, winner of many awards from the local CAMRA branch. Has a front public bar (with WWII memorial), a back lounge/snug (with hatch service) and a stand up drinking area in the passage. Sometimes two or three ciders on at the same time; generally offers seven cask ales that include a mild. Has a beer and cider festival in May.

Palmerston Arms

82 Oundle Road

☎ 01733 565865

12-11; 12-10.30 Sun

🍎**Cider varies**

This two bar music-free pub is an oasis of good drinking and conversation, with a widely drawn clientele. The summer sees a second cider on offer and even the occasional perry. 12 Real Ales on at any one time, including at least one mild. Many awards from the local CAMRA branch.

Cambridgeshire Other Places of Cider Interest

CAMRA's Peterborough Beer Festival

Held in three massive marquees beside the river, this is one of Britain's largest beer and cider festivals. In 1999, 37932 visitors drank 1060 gallons of cider, roughly two-thirds of which had been sourced from the West Country. At the time of writing, the year 2000 event has just topped these impressive 1999 figures, and between the 22nd and 27th of August 39242 visitors drank 1110 gallons of cider and perry. One of the best places to try a range of ciders and perries in the east of England.

For up-to-date information, see the web site at: www.real-ale.org.uk

CHESHIRE

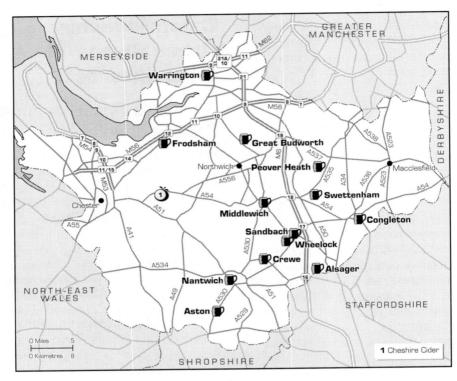

Cheshire Producers

CHESHIRE CIDER

Michael Dykes, Eddisbury Fruit Farm, Yeld Lane, Kelsall, Cheshire, CW6 0TE.

☎ 01829 751255

Email eddisbury@hotmail.com

Web site www.eddisbury.co.uk

Cheshire Cider was founded in 1996, the fruit farm's Diamond Jubilee year, and today produces five or more different ciders.

Cheshire Cider

Grown, Pressed & Bottled at Haworth's of Eddisbury Fruit Farm, Yeld Lane, Kelsall, Cheshire, CW6 0TE.
Tel: 01829 751255

Best before: See base or cap.

Ciders

Unfiltered: Crispin 6.7% abv, Discovery 6.9% abv, Sandy 4.3% abv.

Filtered: Dry 7.4% abv, Medium 7% abv, Sweet 6.3% abv.

(All available in 75cl, 1 litre, 2.5 litre, 1 gallon and 5 gallon containers)

Annual Production

1500 gallons

Visitors

Welcome. During the pressing season (September to November), tours are available Thursdays to Mondays, 10am to 4pm.

Directions

Enter Kelsall village, at the 'House at Top' pub turn into Yeld Lane. Eddisbury Fruit Farm is one mile down the lane on the right.

Sales

Fruit farm shop, 10am to 4pm, 7 days a week.

Other items on sale: Apple juice, apples, pears, fruit.

Outlets

• Tatton Park, at Knutsford.
• Helterskelter at Frodsham (occasional)
• Bhurtpore Inn, Aston, nr Nantwich.
• Wholesaler: Merrylegs (0161 432 6126)

Awards

'Cider of the Festival' at Stockport 1996, Frodsham 1998, 1999 & 2000.

GOOD PUB FOOD
5TH EDITION

by Susan Nowak
380 pages   Price: £9.99

The pubs in the pages of this CAMRA guide serve food as original and exciting as anything available in far more expensive restaurants. And, as well as the exotic and unusual, you will find landlords and landladies serving simple, nourishing pub fare such as a genuine ploughman's lunch or a steak and kidney pudding.

Award-winning food and beer writer Susan Nowak, who has travelled the country to complete this fifth edition of the guide, says that 'eating out' started in British inns and taverns and this guide is a contribution to an appreciation of all that is best in British food...and real cask conditioned ale.

Use the following code to order this book from your bookshop: ISBN 1-85249-151-5

Order directly with your credit card on 01727 867201.

Cheshire Outlets

ALSAGER

Lodge
88 Crewe Road

☎ 01270 873669

11-11; 12-10.30 Sun

⌁**Addlestones**

Busy town pub, popular with both students and locals.

ASTON

Bhurtpore Inn
Wrenbury Road

☎ 01270 780917

12-2.30(3 Sat), 6.30-11; 12-3, 7-10.30 Sun

⌁**Cider Varies**

19th Century pub with four rooms for drinkers and a smoke free dining room for meals. Renowned for its food and beer range (9 Real Ales, many foreign beers). Has an annual beer festival in July during which all the trains stop at Wrenbury Station (normally only a few trains stop or are stopped by request). Has a garden, family room and pool table.

◖ ▶

CONGLETON

Beartown Tap
18 Willow Street

11-2, 4.30-11; 11-11 Fri/Sat; 12-10.30 Sun

⌁**Cider varies**

The Beartown Brewery Tap offering 6 Beartown ales and a good selection of foreign beer. A pleasant, friendly pub much used by both locals and those from further afield. Pork pies and pickled eggs home-made and highly recommended.

CREWE

Monkey
141 West Street

☎ 01270 500079

11-11; 12-10.30 Sun

⌁**Cider varies**

The second pub to have been bought by Stafford micro-brewery Eccleshall, refurbished and reopened in 1999. The cider is usually one from a small producer, and the beer range includes five from Eccleshall and four from other small, independent brewers.

◖ ▶

FRODSHAM

Helter Skelter
31 Church Street
☎ 01928 733361

11-11; 12-10.30 Sun

Cider varies

In the centre of Frodsham, opposite the car park. Good range of guest beers from independent breweries. Restaurant upstairs.

◖ ▶

GREAT BUDWORTH

George & Dragon
High Street
☎ 01606 891317

*11.30-3, 6-11; 11-11 Fri/Sat;
12-10.30 Sun*

Addlestones

Friendly village pub in the centre of picturesque Great Budworth. Public bar at the rear with a pool table, cosy lounge at the front. Welcoming to all drinkers, as well as children and dogs. Good, varied range of guest ales.

◖ ▶

MIDDLEWICH

Kings Lock
Booths Lane
☎ 01606 833537

11-11; 12-10.30 Sun

Addlestones

Right by the Kings Lock at the branch of two canals at the centre of Middlewich. It is a good place to gongoozle! One of the host venues of the annual Middlewich Folk and Boat Festival.

◖ ▶

NANTWICH

Black Lion
29 Welsh Row
☎ 01270 628711

12-11; 12-10.30 Sun

Westons Bounds Brand

Small, old black and white half-timbered pub with a real fire and real ales. Very dog friendly. Chess played, live music at weekends. Food limited to all day breakfasts and toasties.

◖ ▶

PEOVER HEATH

Dog Inn
Well Bank Lane
01625 861421

11.30-3, 5.30-11; 12-4.30, 7-10.30 Sun

Addlestones

One of the three pubs that makes up the Cheshire Inns of Distinction chain, the Dog Inn was converted from a row of 18th century cottages. Friendly, multiroomed and cosy, the good menu has had its desserts especially recommended. Accommodation available.

SANDBACH

Limes

3 Sweet Tooth Lane

☎ 01270 763506

11.30-3, 5-11; 11-11 Fri/Sat; 12-10.30 Sun

Addlestones

Friendly pub with a good local following at the edge of Sandbach town. Bowling green at the front.

Old Black Bear

The Cobbles, High Street

☎ 01270 762388

11.30-11; 12-10.30 Sun

Addlestones

Town centre pub near the famous "Sandbach Crosses", set in the cobbled square. Popular with younger drinkers.

SWETTENHAM

Swettenham Arms

(behind parish church)

☎ 01477 571284

11.30-3, 6-12; 12-4, 7-10.30 Sun

Addlestones

Rural pub with a large beamed interior and a garden. One of the three freehouses in the Cheshire Inns of Distinction chain. Good food. Avoid the road with the ford, it can be 3 feet deep!

WARRINGTON

Wilkies Tavern

25 Church Street

☎ 01925 416564

12-11; 12-10.30 Sun

Cider varies

A single-roomed freehouse with an Irish theme in the town centre. Four ever-changing beers usually from smaller breweries, occasional beer festivals in the back courtyard. The cider is typically, but not always, one of the Westons range.

WHEELOCK

Commercial Hotel ☆

Game Street

☎ 01270 760122

11-11; 12-10.30 Sun

Bulmers Traditional

A Georgian listed building. Four rooms, one of which is no smoking, another of which has a full-sized snooker table and table skittles. Folk music on Thursday nights. Friendly service.

CORNWALL

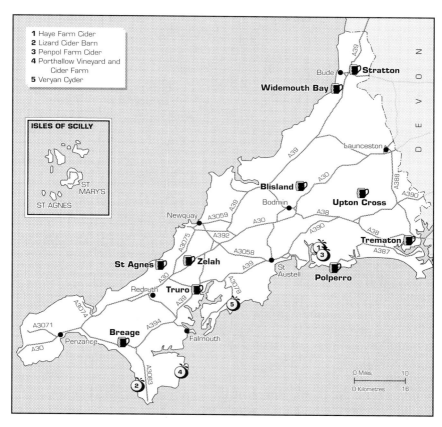

1 Haye Farm Cider
2 Lizard Cider Barn
3 Penpol Farm Cider
4 Porthallow Vineyard and
   Cider Farm
5 Veryan Cyder

ISLES OF SCILLY

ST MARY'S

ST AGNES

Stratton
Bude
Widemouth Bay
Launceston
Blisland
Bodmin
Upton Cross
Newquay
Trematon
St Agnes
Zelah
St Austell
Polperro
Redruth
Truro
Breage
Penzance
Falmouth

N
D E V O N

0 Miles   10
0 Kilometres   16

Cornwall Producers

HAYE FARM CIDER

Haye Farm, St.Veep, Lerryn,
Lostwithiel, Cornwall, PL22 OPB.

☎ 01208 872250

"It's the proper stuff" proclaim
Colin and Rita Vincent referring to
their farm cider, and quite right
they are. Scrumpy-cider has been
made at Haye Farm since the thir-
teenth century, and little has
changed in the method of production. Colin and Rita pick up Cornish
apples from both their own
orchards and others in the locality,
to make a real cider from 100%
juice that is fermented in oak barrels using natural wild yeasts. It's

understandably popular, allowing the Vincents to supply their cider to quite a number of local pubs, shops, caravan parks and farm shops.

Cider

Haye Farm Cider, 7% abv (1, 2.5 and 5 litre plastic containers. 25 litre barrels. 15 litre manucubes)

Visitors

Haye Farm is a working farm. Visitors are welcome for sales, tours for large groups only by prior appointment.

Directions

Sign posted at St.Veep, which is 1¹/₂ miles from Lerryn, 5 miles from Lostwithiel.

OS map reference:
SX1355. 550133.

Sales

Farm house door sales 7 days a week.

Outlets

Many in the local area. A selection:

Pubs:

- Crumplehorn Mill Inn, Polperro.
- City Inn, Truro.
- Caradon Arms, Upton Cross.
- Blisland Inn, Blisland, near Bodmin.

Caravan Park:
- Talland Barton Park, near Looe.

Farm Shop:
- Tamarisk Farm (Old Macdonalds), near Padstow.

Shops:
- Sams Deli, Fowey.
- Lerryn PO & Stores, near Lostwithiel.
- Lostwithiel Stores.
- Lizard Cider Barn, Preddanack.

LIZARD CIDER BARN

Hirvan Lane, Predannack, The Lizard, Cornwall, TR12 7AU.

☎ 01326 241481

Founded on the 1st of August 1999, to sell a range of Cornish ciders, wines and liqueurs. The Cider Barn has links with Porthallow Vineyard (see below), but produces its own Cornish Blacksmith Cider that commemorates An Gof. He led the Cornish protest march in 1497 and was beheaded in London. A contribution is made to the An Gof statue fund from each sale.

Owner Stanley Ward recounted "A green Bentley roared up one day and a gentleman jumped out, 'I'm an industrial chemist from Gloucestershire,' he announced, 'I've analysed your cider and it's made from 100% apple juice. This is most unusual!'"

Cider
Cornish Blacksmith Cider, 7% abv (75cl, 1 litre, 2 litre and 5 litre containers).

Annual Production
20 000 litres.

Visitors
Welcome. Tours available.

Directions
On the main road from Helston to the Lizard Point (A3083), half way between Mullion and Lizard.

Sales
Shop open 11am to 6pm.
Also on sale: Pottery, mead, Cornish liqueurs, country wines.

PENPOL FARM CIDER

Middle Penpol Farm, St. Veep, Lostwithiel, Cornwall, PL22 0NG.
☎ 01208 872017

Keith and Carol Langmaid produce their Cornish farm scrumpy in a very traditional manner, using a variety of apples from local orchards. The apples are pulped and layered with straw to make a 'cheese', and the juice is extracted with an eighteenth-century single-screw press (as shown on their labels). Nothing is added to the juice, which is fermented using natural yeasts in either port or rum oak barrels. Of course traditional methods produce a cider of great quality, and the Langmaids' many loyal customers are able to taste before buying at the farm gate.

Cider
Cornish Scrumpy (2$^1/_2$ and 5 litre containers)

Annual Production

1200-1500 gallons

Visitors

Welcome. Tours by appointment.

Directions

Middle Penpol Farm is situated in the hamlet of Penpol, 5 miles South East of Lostwithiel. From Lostwithiel take the road to Lerryn, then on past Saint Veep church, down the hill (part being a one-way system) and the farm is near the bottom of the hill, just as you enter the hamlet, on the right hand side.

Sales

Farm gate sales all reasonable hours, excluding Sunday pm. Please ring first.

PORTHALLOW

1985, in the centre of Cornwall's 'Landscape Lion'. His cider orchard is a refuge for rare Cornish cider apples – 30 different varieties – including Manaccan Primrose (used by Ted to make an apple wine), Cornish Aromatic (whose skin has a honeyed, spicy aroma), Lady's Finger and the red-fleshed Cornish Wine Apple.

Cider

Porthallow, 7% abv (1 and 2$^1/_2$ litre containers).

Annual Production

1000 gallons

Visitors

Welcome. Tours available.

Directions

On the road from St.Keverne to Porthallow, half a mile from Porthallow beach.

Sales

Shop open 11am-1pm, 2pm-5pm. Also on sale: wines, liqueurs, honey.

Porthallow Vineyard and Cider Farm, St.Keverne, Helston, Cornwall, TR12 6QH.

☎ 01326 280050

Ted Jeffries produces his unfiltered cider from orchards planted in

VERYAN CYDER

Veryan Vineyard & Cyder Farm, Tregenna, Portloe, Near Truro, Cornwall, TR2 5PS.

☎ 01872 501404

George Kington and his family founded Veryan Vineyard in 1983. Wine has influenced their cider making, they use modern wine-making technology and describe their Veryan Dry Cyder as "dry cyder for the wine drinker". Nevertheless proper cyders they most certainly are, using West Country apples (not concentrates) to give a traditional flavour to their range of filtered bottled and unfil-tered draught products. They also produce apple juice from selected apples, bottled and pasteurised on the premises.

Cyders

Unfiltered:

Cornish Gold, 7.3% abv (25 litre polybarrels)

Filtered:

Veryan Dry, 7% abv (75cl bottles)

Veryan Medium, 7% abv (75cl bottles)

Veryan Selected, 8% abv (75cl bottles)

Cornish Summertime, 6% abv (1 litre bottles)

Annual Production

15 000 litres

Visitors

Welcome. Tours by appointment.

Directions

On the South coast of Cornwall between Port Holland and Portloe. Follow our tourist signs from the A3078. OS map refer-ence: SW 946406.

Sales

Shop open 1st May to 31st September, 2pm to 6pm. Wholesale orders by 'phone any-time.

Also on sale: apple juice and other items.

Outlets

• Mounts Bay Wine Co., 22 New Bridge St, Truro.

• • Roseland Stores, Veryan, Near Truro.

• Blisland Inn, Blisland, Bodmin.

Awards

Overall Champion, Hereford Cider Museum 2000.

Cornwall Outlets

BLISLAND

Blisland Inn

☎ 01208 850739

11.30-11; 12-10.30 Sun

🍶**Cider varies**

Traditional, granite free house on the fringe of Bodmin Moor. The traditional cider or perry is ever-changing and always sourced from either Cornwall, Devon or Somerset. The 6-8 real ales also vary, and over 1000 guest beers have been served in five years. Friendly locals and staff.

◖ ◗

BREAGE

Queens Arms

☎ 01326 573485

11-2.30, 6.30-11; 12-10.30 Sun

🍶**Bulmers West Country**

15th century village pub – a good local with a lively atmosphere. Open fires, gardens, children welcome. Accommodation available, jazz Thursdays.

POLPERRO

Blue Peter Inn

Quay Road

☎ 01503 272743

11-11; 12-10.30 Sun

🍶**Haye Farm**

Small, friendly pub by the coastal footpath, reached by a flight of steps from the end of the quay. No food but you may take in your own sandwiches. Entertainment weekend lunchtimes.

ST. AGNES

Driftwood Spars

Quay Road, Trevaunance Cove

☎ 01872 552428

11-11(Midnight Fri/Sat); 12-10.30 Sun

🍶**Addlestones**

Picturesque 17th century hotel in a cove near the beach, welcoming and full of character. Much favoured by locals, there is live entertainment on most weekend evenings. The interesting range of real ales includes those from the pub's own brewery.

STRATTON

Kings Arms

Howells Road

☎ 01288 352396

*12-2.30, 6.30-11; 12-11
Fri/Sat; 12-10.30 Sun*

Winkleigh Sam's Medium

Friendly 17th century pub, well
worth finding. Five real ales and an
enticing menu. Dogs and children
welcome.

◖ ◗

TREMATON

Crooked Inn

Stoketon Cross

☎ 01752 848177

*11-3, 7-11; 12-3, 7-10.30 Sun;
(open all day Fri/Sat/Sun in summer)*

Addlestones

Converted 18th century farmhouse with views over the Lynher
Valley. A goat wanders through the
pub from time to time.

TRURO

City Inn

Pydar Street

☎ 01872 272623

11-11; 12-10.30 Sun

Haye Farm

Busy locals' pub just off the shopping centre. Styles itself as
"Truro's real ale oasis". There are
two bars, the lounge has an
impressive collection of water jugs.

◖ ◗

UPTON CROSS

Caradon Inn

☎ 01579 362391

*11-3.30, 5.30-11; 12-4, 7-
10.30 Sun*

Haye Farm

Old 17th century slate-clad country pub, with granite walls and
beamed ceilings. High on the edge
of Bodmin Moor.

◖ ◗

WIDEMOUTH BAY

Bay View Inn

Marine Drive

☎ 01288 361273

*11-3, 6-11; 12-3, 6-10.30 Sun;
(open all day in the summer)*

Taunton Traditional

Pub with a fine view of a surfing
beach. Excellent value food, three
Cornish real ales plus a guest ale.
Dogs allowed in the children's
room. Look for the frog collection
in the main bar, and the beer
mats and bar towels on the ceiling
of the pool room.

◖ ◗

ZELAH

Hawkins Arms

High Road

☎ 01872 540339

11-3, 6-11; 12-3, 7-10.30 Sun

⌣Westons Old Rosie

Unspoilt old village pub just off the A30 with excellent meals and ever-varied guest ales.

◖ ▶

---

50 GREAT PUB CRAWLS

by Barrie Pepper

256 pages   Price: £9.99

Visit the beer trails of the UK, from town centre walks, to hikes and bikes and a crawl on a train on which the pubs are even situated on your side of the track!

Barrie Pepper, with contributions and recommendations from CAMRA branches, has compiled a 'must do' list of pub crawls, with easy to use colour maps to guide you, notes on architecture, history and brewing tradition to entertain you.

Use the following code to order this book from your bookshop: ISBN 1-85249-142-6

Order directly with your credit card on 01727 867201.

CUMBRIA

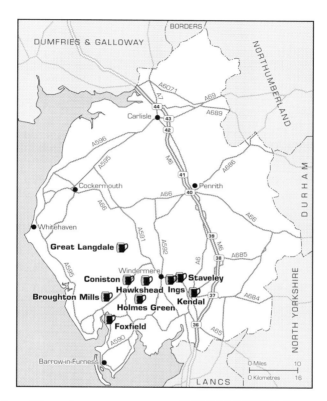

Cumbria Outlets

BROUGHTON MILLS

Blacksmiths Arms ☆
☎ 01229 716824

12-11; 12-10.30 Sun

⌀2 varying ciders (May-Sept only)

A CAMRA Heritage Pub.

◖ ◗

CONISTON

Black Bull Inn
Yewdale Road
☎ 015394 41335

11-11; 12-10.30 Sun

⌀Saxon Platinum Blonde

Home of the Coniston Brewing Company.

◖ ◗

FOXFIELD

Prince of Wales

(Opposite station)

☎ 01229 716238

5(12 Fri & Sat)-11; 12-10.30 Sun; closed Mon & Tues

⌂Draught: cider varies (March-Oct)
Bottled: Dunkertons

Home to the Foxfield Brewery. The Foxfield beers are always on offer, as well as four changing guests that always include one mild. Watch out for Speciality Beer weekends.

◖ ◗

GREAT LANGDALE

Old Dungeon Ghyll

☎ 015394 37272

11-11; 12-10.30 Sun

⌂Westons Old Rosie

Basic walkers/climbers pub adjacent to a well known hotel. Impromptu songs and music are not uncommon.

◖ ◗

HAWKSHEAD

Kings Arms Hotel

The Square

☎ 015394 36372

11-11; 12-10.30 Sun

⌂Saxon or Biddenden (May-Sept)

Traditional Lakeland inn at the centre of this popular tourist destination. Note the earthenware Gaymers Cyder flagon in the alcove by the fire.

◖ ◗

HOLMES GREEN

Black Dog Inn

Broughton Road

☎ 01229 462561

12(11 Sat & Summer)-11; 12-10.30 Sun; closed Mon lunch winter

⌂Draught: Biddenden range; Gwatkin cider range, perry; Westons Old Rosie
Bottled: Biddenden   Special Reserve

The premier cider outlet in the Furness area. Also offers seven constantly changing guest ales. Furness CAMRA Pub of the Year 1998 & 1999. Handy for the South Lakes Wildlife Park.

◖ ◗

INGS

Watermill Inn

☎ 01539 821309

12-2.30, 6-11; 12-3, 6-10.30 Sun

⌂Westons Old Rosie

Award-winning family run pub with

a warm welcome and a huge range of guest beers.

ᐊ ▶

KENDAL

Burgundy's

19 Lowther Street

☎ 01539 733803

11-3.30 Thurs-Sat; 6.30-11 Tues-Sat; 7-10.30 Sun; closed Mon

Saxon

A town centre bar with a wide choice of continental beers on draught and in bottle. Hosts specialist beer festivals.

ᐊ ▶

STAVELEY

Eagle & Child

Kendal Road

☎ 01539 821320

11-11; 12-10.30 Sun

Addlestones

Village pub with a function room and a riverside garden across the road.

ᐊ ▶

HERITAGE PUBS OF GREAT BRITAIN

by Mark Bolton and James Belsey
144 pages hard back
Price: £16.99

It is still possible to enjoy real ale in sight of great craftsmanship and skill. What finer legacy for today's drinkers? Feast your eyes and toast the architects and builders from times past. This full colour collectible is a photographic record of some of the finest pub interiors in Britain. Many of the pubs included have been chosen from CAMRA's national inventory of pub interiors which should be saved at all costs. As a collector's item. As such it is presented on heavy, gloss-art paper in a sleeved hard back format. The pub interiors have been photographed by architectural specialist Mark Bolton and described in words by pub expert James Belsey. Available only from CAMRA with your credit card – call 01727 867201 (overseas +44 1727 867201)

DERBYSHIRE

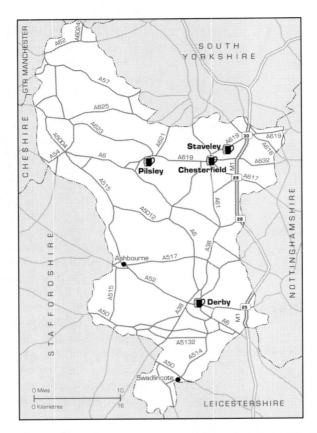

Derbyshire Outlets

CHESTERFIELD

Derby Tup

387 Sheffield Road, Whittington Moor

☎ 01246 454316

11.30-3, 5-11; 11.30-11

Fri/Sat; 12-4, 7-10.30 Sun

🍺Westons Old Rosie, Traditional Scrumpy

Friendly Tynemill pub, with an excellent range of ten real ales. Good value menu, specialising in Thai cuisine. Themed food nights once a month, evening meals Thursday to Saturday only.

◖ ◗

Rutland Arms

16 Stephenson Place

☎ 01246 205857

11-11; 12-10.30 Sun

Westons Old Rosie

Town centre split-level Hogshead pub, popular with all ages. Built c1700, it's right next to Chesterfield's famous crooked spire. Holds around four beer festivals per year, each with a couple of guest ciders.

◖ ◗

DERBY

Alexandra Hotel

203 Siddals Road

☎ 01332 293993

11-11; 12-3, 7-10.30 Sun

Cider range varies

Traditional real ale free house, offering two ever-changing ciders. The excellent range of 11 real ales is complemented by at least 5 draught foreign beers, plus a selection of continental bottled beers. Patio beer garden at the back, Bed & Breakfast available. Close to the railway station.

◖ ◗

Brunswick Inn

1 Railway Terrace

☎ 01332 290677

11-11; 12-10.30 Sun

Westons Old Rosie; guest cider (occasional)

Classic free house. A grade II listed building constructed in the 1840s, it is reputed to have been the first purpose-built railwayman's pub. Home of the Brunswick Brewery (est. 11.6.91), so 5/6 of the 17 handpumps serve Brunswick's beers, with the remainder offering ales from independent brewers. Multi-roomed with a flagstone floor and no background music, it's a place for people to drink and talk. Guest ciders offered at the pub's beer festivals. Jazz Thursdays, evening food by prior arrangement only.

◖

Flowerpot

25 King Street

☎ 01332 204955

11-11; 12-10.30 Sun

Westons

Lively pub which frequently has live music in its function room. Offers 3 permanent real ales and up to 17 guests, and customers in the ground floor Cellar Bar can view the stillaged beer barrels through a viewing window. Home-made specials can be found on the menu, which is available until 6.45pm.

◖ ◗

PILSLEY

Chatsworth Farm Shop
Stud Farm
☎ 01246 583392
Web site www.chatsworth-house.co.uk

9-5(5.30 summer); 11-5 Sun

⌕Bottled: Dunkertons range

Excellent farm shop on the Chatsworth House Estate. Sells a range of quality, speciality food and drink, much of which is either produced on the estate or sourced locally. Two own label beers – Apostle Ale (8.5% abv) and Gardener's Tap (5% abv) – are brewed by Springhead Brewery, and based on ales once brewed at the House itself. They also have their own bakery and butchers. Mail order service available.

STAVELEY

Speedwell Inn

Lowgates
☎ 01246 472252

6-11; 6-10.30 Sun

⌕Cider varies

Chesterfield CAMRA Pub of the Year 2000, in a former mining village on the outskirts of Chesterfield. The home of Townes Brewery, four Townes beers are offered (plus an ever-changing guest from a micro-brewery), and brewery trips are available by appointment. The cider varies, but is usually Westons 1st Quality. Range of bottled Belgian beers.

PUBS FOR FAMILIES

by David Perrott
308 pages   Price: £8.99

Traditional pubs with CAMRA-approved ale and a warm welcome for the kids! Nothing could be better. But where to find such a hospitable hostel on home patch, let alone when out and about or on holiday? This guide provides invaluable national coverage with easy to use symbols so that you know what facilities are available and where. The regional maps show you how to get there. Get the best of both worlds with Pubs for Families.

Use the following code to order this book from your bookshop:
ISBN 1-85249-141-8. Order directly with your credit card on 01727 867201.

DEVON

Devon Producers

BOLLHAYES CIDER

Bollhayes Park, Clayhidon, Devon, EX15 3PN.

☎ 01823 680230

Alex Hill founded Bollhayes Cider in 1988, and initially produced draught cider only. However in 1992, following the example of Gospel Green's James Lane, he took the plunge and produced the first vintage of his champagne-like Bottle Fermented Cider – the cider that has made his reputation. It's a classy drink – the looks, froth and smoothness of a champagne – complemented by the distinctive aroma and flavour of tannic cider apples. A second bottle fermented cider, Total Eclipse, was released in 1999.

Alex's principle occupation is running Vigo Vineyard Supplies (see advert inside this book's cover),

from which the small-scale cider maker can purchase all necessary equipment plus supplies of Bollhayes Cider!

Ciders
Bollhayes Draught, 7% abv (15 litre manucubes)
Bollhayes Dry Bottle Fermented, 8% abv (750ml champagne bottles)
Total Eclipse Medium Dry Bottle Fermented, 8% abv (750ml champagne bottles)

Annual Production
1500 gallons

Visitors
By appointment only.

Sales
Available from Vigo Ltd, Station Rd, Hemyock, Devon, EX15 3SE. Also on sale: Full range of cider making equipment.

Outlets
• The Blue Ball Inn, Triscombe, Bishops Lydeard, Taunton, Somerset.
• The Drewe Arms, Broadhembury, Devon.
• The York Inn, Churchinford, Somerset.

Awards
Several firsts at both the Royal Bath & West Show and Devon County Show.

BRIMBLECOMBE'S FARMHOUSE CIDER

Farrants Farm, Dunsford, Devon.

☎ 01647 252783

Farrants Farm boasts what must be one of the most ancient and traditional cider making operations in Britain. The cider barn was once a farmhouse that dates back to at least the Saxon age. Some 450 years ago the present farmhouse was built next door and a cider press was installed in the barn. Little has changed since, and today Mr and Mrs Barter still press through straw. Customers can sample the range of ciders directly from the old oak barrels.

Ciders

Regular (Sweet, Dry or Medium), 7% abv.

Vintage (Sweet, Dry or Medium), 7% abv.

(All available in 1, 2, 2¹/₂ or 4 litre plastic containers).

Annual Production

1200 gallons.

Visitors

Welcome. Tours available.

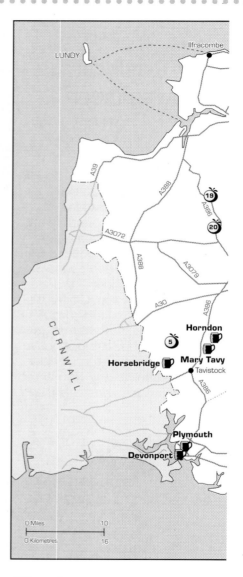

Directions

On the B3212 from Exeter to Mortenhamstead, at the junction of the B3193.

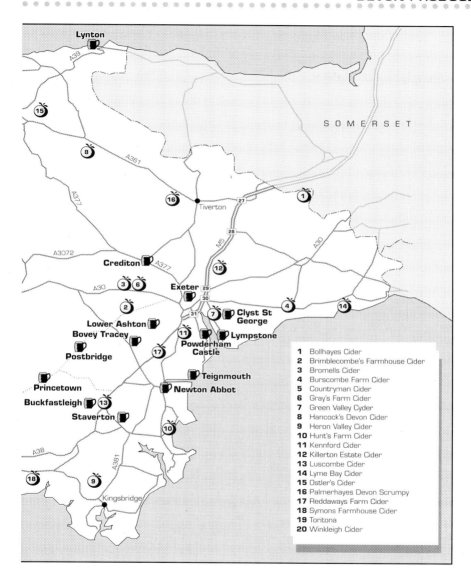

Lynton

SOMERSET

15

8

A39

A361

A377

16

Tiverton

27

28

M5

A30

1

A3072

Crediton

A377

12

A30

3 6

Exeter

29

30

2

31

7

Clyst St George

4

14

Lower Ashton

Bovey Tracey

11

Lympstone

Powderham Castle

Postbridge

17

Princetown

Teignmouth

Newton Abbot

Buckfastleigh

13

Staverton

10

A38

A381

18

9

Kingsbridge

1 Bollhayes Cider
2 Brimblecombe's Farmhouse Cider
3 Bromells Cider
4 Burscombe Farm Cider
5 Countryman Cider
6 Gray's Farm Cider
7 Green Valley Cyder
8 Hancock's Devon Cider
9 Heron Valley Cider
10 Hunt's Farm Cider
11 Kennford Cider
12 Killerton Estate Cider
13 Luscombe Cider
14 Lyme Bay Cider
15 Ostler's Cider
16 Palmerhayes Devon Scrumpy
17 Reddaways Farm Cider
18 Symons Farmhouse Cider
19 Toritona
20 Winkleigh Cider

Sales

Shop open 10am to 6pm, all week April to November. Please ring when out of season.

Also on sale: honey, mustard, eggs, handcream and other 'bee' products, tea towels and post-cards.

Outlet

Nobody Inn, Doddiscombsleigh, Devon.

BROMELLS CIDER

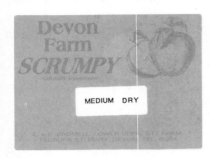

E, P & I Bromell, Lower Uppacott Farm, Tedburn St. Mary, Exeter, Devon.

☎ 01647 61294

Bromells cider is made at the family farm on the edge of Dartmoor National Park. Eric Bromell's Grandfather was making cider in Tedburn in 1910, and his father delivered cider in 54 gallon barrels to Exeter and Chagford by horse and cart.

Ciders

Sweet, Dry and Medium Dry, 6% abv (Demi johns. 1, 2, 2^1/$_2$ & 4 litre plastic containers. 5 gallon barrels)

Annual Production

4000 gallons

Visitors

Welcome. Tours available.

Directions

Leave A30 at Fingle Glen. Come into Tedburn St. Mary, take first right Whitestone Rd, and the farm is 300 yards down on the right.

Sales

Farm gate sales, 8am to 8pm. Also sell: veg, fruit, milk, cider vinegar.

Outlets

• Dartington Cider Press Centre, Dartington.

• Old Coach House, Linton.

• The Village Store, Tedburn.

Awards

A number at the Devon County Show.

BURSCOMBE FARM CIDER

Burscombe Farm, Sidford, Sidmouth, Devon, EX10 0QB.

☎ 01395 597648

Email
burscombefarm@sidbury.fsbusiness.co.uk

Robert and Annette Pearse make a traditional, unfiltered cider just a couple of miles outside Sidford. Their cidermaking predecessor at Burscombe Farm was Spillers Cider, reputed to have once made cider for Inch's before they themselves started up in production.

The Pearses no longer use their own cider apples, but instead source them from neighbouring orchards that include those belonging to Whiteways. The apples are pulped with an electrically-powered belt-driven mill, hand-pressed with barley straw, and then fermented in oak barrels.

Cider

Farmhouse (Sweet, Medium & Dry), 6% abv (2, 2$^1/_2$ & 5 litre plastic containers).

Annual Production

800 gallons.

Visitors

Welcome.

Directions

From Honiton, go through Sidbury on the A375 and turn right at the war memorial. You will see the cider sign on the left.

Sales

Farm gate sales Monday to Saturday 8am to 9pm, Sunday 10am to 9pm.

COUNTRYMAN CIDER

Felldownhead, Milton Abbot, Tavistock, Devon.

☎ 01822 870226

The Lancaster family first made cider in 1858, and four generations later Horace Lancaster developed this family tradition into a commercial concern with the installation of a hydraulic press and mill in the late 1960s. Today the family business is run by Vernon and Teresa Shutler, and their visitors can take a tour of the orchard, apple silo, mill and press, followed by some free tasters in the shop.

Ciders

Countryman Dry, Medium, Sweet (all 6.5% abv)

Gold Label Special (7% abv)

(Containers: 2 pints, 2 litre PET bottles, 2$^1/_2$ litre plastic jars, 1 gallon, 75cl wine bottles and stone jars.)

Annual Production

10 000 gallons

Visitors

Welcome. Tours on request.

Directions

From Tavistock take the B3362 to Launceston and pass through Milton Abbot and take the turning to Bradstone and Kelly. From Launceston take the B3362 to Tavistock and turn left after Greystone Bridge.

Sales

Shop open Mon-Sat, 9am-6pm.

Also on sale: country wines, meads, apple brandy aperitif, apple juice, perry, cider vinegar, stone jars and recipe books.

Outlets

Countryman cider can be found in a variety of outlets in the area. A selection:

Pubs:

• Warren House Inn, Postbridge, Dartmoor.

• Harris Arms, Lewdown, Okehampton.

• Countryman Inn, Langdon Cross, Launceston.

• Pym Arms, Devonport,

DEVON PRODUCERS

Plymouth.
- Queens Head, Albaston, Gunnislake.
- Rising Sun, Gunnislake.
- Tavistock Hotel, Gunnislake.

Off-licences:
- Chillaton Stores, Chillaton, Tavistock.
- Milton Abbot Stores, Milton Abbot, Tavistock.
- Upton Cross Stores, Upton Cross, Liskeard.

Distributor:
- St. Austell Brewery.

GRAY'S FARM CIDER

Halstow, Tedburn St. Mary, Exeter, Devon, EX6 6AN.

☎ 01647 61236

One of the oldest and largest cider makers in Devon. The Gray family have been making cider throughout their occupation of Halstow, a period in excess of 300 years.

Cider

Sweet, Medium, Med Dry, Dry; 6.5% abv ($^1/_2$, 1 litre glass bottles. $2^1/_2$ litre "horrible mock stone kegs for grockles". $2^1/_2$ & 5 litre plastic containers. 25 litre polypins. Can provide your own container.)

Annual Production

Slightly less than 20 000 gallons.

Visitors

Welcome, tours by special arrangement only.

Directions

Turn off the A30 at the Tedburn St. Mary junction. Head about two miles south towards Dunsford. OS map ref 823 923.

Sales

Farm gate sales daylight hours Monday to Saturday (not Sunday).

Outlets

- Powderham Farm Shop, Kenton Old Inn, Widecombe in the Moor, Newton Abbot
- Lee's Wine Store, Crediton
- Fermoy's Farm Shop, Newton Abbot
- Dartington Cider Press Centre, Dorset

GREEN VALLEY CYDER

Darts Farm, Clyst St. George,
Exeter, Devon, EX3 0QH.

☎ 01392 876658

Green Valley Cyder was founded in
1989 by Chris Coles with the
backing of several other former
Whiteway employees. They use
only juice from freshly pressed
local Devon apples, whenever possible buying from orchards where
chemical sprays and artificial fertilisers are not used. The juice is
fermented using wild yeasts,
before being matured over the
winter in ancient oak vats.
Traditional craft methods always
produce full flavoured ciders, and
the comprehensive range of Green
Valley Cyders on sale at Darts
Farm are no exception.

Ciders

Unfiltered:

Traditional, 7% abv

Rum Tiddly Tum, 7-8% abv (winter
only).

(1, 1.7, 2.5 and 5 litre containers)

Filtered:

Standard Dry, Medium and
Sweet, 7% abv (1, 1.7, 2.5 and 5
litre containers)

Stillwood Vintage Dry, 8.3% abv
(75cl glass bottles)

Table Cyder, Medium Sweet, 8.3%
abv (75cl glass bottles)

Annual Production

10 000 gallons

Visitors

Welcome. Tours by arrangement.

Directions

Leave M5 at Junction 30. Follow
directions towards Exmouth
(A376). When you reach Clyst St.
George (2 miles) go straight over
first roundabout and turn right at
second (mini) roundabout. Darts
Farm is 150 yards down the hill
on the right-hand side.

OS map reference: SX 978883.

Sales

Shop open Mon-Sat 9am-6pm,
Sun 10am-5pm.

Also on sale: wide range of bottled beers and West Country
apple juices.

Darts Farm also has a Farm
Shop, Delicatessen, Butchers and
Café.

Outlets

Pubs:

• Fountain Head, Branscombe.

• Turf Hotel, Exminster.

• Journey's End, Ringmore.

Off-licences: A wide range in
North and South Devon.

Wholesaler:

An informal link with RCH brewery.

Awards

Champion Farmhouse Cider, Devon County Show 1999 (2 First Prizes, 1 Second).

Taste Of The West, Gold Medal 1999 (for Stillwood Vintage Cyder).

HANCOCK'S DEVON CIDER

Clapworthy Mill, South Molton, North Devon, EX36 4HU.

☎ 01769 572678

Five generations of the Hancock family have been making their natural, traditional cider. They were amongst the first to use hydraulic presses – starting over 50 years ago – and have won many prizes for their ciders at the local agricultural shows.

Ciders

Sweet, Medium, Dry and Extra Dry, all 6-8% abv.

(Medium and Dry available on draught, all available in a variety of bottles and plastic jugs)

Annual Production

15 000 gallons

Visitors

Welcome. Self-conducted tours, including a video on cider making, available.

Directions

3 miles from South Molton, on the B3226 to Exeter. Follow the brown tourist signs.

Sales

Shop open 9-1 & 2-5, Monday to Saturday, Easter to the end of October. Winter opening: 9-1 & 2-5, Thursdays and Saturdays only.

Also on sale: Apple juice, apple wine (10-12% abv), cream, cheese, butter, eggs, gifts.

Outlets

• English Farm Cider Centre, Lewes, Sussex.
• Bee Hive Wine Stores, South Molton, Devon.
• Old Coach House, Lynton, Devon.
• Caravel, Lynmouth, Devon.
• Woolacombe Off-Licence, Woolacombe, Devon.
• Post Office, Exford, Somerset.

HERON VALLEY CIDER

Heron Valley Cider Ltd,
Crannacombe Farm, Hazelwood,
Loddiswell, Kingsbridge, Devon,
TQ7 4DX.

☎ 01548 550256

Heron Valley Cider was founded by
the enterprising Steve Bradley in
1997. Aside from making and
marketing his own organic cider,
non-organic cider and organic
apple juice, Steve is Director of
Orchard Link (sponsored by South
Hams District Council), and
Director of South Hams Food and
Drink Association. In 1998 he
formed an organic producers
group, and both his organic cider
and apple juice carry the Soil
Association Organic Standard.

Steve uses only traditional cider
apple varieties – both from his own
farm in the Avon valley and from
other old South Devon orchards –
and their ancient names are
proudly displayed on his labels.

Ciders
Heron Valley Farmhouse, 6.2%
abv (unfiltered)
Ruddy Turnstone, 6.0% abv (fil-
tered)
(Also available: Café cider, 6.2%
abv (lightly carbonated, medium))
Annual Production
7000 gallons approx.
Visitors
Welcome
Directions
Leave A38 at Wrangaton. Turn
left, staight on to California cross

roads, fork left to Loddiswell.
Third council lane on left marked
'Hazelwood 1 mile'. Second farm
down long lane.
Sales
Farm gate sales, telephone first.
Also on sale: organic apple juice,
organic grapefruit juice with
apple.
Outlets
Available widely in South Devon.
Wholesalers: Wilkinson Quality
Drinks (01626 334963)
• Dartmouth Vintners (01803
832602)

HUNT'S FARM CIDER

W.G.F.Hunt & Son, Higher
Yalberton Farm, Paignton, Devon,
TQ4 7PE.

☎ 01803782309

A small, traditional family business
that has made cider since 1954.
No concentrate is used, just juice
from their own 20 acre orchard.
Cider
Hunt's Devon Cider, 6% abv (2
and 4 litre containers)
Annual Production
6000 gallons
Visitors
Welcome. Tours sometimes avail-
able.

Directions

Take the Totnes-Paignton road from the Torbay ring road. At the Parkers Arms turn left into Stoke Road. Towards Stoke Gabriel take the second left by the Big Cider Barrel. First house on the right.

Sales

Shop open 9-5 Mon-Sat, 12-1 Sun.

Outlets

• Albert Inn, Totnes

• Culinaria, Brixham

INCH'S CIDER

(See Bulmers, Herefordshire)

KENNFORD CIDER

Lamacraft Farm, Kennford, Exeter, Devon, EX6 7TS.

☎ 01392 832298

Roy Baker's family have been making their unfiltered farm cider, by wholly traditional methods, since 1945. Visitors can buy the cider, poured directly from oak barrels, in the splendid surroundings of a traditional cider barn – built in 1662 – complete with cobbled floor and oak beams.

Ciders

Dry, Medium and Sweet ($^1/_2$ and 1 gallon plastic containers).

Annual Production

1200 gallons

Visitors

Welcome

Directions

Off the A38 at Kennford Services. Farm is in the centre of Kennford village, next to the village hall.

Sales

Farm gate sales, 9am – 6pm, seven days a week.

Also on sale: honey.

KILLERTON ESTATE CIDER

The Stables Gift Shop, Killerton House, Broadclyst, Exeter, EX5 3LE.

☎ 01392 881912

Cider made at the National Trust's Killerton House, with profits going towards the upkeep of the estate. The estate wardens make the cider using an old mill and press, and it is bottled filtered and still by Green Valley Cider.

Cider

Killerton Estate Cider, 5.1% abv (75cl bottles)

Annual Production

1000 litres

Visitors

Welcome to the shop and house.

Directions

6 miles north of Exeter on the B3181, follow the brown signs to Killerton House.

Sales

National Trust shop is open 11-5 Mon-Sun April-Oct; 11-4 Wed-Sun Nov-Dec; 11-4 Sat-Sun Jan-March.

Also on sale: cider chutney, cider mustard, local beer, local crafts, plus the usual range of NT gifts.

Outlets

All 6 National Trust licensed restaurants in Devon.

LUSCOMBE CIDER

Luscombe Cider Ltd, Luscombe Farm, Colston Road, Buckfastleigh, Devon, TQ11 OLP.

☎ 01364 643036

Email luscombeltd@freeserve.net

Web site www.luscombe.co.uk

Cider making was incorporated into Luscombe Farm's activities 25 years ago, and production was scaled up in 1987. Cider maker David Gabriel ferments his ciders with their own natural yeasts, and keeps metabisulphite to an absolute minimum.

Ciders

Draught: Traditional Devon Cider, 6% abv (1 to 4 litre containers).

Bottled: Organic Devon Cider, 5% abv (33 to 100cl bottles).

Annual Production

10-20 000 gallons.

Visitors

Welcome by prior arrangement.

Directions

Very twisty lanes, call for directions when making your plans.

Sales

Farm gate sales 9am to 1pm. Please telephone first.

Outlets

• The Cider Press Centre, Dartington, Totnes.
• Riverford Farm Shop, Staverton, Totnes.
• Tuit Centre, Lewdown, Okehampton.
• Tuckers Maltings, Newton Abbot.
• Church House, Holne.
• Smugglers, Totnes.
• Tradesmans, Scorriton.

- Tors Hotel, Belstone.
- Sloop, Bantham.
- White Hart, Dartington.

Wholesaler: The Beer Seller, Paignton (01803 559826).

Awards

Devon County Show 1998.
Great Taste Awards 1999.

LYME BAY CIDER

Lyme Bay Cider Co Ltd, Manor Farm, Seaton, Devon, EX12 2TF.

☎ 01297 22887

Email lymebay@btinternet.com

London stockbroker Nigel Howard decided to start a new life in Devon, and in 1994 Lyme Bay Cider was born. The gamble paid off, and today Nigel and his wife Jacqui Barker preside over one of Devon's most thriving cider companies. Their ciders are made in the traditional Devon manner and with local Devon fruit. This local connection continues with the name used for their draught and still ciders – 'Jack Ratt' – after Jack Rattenbury, the notorious nineteenth-century Lyme Bay smuggler.

Ciders

Unfiltered: Jack Ratt Scrumpy, 6% abv, medium (2.5 and 5 litre plastic containers).

Filtered: Jack Ratt Scrumpy, 6% abv, medium (1 litre glass bottles, 1 litre glass flagons, 2.5 litre plastic containers).

Jack Ratt Vintage, 7.4% abv, dry or medium-sweet (1 litre glass bottles/flagons, 2.5 litre plastic containers).

(Also available, two sparkling bottled ciders:

Lyme Bay Cider, 6% abv, medium-sweet or dry.

Lymelight, 6% abv, sweet.)

Annual Production

20 000 plus gallons.

Visitors

Welcome. No formal tours, but visitors are welcome to look at the press room and vat room.

Directions

Lyme Bay Cider is directly behind Seaton on the main A3052 (runs from Lyme Regis to Sidmouth). Follow the brown tourist signs.

Sales

Shop open Mon-Sat 10am-5pm (summer), Mon-Fri 10am-4pm (winter).

Also on sale: country wines, traditional liqueurs, apple juice, cider vinegar, chutney, jam, honey, etc.

Outlets

Available throughout the West Country at selected pubs, off-licences and speciality stores.

OSTLER'S CIDER

The Cider Mill, Eastacott Lane, Norleigh Hill, Goodleigh, Near Barnstaple, Devon, EX32 7NF.
☎ 01271 321241

Peter Hartnoll is a remarkable man – managing a five acre orchard and running his own cider making company – all despite a serious disability inflicted by a car crash that left him unconscious for three months when he was 18. Peter can trace his North Devon farming ancestry back to the 1530s, and initially trained in horticulture, learning all he could from master cidermaker Keith Goverd. He took a number of self employed jobs away from farming, but yearned to return to the land, and managed to do so by buying 14 acres of land on which to make cider.

Grants from the Access To Work scheme have provided specially adapted equipment – a cider press he can operate from a sitting position, a hoist and a bottle labeller which is operated by a foot pedal – and a support worker. Alongside his Dry and Sweet Scrumpys, Peter produces Scrumpy Black, a mixture of cider and blackcurrant.

Ciders

Traditional Scrumpy, 7% abv, dry. Sweet Scrumpy Cider, 7% abv, sweet.
(25 litre barrels; 2¹/₂ and 2 litre plastic; 1 litre, ¹/₂ litre and 330ml bottles)

Annual Production
2000 gallons

Visitors
Welcome. Tours available.

Directions
Find the New Inn on your right in Goodleigh village. Take the next left, signposted Norleigh. Turn right into a rough lane just before a 12'9" signpost. Ostlers Cider Farm entrance is on the right.

Outlets
• Coach House, Lynton, Devon.
• Caravelle, Lymouth, Devon.

PALMERHAYES DEVON SCRUMPY

C.J. & A.W. Greenslade, Palmerhayes Farm, Calverleigh, Tiverton, Devon.
☎ 01884 254579

Cider has been traditionally made at Palmershayes Farm for over 100 years.

Cider

Palmerhayes Devon Scrumpy, 6-8% abv (1, 2, 2^1/$_2$ and 4 litre containers).

Annual Production

4000 gallons

Visitors

Welcome

Directions

On the Tiverton to Rackenford road.

Sales

Farm gate sales 9am to 10pm.

Outlets

Off-licences in Woolacombe, Mortehoe, Ilfracombe, Lynmouth, Tiverton and Westward Ho.

REDDAWAYS FARM CIDER

Lower Rixdale Farm, Luton, Chudleigh, Newton Abbot, Devon.

☎ 01626 775218

John Reddaway makes cider as his father and grandfather once did – using traditional methods and with apples grown on the working family farm.

Cider

Reddaways Farm Cider, 6% abv (2 litre, 4 litre and 5 gallon containers)

Annual Production

1000-1500 gallons.

Visitors

Welcome

Directions

From the village of Luton take the road opposite the phone box and follow for half a mile to the farm.

Sales

Farm gate sales any time within off-licence hours.

Outlets

• Elizabethan Inn, Luton.
• Lord Nelson Inn, Kingskerswell, Torquay.

Awards

Champion Prize, Devon County Show 1982. Other prizes at local shows.

SYMONS FARMHOUSE CIDER

Borough Farm, Holbeton, Plymouth, PL8 1JJ.

☎ 01752 830247

John Walters-Symons has made cider at Borough Farm for 13 years, and prior to that at another farm in the locality. He sources many varieties of apple from a number of local traditional orchards. His cider is made from 100% fresh juice, with some batches being fermented by the local natural yeast, others requiring a dose of commercial yeast. The cider is allowed to ferment out to dryness, with some being sweetened up to a medium.

Cider

Symons Farm Cider (Medium or Dry), 6% abv (1, 2$^1/_2$ & 5 litre plastic containers).

(At the time of writing John was experimenting with filtering some of his cider.)

Annual Production

1400 gallons.

Visitors

Welcome, but please ring first.

Sales

Farm gate sales, please ring ahead.

Outlets

A number of local outlets are supplied, including:

• Mildmay Colours, Holbeton.
• Dartmoor Union Inn, Holbeton.
• Kitley Farm Shop, Yealmpton.
• Macgills Delicatessen, Modbury.

TORITONA

126 Mill Street, Great Torrington, North Devon, EX38 8AW.

☎ 01805 624746

Rob Wilson was on the first ever APPLE committee, and today is a distributor and wholesaler of Real Cider. His cidermaking is more of a hobby, and started in Somerset in 1996 under the name of Asney Cottage. The name was changed to Caddywell in 1998 after a move to Devon, and then changed again in 1999 to Toritona (the Domesday Book spelling of Torrington). Rob owns no cider making equipment, and buys and presses his apples in Somerset. Nothing is added to the juice, which is brought home to ferment and mature in oak barrels. Toritona specialises in single apple variety ciders, Rob's current favourite being Yarlington Mill.

An active revivalist of the custom of Wassailing the apple trees, Rob leads the Wassail at a nearby orchard in Taddiport in January (usually on the Tuesday evening following January 17th, the traditional date for Wassailing). For details of this event, please phone 01805 624746 or 01805 624245.

Cider

Yarlington Mill (rum flavoured), 8% abv, (5 gallon polycasks).

Annual Production

90 gallons.

Awards

'Cider of the Festival', Doncaster Beer and Cider Festival 1997.
'Cider of the Festival', Nottingham Beer and Cider Festival 1997.
1st and 2nd Prizes at the Cider Making Competition, Theale Show, Somerset, 1997.

WINKLEIGH CIDER

Western Barn, Hatherleigh Road, Winkleigh, Devon, EX19 8AP.

☎ 01837 83560

Email winkleighcider@freeuk.com

From the ashes of Inch's demise, Winkleigh Cider Company was born on the 26th January 1999. Winkleigh's owner, David Bridgman, came to work for Sam Inch as a 15 year old apprentice in 1967. Thirty years later, after Bulmers decided to close the factory down, David bought part of the site and started the business up again. David's 30 years of cider making experience have been far from wasted, and already Winkleigh's ciders have built up an enviable reputation and sales have risen quickly. All of the cider is fermented and matured in 100 year old oak vats, although only 4 of the original 30 vats owned by Inch's remain.

Ciders

Sam's (Dry, Medium or Sweet) 6% abv

Autumn Scrumpy (Medium Dry and Medium Sweet) 7.4% abv

(all available in $1/2$ & 1 litre plastic containers, 20 litre manucubes and 5 gallon polykegs)

Annual Production

200 000 litres, set to increase.

Visitors

Welcome. Tours may be available in the future, please ring to enquire.

Directions

Take the Hatherleigh Road out of Winkleigh village, Winkleigh Cider is 500 yards from the village outskirts.

Sales

Shop open 9-5, Monday to Saturday.

Outlets

A selection:

• Ye Olde Cider Bar, Newton Abbot.
• Kings Arms, Winkleigh.
• Seven Stars, Winkleigh.
• Duke of York, Hatherleigh
• Tally Ho!, Hatherleigh.
• George, Hatherleigh.
• Bridge, Hatherleigh.
• Locomotive, Newton Abbot.
• Dartmouth Inn, Newton Abbot.
• Admiral Vernon, Torrington.

• Wholesaler: Beer Seller

Devon Outlets

BOVEY TRACEY

Queens of Bovey

50 Fore Street

☎ 01626 834213

Mon-Sat 10-9

⬦**Old Buckys Cider**

Off-licence selling Old Buckys in 2.5 litre plastic jugs.

BUCKFASTLEIGH

Buckfastleigh Wines and Spirits

3-4 Fore Street

☎ 01364 643790

10.30-9; 12-2, 7-9 Sun

⬦**Draught: Heron Valley Dry, Medium; Luscombe Dry, Medium; Sams Dry, Medium-Dry, Medium, Medium-Sweet.**

The friendly licensee has been selling cider from polycask for 15 years. Good selection of premium bottled ciders.

CLYST ST GEORGE

Green Valley Cider

Darts Farm

☎ 01392 876658

9-6; 10-5 Sun

⬦**Draught: Green Valley Traditional, Devon Farm, Rum Tiddly Tum (winter only).**

Plastic containers: Grays Dry, Medium, Sweet.

Bottles: Bollhayes Perry; Countryman Medium, Sweet; Hecks Cider, Perry; Westons Perry.

Farm Shop adjacent to the Green Valley Cider Company, and part of the Darts Farm complex.

CREDITON

Lees Wine Store

21 High Street

☎ 01363 772561

9-5.30 Mon-Sat

⬦**Grays Dry, Medium, Sweet; Winkleigh Sams Medium, Medium Dry**

Family business in the centre of Crediton selling local ciders and a good selection of bottle-conditioned beers.

DEVONPORT

Pym Arms

16 Pym Street

☎ 01752 561823

11-11; 12-10.30 Sun

⬦**Countryman**

Basic but friendly students and locals pub.

EXETER

Double Locks

Canal Banks

☎ 01392 256947

11-11; 12-10.30 Sun

Grays

Large and well-known canalside pub with a huge garden. Built originally as a combined pub and lock-keepers cottage.

HORNDON

Elephants Nest

☎ 01822 810273

11.30-2.30, 6.30-11; 12-2.30, 7-10.30 Sun

Thatchers

16th century pub with views of the moors. Good food.

HORSEBRIDGE

Royal Inn

☎ 01822 870214

12-3, 7-11; 12-3, 7-10.30 Sun

Rich's

15th century converted nunnery.

LOWER ASHTON

Manor Inn

☎ 01647 252304

12-2.30, 6.30-11; 12-2.30, 6.30-10.30 Sun; (closed Mondays except Bank Holidays)

Grays

Lovely, unspoilt, traditional rural pub in the Teign Valley. Public bar, lounge and "outdoor family room" (ie the garden). Five interesting real ales, including a varying guest spot that has been filled by 1500 ales in the last 8 years, plus a range of foreign beers. CAMRA's South West Pub of the Year in 1994. No music, a place to sit and chat.

LYMPSTONE

Redwing

Church Road

☎ 01395 222156

11.30-3.30, 6-11; 11.30-11 Sat; 12-10.30 Sun

Thatchers Dry

Lively village free house at the lower end of the village. No evening meals Sunday.

◖ ◗

LYNTON

Old Coach House

Church Hill

☎ 01598 753662

9am-11pm, Mon-Fri; 10-10 Sat

Bottled: Hancocks; Lyme Bay; Ostlers

Traditional, independent off-licence, specialising in Devon produce. Aside from the large range of Devon ciders, there's also honey, clotted cream, goat's cheese and a good selection of bottled beers.

MARY TAVY

Mary Tavy Inn

Lane Head

☎ 01822 810326

11.45-3, 6-11; 12-3, 7-10.30 Sun

Winkleigh Sams

Cosy and friendly pub on the edge of Dartmoor. Serves good-value food.

◖ ◗

NEWTON ABBOT

Horwells Grocery

97 East Street

☎ 01626 203335

8-7.30; 10-1.30 Sun

Thatchers Medium

Cornershop off-licence selling Thatchers in 2.5 litre plastic jugs.

 CIDER HOUSE

national treasure – sells draught cider but no draught beer

Ye Olde Cider Bar

99 East Street

☎ 01626 354221

11-11; 12-10.30 Sun

Winkleigh Sams Dry, Medium; Thatchers Cheddar Valley Dry, Dry, Sweet; Westons Traditional Scrumpy, Perry; occasional Guest Cider (summer).

An absolutely superb cider house selling cider and country wines, but no beer or spirits. The cider is all served by gravity from barrels behind the bar, most of which are made from oak. Very reasonable prices. Run for 30 years by the same excellent landlord – Richard Knibbs. Room at the rear for children with responsible parents, outside patio. Tables and chairs fashioned from oak barrel staves. Do not miss this English classic.

 REAL ALE

PLYMOUTH

Borringdon Arms

Borringdon Terrace, Turnchapel

☎ 01752 402053

11-11; 12-10.30 Sun

⌣**Addlestones; guest cider (summer)**

Unique and very friendly pub in a waterside village on the South West Coastal Footpath. Bi-monthly beer festival.

◖ ▶

Clifton

35 Clifton Street

☎ 01752 266563

⌣**Addlestones**

Small, friendly locals pub with lots of pub teams.

POSTBRIDGE

Warren House Inn

☎ 01822 880208

11-3, 6-11(11-11 Fri/Sat summer); 12-3, 6-10.30(12-10.30 summer) Sun

⌣**Countryman**

The third highest pub in the UK, isolated on Dartmoor, whose log fire has burned continuously since 1845.

◖ ▶

POWDERHAM CASTLE

Powderham Castle Farm Shop

☎ 01626 891883

9-6; 10-4 Sun

⌣**Grays; Luscombe; Sheppys; West Monkton.**

Farm shop whose cider range (all in glass, plastic or ceramic) has increased steadily since opening in May 1999. Also sells an interesting selection of West Country wines.

◖

PRINCETOWN

Plume of Feathers

The Square

☎ 01822 890240

11-11; 12-10.30 Sun

⌂**Countryman**

Princetown's oldest pub (1785), popular with Dartmoor walkers. Slate floors, good disabled facilities.

STAVERTON

Riverford Farm Foods

Riverford Farm

☎ 01803 762523

9(10 Wed)-6; 10-4 Sun

⌂**Luscombe Organic Young Devon Cider (Feb-May), Traditional Devon Cider.**

Organic farm shop run by a family of organic farming sons. Cider sold in either glass bottles or plastic containers.

TEIGNMOUTH

Teign Brewery

20 Teign Street

☎ 01626 772684

11-11; 12-10.30 Sun

⌂**Thatchers Dry**

Pub in a building that once housed a brewery. The friendly landlord also sells keg Thatchers, so ask for the Real Cider by name.

~~REAL ALE~~

Photographs

Cider Cellar sign at Gray's Cider.

Photo: Dave Matthews

Larry Pope of Green Valley Cyder Ltd. with the Devon County Show Championship Cup (from 1999 show).

Photo: Nigel Albright

Kennford Cider Farm.

Photo: Dave Matthews

Manor Inn, Lower Ashton, Devon.

Photo: Dave Matthews

Ye Olde Cider Bar, Newton Abbot.

Photo: Dave Matthews

DORSET

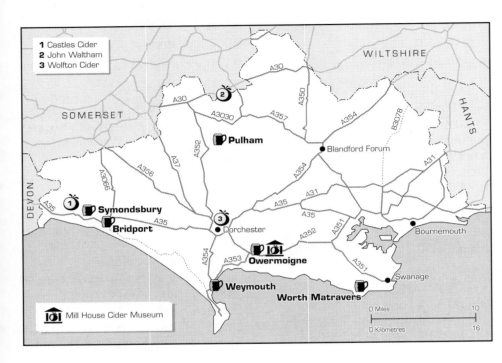

1 Castles Cider
2 John Waltham
3 Wolfton Cider

WILTSHIRE

SOMERSET

HANTS

Pulham

Blandford Forum

DEVON

Symondsbury

Bridport

Dorchester

Bournemouth

Owermoigne

Swanage

Weymouth

Worth Matravers

Mill House Cider Museum

0 Miles   10
0 Kilometres   16

Dorset Producers

CASTLES CIDER

Crabbs Bluntshay Farm,
Whitchurch, Canonicorum, Near
Bridport, Dorset, DT6 6RN.

☎ *01297 489064*

Although founded as recently as
1997, Castles Cider is steeped in
history with a press dating from
1850, an apple mill dated circa
1890, and a 250 year old Cider
Cellar under Crabbs Bluntshay
Farm itself.

Cider
Castle's Dorset Cider, 7% abv
(.75 litre bottles or on draught,
unfiltered)

Annual Production
750 gallons

Visitors
Welcome, tours available but no
coaches please.

Directions
Approach from Broad Oak, turn
left at Shave Cross, 800 yards
down lane on the left.
OS map reference: SY 415974.

JOHN WALTHAM

Manor Farm, Purse Caundle,
Sherborne, Dorset, DT9 5QY.

☎ 01963 250239

John's cider must be good, for
when it won the Dry Cider class at
the Bath & West Show (c. 1993)
it was stolen from the showground! Five generations of John's
family have made cider at Manor
Farm, but sadly John plans to
leave farming. He hopes to set up
his cidermaking elsewhere, please
contact Manor Farm for details.

Cider
Dry, 7-8% abv (5 & 25 litre containers).

Annual Production
1700 gallons.

Visitors
Welcome, by appointment only.

Directions
Head out of Sherbourne on the
A30 and take the Purse Caundle
turn on the right. In the middle of
the village, turn right to Manor
Farm.

Sales
Farm gate sales by appointment
only.

Outlets
Trooper, Stourton Caundle.

WOLFETON CIDER

Wolfeton House, Near Dorchester,
Dorset, DT2 9QN.

☎ 01305 263500

Wolfeton House is the fine mediae-
val and Elizabethan home to the
Thimbleby family. Cider is made in
the old cyder house, which is open
to the public during the summer
months.

Cider
Wolfeton Cider (in bottles or on
draught)

Visitors
During house opening hours (see
below) or by appointment.

Directions
1½ miles from Dorchester on
the A37 towards Yeovil.

Sales
July 15th-September 15th,
Mondays and Thursdays 2-6pm.

Dorset Outlets

BRIDPORT

Hope & Anchor

13 St Michaels Lane

☎ 01308 422160

11-11; 12-10.30 Sun

🍎**Burrow Hill; Taunton Traditional; Thatchers Cheddar Valley**

Unpretentious single-bar town local. Varying range of ales from West Country micros.

OWERMOIGNE

Mill House Cider Museum

The Mill House

☎ 01305 852220

10-5; closes at 4pm and all day Monday, Nov-March

🍎**Burrow Hill**

The shop at the Cider Museum sells both the cider and cider brandy from Burrow Hill, as well as Lyme Bay wines and West Country cheeses. The museum's collection includes around 18 presses and the same number of mills, some of which have been restored to working order. There's also a nursery and clock museum. Well worth a visit.

PULHAM

Halsey Arms

☎ 01258 817344

11.30-2.30, 6-11

🍎**Cider varies**

Traditional Dorset pub with a pleasant atmosphere. Cider festival (with some 10-12 ciders) over one summer weekend. At least four guest ales.

◖ ◗

SYMONDSBURY

Ilchester Arms

☎ 01308 422600

11-3, 6-11; 12-3, 7-10.30 Sun

🍎**Taunton Traditional**

Low beamed country inn with a good food reputation.

◖ ◗

WEYMOUTH

Boot

High Street West

☎ 01305 770327

11-11; 12-10.30 Sun

🍎**Thatchers Cheddar Valley**

Weymouth's oldest inn, a true pub where conversation reigns. Difficult to find, look behind the fire station.

◖ ◗

Dorothy Inn

The Esplanade

☎ 01305 766996

11-11; 12-10.30 Sun

⌂Taunton Traditional

Seafront bar with a nightclub above. Late licence in the club until 2am, but with access to the bar.

◖ ◗

WORTH MATRAVERS

Square & Compass ☆

☎ 01929 439229

12-3, 6-11; 11-11 Sat; 12-3, 7-10.30 Sun

⌂Bulmers Traditional; Burrow Hill Dry, Medium; Thatchers Dry, Medium

A traditional old pub run by the same family since 1907. Food limited to home-made pasties only.

◖ ◗

Other Places of Cider Interest in Dorset

Mill House Cider Museum

Owermoigne, Nr Dorchester, Dorset, DT2 8HZ.

☎ 01305 852220

A fine collection of between 30-40 cider-making mills and presses, all dating from the 18th and 19th centuries, some of which have been restored to working condition. There's also a video on the cider-making process, and the shop sells both cider and cider brandy.

Open

April-October,   10am-5pm, Monday to Sunday.

November-March,   10am-4pm, Tuesday to Sunday.

(Closed   December   25th   to January 14th)

DURHAM

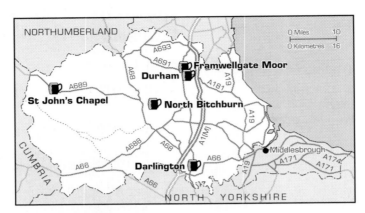

Durham Outlets

DARLINGTON

Binns Department Store
1-7 High Row

☎ 01325 462606

9-5.30(6 Sat); 11-5 Sun

☃**Westons In Bottle Conditioned**

Established off-licence in the basement of a large department store
selling a wide range of English and
Belgian bottle-conditioned products.

Oddbins
24 Grange Road

☎ 01325 468884

11-9 Mon-Thur; 10-9 Fri/Sat

☃**Westons In Bottle Conditioned**

National off-licence chain selling a
range of bottle-conditioned products.

Tanners Hall
64 Skinnergate

11-11; 12-10.30 Sun

☃**Addlestones**

Large Wetherspoons pub selling
cheap food and drink all day.
Building formerly a shop premises.
Numerous beer festivals throughout the year.

◖ ◗

Tap & Spile
99 Bondgate

☎ 01325 381679

11-11; 12-10.30 Sun

☃**Westons Old Rosie**

Large town house now run by the
local Castle Eden brewery, offering
a range of Castle Eden beers and
guest ales.

◖

DURHAM

Market Tavern

27 Market Place

☎ 0191 386 2069

11-11; 12-10.30 Sun

◠Bulmers Traditional

Narrow T&J Bernard alehouse near the market which dates from 1850. The selection of Scottish Courage beers and guest ales help to satisfy the thirst of the many shoppers that pile in during the day. Food limited to pies after 2pm.

◖ ◗

Oddbins

73-75 Saddler Street

☎ 0191 386 1079

10-8; 11-5 Sun

◠Westons In Bottle Conditioned Cider

National off-licence chain selling a range of bottle-conditioned products.

FRAMWELLGATE MOOR

Tap & Spile

27 Front Street

☎ 0191 386 5451

11.30-3, 6-11; 12-3, 7-10.30 Sun

◠Westons Old Rosie

Popular two roomed village pub on the A167 by-pass 1¹/₂ miles north of Durham city centre. Offers a choice of guest ales.

◖

NORTH BITCHBURN

Famous Red Lion

North Bitchburn Terrace

☎ 01388 763561

12-3, 7-11; 12-3, 7-10.30 Sun

◠Addlestones

Rural pub with a reputation for excellent food and fine ales. The two house beers 'Mane Brew' and 'Weird Ale' are brewed by Hambleton. Note the interesting pub sign.

◖ ◗

ST JOHN'S CHAPEL

Blue Bell Inn

12 Hood Street

☎ 01388 537256

5(11 Sat)-11; 12-3, 6.30-10.30 Sun

◠Addlestones

Village local dating from 1840. High in the Pennines with excellent country walking on the doorstep, hence popular with ramblers.

ESSEX

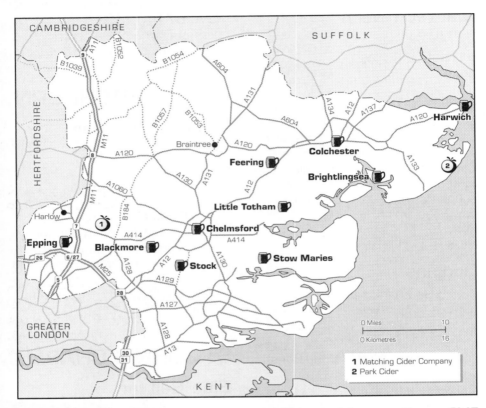

1 Matching Cider Company
2 Park Cider

ESSEX Producers

MATCHING CIDER COMPANY

4 Mill Lane, Moreton, Essex, CM5 0DN.

☎ 01277 890519

Steve DeLarre has been making Old Moulder cider for some ten years now, using culinary apple varieties Cox and Bramley, and when available Spartan and Hawgate Wonder. Molly Dancer cider is a more recent addition to Matching's portfolio and has a much higher tannin content than

Old Moulder, similar to a West Country cider.

Both of Steve's ciders are fermented with a commercial yeast, and neither contains any added water, colouring or sweetener. Due to planning regulations Steve regrets that visitors are not allowed at the cider barn. Instead, find his ciders at selected local free houses and beer festivals.

Ciders

Old Moulder, 7.5% abv

Molly Dancer, 7% abv

(Both available on draught or in 4 pint containers)

Annual Production

1500 gallons

Outlets

• White Horse, Hatfield Heath, Essex.

• White Hart, Moreton, Essex.

• Wholesaler: Jon Hallam, tel 01179 660221.

PARK CIDER

7.5% ABV   75cl

Cider

Serve Chilled

Naturally Dry and Still Cider
fermented in oak barrels
Consume within 4 days of opening
• Park Fruit Farm • Gt Holland • Frinton • Essex •

G.E.Elsworth & Son, Park Fruit Farm, Pork Lane, Gt Holland, Frinton-on-Sea, Essex.

☎ 01255 674621

Formerly known as 'Hogshead Cider', cider production is now an integral part of Park Fruit Farm. The dry unfiltered cider is made in the traditional East Anglian way from Bramleys and dessert apples, and is fermented on its own yeasts, without additives, in oak barrels. They also produce fresh, unpasteurised apple juice, from apples pressed 2-3 times a week in season.

Cider

Park Cider, 7% abv (75cl bottles. Please 'phone ahead if you wish to provide your own container.)

Visitors

Welcome

Directions

Take A133 from Colchester to Weeley, then B1033 to Thorpe-le-Soken. Keep on B1033 for about 2 miles (towards Frinton & Kirby), turn right into Pork Lane, the farm is about one mile ahead.

Sales

Farm Shop open: Mon-Sat 9-5, Sunday 10-4, August – December. Mon-Sat 9-5, closed Sunday, January – March.

Other items on sale include: many varieties of apples, other fruit, fresh apple juice, honey, vegetables and eggs.

Essex Outlets

BLACKMORE

Leather Bottle

The Green

☎ 01277 821891

11-11; 12-10.30 Sun

🍺Addlestones

A village pub with two bars and a restaurant area. Attractions include a real fire, monthly jazz, quiz evenings, and a beer festival every six weeks. Allegedly haunted by five ghosts.

◖ ◗

BRIGHTLINGSEA

Railway Tavern

Station Road

☎ 01206 302581

5(3 Fri)-11; 12-11 Sat; 12-3, 7-10.30 Sun

🍺Cider varies

Excellent two-bar local offering five guest ales and varying cider. Five day cider festival every year over the first weekend in May. The land-lord brews his own beer 'Crab and Winkle Mild' on the premises.

CHELMSFORD

Globe

65 Rainsford Road

☎ 01245 350232

11-11; 12-10.30 Sun

🍺Addlestones

Large open-plan Wetherspoons pub, popular with all ages. Several guest beers.

◖ ◗

COLCHESTER

Odd One Out

28 Mersea Road

☎ 01206 578140

4.30-11; 11-11 Fri/Sat; 12-10.30 Sun

🍺**Crones User Friendly Organic; Thatchers Medium; Theobolds Strong Kentish**

A Georgian conversion of two 18th Century cottages, this friendly, basic local is just 200 yards from Colchester railway station. The ciders are served by gravity from the cask, and the five guest ales on offer always include a dark beer. Spirits available include fifty malt whiskies, twelve Irish whiskies, and madeira on optic.

EPPING

Forest Gate

Bell Common

☎ 01992 572312

10-3, 5.30-11; 12-3, 7-10.30 Sun

⌒**Bulmers Traditional**

On the edge of Epping Forest, this single-bar, traditional, 17th century pub has been run by the same family for many years. The lunchtime turkey broth is highly recommended.

◖ ◗

FEERING

Sun Inn

Feering Hill

☎ 01376 570442

11-3, 6-11; 12-3, 6-10.30 Sun

⌒**Cider varies**

Originally part of a 16th century gentleman's residence known as "Feering House", the Sun Inn today is a classic free house. The cider is served by gravity from the cellar, and up to twenty real ales make an appearance each week, with six on at any one time. There are forty single malts, two log fires and a large range of home-cooked food. Recommended by all the leading guides.

◖ ◗

HARWICH

Hanover Inn

65 Church Street

☎ 01255 502927

10.30-2, 6.30-11; 12-10.30 Sun

⌒**Addlestones**

A Grade II listed regulars pub in "Old Harwich".

LITTLE TOTHAM

Swan

School Road

☎ 01621 892689

11-11; 12-10.30 Sun

⌒**Westons Old Rosie, Perry; two guest ciders**

16th century beamed village pub in relaxing surroundings with friendly clientele. Essex CAMRA Pub of the Year 2000, the Swan holds a beer and cider festival each June. All year round there is an ever-changing range of five guest ales. No food Mondays and Tuesdays.

◖ ◗

STOCK

Hoop

21 High Street

☎ 01277 841137

11-11; 12-10.30 Sun

◌**Cider range varies.**

Great pub to which people travel from miles around. Offers between 6 and 12 varying real ales, plus 2 or 3 changing ciders. Good food. The May beer festival is held in the large back garden.

STOW MARIES

Prince of Wales

Woodham Road

☎ 01621 828971

11-11; 12-10.30 Sun

◌**Cider varies**

Renowned ale house with real fires and stone floors. Proprietor Rob Walster keeps around 5 real ales plus a large range of draught and bottled foreign beers. The Greek chef is an enthusiastic proponent of beer cuisine, and on Sunday nights between May and September he holds a Greek fish barbecue. The old Victorian bakery is put to good use (on Thursday nights between October and April) to bake pizzas. A real perry may occasionally accompany the changing cider on offer.

GLOUCESTERSHIRE & BRISTOL

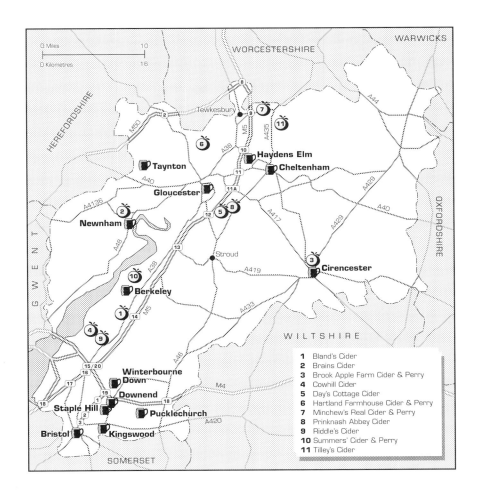

WARWICKS

WORCESTERSHIRE

HEREFORDSHIRE

0 Miles 10
0 Kilometres 16

Tewkesbury

Haydens Elm

Taynton

Cheltenham

Gloucester

Newnham

Stroud

Cirencester

Berkeley

GWENT

OXFORDSHIRE

WILTSHIRE

Winterbourne
Down

Downend

Staple Hill

Pucklechurch

Bristol

Kingswood

SOMERSET

1 Bland's Cider
2 Brains Cider
3 Brook Apple Farm Cider & Perry
4 Cowhill Cider
5 Day's Cottage Cider
6 Hartland Farmhouse Cider & Perry
7 Minchew's Real Cider & Perry
8 Prinknash Abbey Cider
9 Riddle's Cider
10 Summers' Cider & Perry
11 Tilley's Cider

Gloucestershire & Bristol Producers

BLAND'S CIDER

Heneage Farm, Moorslade Lane, Falfield, Glos, GL12 8DJ.

☎ 01454 260019 (Heneage Farm, sales)

☎ 01453 811004 (Vernon Bland, cider maker)

Vernon Bland made his first cider at Frampton on Severn in 1970. By the time he sold his company to Hazlewood's Cider in 1983, his annual production had risen from 2 thousand to 2 million gallons a year. But he couldn't keep away, so after a gap of 16 years, Bland's Cider is back, and being sold for him at a local farm. Vernon is a great believer in using stainless steel, for both fermentation and storage, and as a result he claims "I've never lost a gallon in my life!".

Ciders

Dry, Medium and Sweet (2¹/₂ litre, 5 litre, 2 gallon and 5 gallon containers)

Annual Production
5000 gallons

Visitors
Welcome

Directions
Leave the M5 at Junction 14, and head for the A38. Turn right onto the A38 towards Gloucester, then take the first turning on the left (look for the 'cider' sign).

Sales
Farm gate sales. Most reasonable hours, please ring ahead.

BRAINS CIDER

The Orchards, Edge Hills, Littledean, Cinderford, Glos.

☎ 01594 822416

Dave Brain makes cider in one of England's most idyllic spots – a secluded clearing deep in the Forest of Dean, only accessed by an unmetalled road through the forest, with views towards Gloucester and beyond. Cider has been made at The Orchards for over one hundred years, and today Dave uses his own cider apples and an old twin screw press with forest stone base and run off trough. The mill is modern and electric, because Dave's father broke up the horse-drawn one in the 1950s and used the stone to build the shed now housing the mill and press.

Dave recounts a local story: "On a steep wooded bank about half a mile from the house, a horse drawn cider press base stone was being chipped out of a large piece of stone. When nearly finished it cracked and was left where it was, and can be still seen there today. No doubt there were some choice remarks when this happened. No one knows the exact date that this occurred, but it was probably over 120 years ago."

Brains Ciders are full-flavoured and traditional in style, with plenty of tannin from the use of apple varieties such as Vilberie.

Cider

Farmhouse Dry/Medium (5 litre containers or manucubes, or bring your own)

Annual Production

400-600 gallons

Visitors

Welcome

Sales

Farm gate sales any reasonable time, but please ring first.

Other items on sale: Perry pears, several varieties, can be milled and pressed if required.

Awards

'Cider of the Festival', Cardiff Beer & Cider Festival 1998.

BROOK APPLE FARM CIDER AND PERRY

'New Season'
PERRY

7.0% abv   75cl
BROOK APPLE FARM
Rendcomb
Cirencester
GLOUCESTERSHIRE
01285 831479   L61

24 Rendcomb, Cirencester, Gloucestershire, GL7 7HF.
☎ 01285 831479

Email bob@cook.freeuk.com

Brook Apple Farm Cider and Perry was born in 1998. Like most enthusiasts, Bob Cook started by making a single 40 gallon barrel, but has since increased his output of bottled ciders and perries. After unprecedented success in his first competition – Putley 2000 – Bob plans to both increase production and to diversify towards supplying draught cider and perry to local pubs.

Ciders

New Season Cider, 8.2% abv
New Season Perry, 7% abv
(The name of the cider or perry changes with every bottling – about 200 bottles each time.)

Annual Production

360 gallons

Outlets

Cirencester's Farmer's Market, every 2nd Saturday in the month. Contact Simon Smith 014353 834777.

Awards

Big Apple Cider Trials at Putley 2000: 1st and 3rd for Draught Cider (Dry and Medium Sweet), 1st for Bottled Cider and 1st for Bottled Perry.

COWHILL CIDER

Fishermans Cottage, Cowhill, Oldbury-on-Severn, South Gloucestershire, BS35 1QS.

☎ 01454 412152

John Tymko produces his rich, ripe and tasty ciders (and occasional perries) virtually in the shadow of the old Severn Bridge. Cowhill Cider was started by John's Father-in-Law in 1960, and the cider is made entirely from local organic cider apples. The twin-screw hand press (1/3 ton capacity) has no gearing system and is described by John as "probably obsolete when Victoria came to the throne, and must be one of the oldest working presses in the country." The juice is fermented naturally in oak casks, from which customers' containers are filled directly.

Ciders

Dry and Medium, both 6.5% abv.

Annual Production

1500 gallons

Visitors

Welcome. Tours available.

Directions

Cowhill Cider is 5 miles from Junction 14 on the M5, and 4 miles from Junction 1 on the M48 (the old Severn Bridge). Near the village of Oldbury-on-Severn.

Sales

Farm gate sales during daylight hours. Best to phone first.

DAY'S COTTAGE CIDER

Day's Cottage Apple Juice & Cider Co., Day's Cottage, Upton Lane, Brookthorpe, Gloucestershire, GL4 0UT.

☎ 01452 813602

Email applejuice@care4free.net

Dave Kaspar and Helen Brent-Smith live and work on an organic small-holding that has been in Helen's family for many genera-tions. They have restored the old orchard – established in 1912 by Helen's Great Aunt – and have planted around 250 standard apple trees during the past 8 years, mostly old cooking and eat-ing varieties that supply the raw material for their successful apple juice business. But they have also started to make and sell small amounts of cider, and so have planted some Kingston Black, Dunkertons Late Sweet, Broxwood Foxwhelp and Severn Bank cider apple trees.

The cider is fully traditional, fermented with the natural yeasts, and production levels are likely to rise in the future. Dave is also currently developing a perry.

Ciders

Day's Cottage Cider, 7% abv

Mrs Sylvie's Cow, 7% abv (apples from Mrs Sylvie's orchard, including her big, pale, yellow Severn Bank "Cow Apples"!)

(Both available in 1 and 2¹/₂ litre plastic containers)

Annual Production

400 gallons cider; 15 000 75cl & 10 000 25cl bottles of apple juice.

Visitors

Welcome.

Directions

Take the A4173 south from Gloucester towards Stroud. After crossing the M5, take the first turn on the left (Upton Lane). Day's Cottage is 400 yards down on the right.

Sales

Farmgate sales at any reasonable time, but please ring ahead.

Also on sale: apple juice, cider vinegar, vegetables, free-range eggs.

Outlets

Farmers Markets: Corn Street, Bristol (Wednesdays); Stroud (1st & 3rd Saturday of the month); Cirencester (2nd Saturday); Dursley (4th Saturday).

Wholesaler: Jon Hallam

HARTLAND FARM-HOUSE CIDER AND PERRY

Tirley Villa, Tirley, Gloucestershire, GL19 4HA.

☎ 01452 780480

In making his traditional Farmhouse cider, Dereck Hartland continues a long family tradition. Dereck reports that his late father Ray (by all accounts a real character, and the subject of an article by Roy Bailey that can be found on Roy's website), was making cider with Ray's Father-in-Law Arthur Strawford at Flat Farm back in the 1950s. The family stepped-up production in 1982, and moved to Tirley Villa in 1994. Today Dereck welcomes customers into his Cider Shed and Shop, where the Dry and Sweet ciders can be poured from his row of oak barrels and may be blended to produce a Medium to suit individual tastes.

Hartland's Ciders are made from a blend of cider apples that include Yarlington Mill and a rare local variety named Corse Hill. They are fully traditional and have a beautiful balance of fruitiness and tannin.

Ciders

Sweet, Medium and Dry Cider, 5.5-6.5% abv.

Perry, 5.5-6.5% abv.

(All available in 5 litre containers)

Annual Production

3300 gallons

Visitors

Welcome. Tours available, but please phone first.

Directions

From Tewkesbury take the A38 towards Gloucester. Turn right at the traffic lights for Apperley (B4213), go through Apperley over Haw Bridge, through Tirley village. Take first left after village, Tirley Villa is just on the right.

Sales

Shop open 9am to 6pm.

Also on sale: chutneys, pickles, eggs, vegetables.

Outlets

English Farm Cider Centre, Sussex.

Plans to supply The Boat, Ashleworth at the time of writing.

Wholesalers: Jon Hallam, 0117 9660221.

Inn Cider.

Awards

Cider: Putley 'Big Apple' 1994.

Perry: GBBF 1989, Norwich 1994, St Albans 1999.

MINCHEW'S REAL CYDER & PERRY

Rose Cottage, Aston Cross, Tewkesbury, Gloucestershire, GL20 8HX.

☎ 01684 773427 or 0797 4034331 (mobile).

Email kevinornikki@minchewscyderandperry.freeserve.co.uk

Web site http://members.tripod.co.uk/Minchews/index-3.html.

Founding his company as recently as 1993, Kevin Minchew has already become one of the most successful and respected craft cider makers in the UK. A passionate ambassador for his art and its threatened culture, he was presented with APPLE's Pomona Award in 1999 for his work in searching for, grafting and conserving rare perry pear varieties. Rare varieties of perry are once again being planted in Gloucestershire's orchards, due in no small part to the publicity given to them by Kevin's range of single variety bottled and draught perries. Kevin also produces a number of single variety cyders, which together with his perries (and occasional blends) form the largest range produced by a single cidermaker anywhere in the world.

Production techniques are fully traditional to ensure a top-quality product. Most of the cider apples, and all of the perry pears, are sourced from unsprayed orchards. The fruit is picked, washed and any damaged areas cut out – all by hand. After milling the juice is extracted with an ancient stone-bedded twin-screw press, then fermented with its natural yeasts in small oak barrels. Kevin's cyders and perries are strong, smooth and have an appealing depth of flavour. At the time of writing he has plans to release some of his vintages in bottle-fermented form.

Ciders

Single variety ciders: Kingston Black, Dabinett, Stoke Red, Somerset Redstreak, Sheeps Snout, Medaille d'Or, Foxwhelp, Rienne de Hative, Yarlington Mill. Occasional blends.

Perries

Single variety perries: Malvern

Hills, Rock, Gin, Dumbleton Huffcap, Blakeney Red,

Oldfield, Walton Cardiff Huffcap, White Longdon.

Occasional blends

• The precise range of single varietal cyders and perries varies from year to year, depending on the availability of fruit.

• Alcoholic strength also varies from vintage to vintage, but typically approaches 8.4% abv.

• Cyders and perries are available filtered in 75cl bottles, or draught in 2 pint, 4 pint and 1 gallon containers, 5 gallon polykegs and 9 gallon metal kegs.

Annual Production

7000 litres.

Visitors

Welcome, by appointment only. Tours available.

Sales

Farm gate sales, wholesale only. Please ring ahead.

Outlets

• Orchard, Hive & Vine, Leominster, Herefordshire. Tel: 01568 611232.

• Green Valley Cider Ltd, Clyst St George, Devon. Tel: 01392 876658.

• York Beer Shop, York. Tel: 01904 647136.

• Pam's Pantry, Cheltenham, Glos. Tel: 01242 515661.

• English Farm Cider Centre, Lewes, Sussex. Tel: 01323 811324.

• Goodfood Shop, Newcastle-under-Lyne, Staffs. Tel: 01782 710234.

• Bromfords, Cricklade Street, Cirencester, Glos.

• Wayside Farm Shop, 50 Pitchers Hill, Wickhamford, Evesham, Worcs.

• Beehive Inn, Cheltenham, Glos. Tel: 01242 579443.

Wholesaler: John Reeke, Merrylegs.

Awards

A great many, including:

The Big Apple Trials, Putley: 1st 1993 and 1995.

Hereford Museum of Cider: 1st 1995 and 1997, 1st and Overall Champion 1999.

Stockport Beer and Cider Festival: Perry of the Festival and Overall Champion 1997.

CAMRA National Cider and Perry Championships: Silver Medal, Perry, 1999 (and voted Overall Champion by the public).

PRINKNASH ABBEY CIDER

Prinknash Abbey Enterprises, Prinknash Abbey, Cranham, Gloucestershire, GL4 8EX.

☎ 01452 812455 (Abbey)

☎ 01452 812066 (Gift Shop).

Email Pabbey@Waitrose.com

Prinknash Abbey is home to a Benedictine Roman Catholic community, and has extensive facilities for visitors including a gift shop selling their cider. Perry was made at the abbey at least as early as 1945, using a horse-powered mill, for consumption by the community and its guests. A cider orchard was planted in 1972, and good crops persuaded the Brothers to change from perry to cider making. Nowadays an electric mill and press are used, and sales are exclusively from the gift shop.

Cider

Prinknash Abbey Cider (25cl & 75cl glass bottles, 2.5 litre plastic containers. 5 litre plastic containers available by prior arrangement).

Annual Production

1400 gallons.

Visitors

Visitors are welcome to see the cider department when production is in progress (during

October & November), or by arrangement. Please contact the manager of the shop.

Directions

On the A46 between Cheltenham and Stroud, follow the tourist signs.

Sales

Gift shop open 7 days a week, 9am to 5.30pm summer, 9am to 4.30pm winter.

Also on sale: Apple juice, pottery, gifts, religious items (e.g. rosaries, incense, books).

RIDDLE'S CIDER

Oak Farm, Oldbury Lane, Thornbury, South Gloucestershire.

☎ 01454 413263

Matthew Riddle gathers his cider apples from the parishes of Thornbury, Tytherington and Oldbury-on-Severn, all in the Vale of Berkeley. Milled and pressed using machinery dating from the early 1900s, then matured in oak barrels, the result is a fully traditional farmhouse cider that has been compared (by cider wholesaler Jon Hallam) to a fine, dry Belgian gueuze.

Cider

Riddle's Cider, 6-7% abv (1 gallon or 5 litre plastic containers).

Annual Production

1500 gallons.

Visitors

Welcome.

Directions

Come out of Thornbury towards Oldbury-on-Severn, second house on the right in Oldbury Lane.

Sales

Farm gate sales daylight hours, closed Sundays.

Also on sale: free range eggs.

SUMMERS' CIDER & PERRY

Slimbridge Lane, Halmore, Near Berkeley, Glos, GL13 9HH.
☎ 01453 811218

Rodney Summers started his cider company in 1982, after inheriting orchards that had belonged to the Apple Tree Inn, a noted cider house that once traded at Halmore. The apples and pears used are all grown in the Vale of Berkeley, and are free from artificial fertilisers, pesticides and fungicides. When the pears are available, Rodney makes a single variety perry from the Green Horse pear tree, one of the oldest perry varieties on record.

Cider
Breadstone Dry Cider, 6.5% abv
Medium Cider, 6.5% abv
Medium Perry, 5.5% abv (all three available in 1 gallon containers or 5 gallon kegs)
Green Horse Perry (when pears available)

Visitors
Welcome

Sales
Farm gate sales 9am-1pm, 2pm-6pm.

Awards
Overall Winner, National Cider and Perry Championships 1997, Great British Beer Festival, London.

TILLEY'S CIDER

Moat Farm, Malleson Road, Gotherington, Cheltenham, Gloucestershire, GL52 4ET.
☎ 01242 676807.
Email jo@moatfarm.free-online.co.uk

Peter Tilley is a retired musician who has been making cider at Moat Farm for 35 years. Peter and his family also offer holiday cottages, a riding school and B&B; and Peter says that he makes cider really just for the fun of it. Cider is sold from the barn, with free tastings available. Peter also offers a contract apple-pressing service.

Ciders
Tilley's Sweet, Medium & Dry, 4.5% abv ($2^1/_2$ & 5 litre plastic containers).

Annual Production
3000 to 4000 gallons.

Visitors
Welcome, but tours not available.

Directions
Turn off the A46 Cheltenham to Evesham road towards Gotherington. Follow the road

past the Shutters pub, Moat Farm is about 400 yards further on the left in the centre of the village.

Sales

Farm gate sales 7am to 7pm, Monday to Saturday. 7am to 1pm, Sunday.

Outlet

English Farm Cider Centre, Lewes, Sussex.

Photographs

Dereck Hartland in his cider house.

Photo: Dave Matthews

Hartland's Farm House Cider Sign.

Photo: Dave Matthews

Bottle of Minchew's Classic Perry.

Photo: Dave Matthews

Gloucestershire & Bristol Outlets

BERKELEY

 CIDER PUB

sells more cider than beer!

Mariners Arms
49 Salter Street

☎ 01453 811822

11-11; 12-10.30 Sun

Bulmers Traditional Medium

A very traditional drinkers pub, popular with the locals. Public bar, lounge bar, snug and skittle alley – with real beams and open fires. No juke box, fruit machines or pool, just traditional pub games. Live music Saturdays, quiz once a month.

BRISTOL

 CIDER PUB

sells more cider than beer!

Apple Tree
27 Philip Street, Bedminster

☎ 0117 966 7097

10.30-11; 12-10.30 Sun

Taunton Traditional

Cracking backstreet single-roomed cider house. Probably the smallest pub in Bristol, packed full of friendly characters. The cider is drunk from handled glass mugs with a slice of lemon to "take the acid out of the cider", a habit possibly unique to Bristol's cider drinkers! Don't miss this little gem.

REAL ALE

Avon Packet

185 Coronation Road, Bedminster

☎ 0117 987 2697

11-11; 12-10.30 Sun

⌂Taunton Traditional; Thatchers Traditional, Cheddar Valley

Very friendly, characterful pub. Outdoors there's a duck pond, children's play area, patio used for barbeques, and the site of a bear pit that was once used for bear baiting. The home-cooked and competitively priced food is available right up to closing time.

◖ ▶

 CIDER PUB

sells more cider than beer!

Bridge

Main Road, Shortwood

☎ 0117 937 2328

11-11; 12-10.30 Sun

⌂Taunton Traditional

Large two-bar cider house next to the final phase of the Avon Ring Road (and the Avon Cycleway). Very traditional, with friendly bar staff and locals. Built in the 1880s, and named after the adjacent 150 year old rail bridge – sadly demolished and replaced with a concrete bridge in June 2000. Cribb (league team) and darts played.

 CIDER PUB

sells more cider than beer!

Coronation Tap

8 Sion Place, Clifton

☎ 0117 973 9617

12-3, 5.30-11; 12-3, 7-11 Sat; 12-3, 7-10.30 Sun

⌂Bulmers Traditional Medium, West Country, Inch's Harvest Scrumpy; Taunton Traditional; Exhibition

A single room with rustic decor, the Coronation Tap is Bristol's most famous cider house. It once sold nothing but cider, and today has a house cider – the sweet, full-bodied Exhibition (8.4% abv) – made especially for the Coronation Tap by a West Country cider maker. Popular with both students and locals, it is a good place to see "faces" from TV.

Tremendous, traditional , narrow cider house with a tiny snug at the front. Full of characters, aged 18 to 130, many of whom drink from their own personal cider mugs. Cider outsells beer by some 7 or 8 times, and the pub is one of the, if not *the* highest volume outlet for Thatchers traditional ciders. The character drinking cider on the pub sign is a customer called Gypsy John, and the cider frieze on the wall inside the pub was painted by customers some 30 to 40 years ago. Back in the 19th century, the building was used as a store for porter beer, and hence the pub's name. Occasional guest ciders, hot cider at Christmas, happy hour 2-5pm. A "must visit" cider house.

 CIDER PUB

sells more cider than beer!

Cotham Porter Stores

15 Cotham Road South, Cotham

☎ 0117 903 0689

12-11, 12-10.30 Sun

⌂Thatchers Dry, Cheddar Valley; Westons Traditional Scrumpy

Elstons

509 Wells Road, Hengrove

☎ 0117 977 5957

10-1, 4-10

⌂Draught: Broadoak Kingston Black, Special; Thatchers Dry, Medium

Off-licence selling both cider and beer on draught.

Long Bar

70 Old Market Street

☎ 0117 927 6785

11-11; 12-10.30 Sun

⌂Taunton Traditional; Thatchers Traditional

Hugely popular freehouse within half a mile of Broadmead Shopping Centre. Very competitively priced on all drinks, sells a great deal of cider.

CIDER PUB

sells more cider than beer!

Orchard

12 Hanover Place, Cumberland Road

☎ 0117 926 2678

12-3, 5-11; 12-4, 7-10.30 Sun

⌂Taunton Traditional; Thatchers Traditional Dry

Popular single-bar pub near Bristol's "Historic Harbour". Superb value lunches.
⌇

CHELTENHAM

Beehive

1-3 Montpellier Villas

☎ 01242 579443

12-11; 12-10.30 Sun

⌂Minchews

An old coaching house, the "village pub of Montpellier". Minchews Real Cyders available both on draught and bottled. The restaurant – "Upstairs at the Beehive" – is open 7-10pm, Thursday to Saturday.

⌇ ▶

Pam's Pantry

182 Bath Road

☎ 01242 515661 (Fax 01242 525842)

Web site www.pamspantry.co.uk

9-5.30, Mon-Sat

⌂Bottled: Minchews range

Independent delicatessen selling many locally produced quality foods and drinks, including most of the Minchews range of bottled cyders and perries. Hook Norton and Goffs bottled beers are also available, as well as polypins and firkins to order.

CIRENCESTER

Bomfords Deli

61A Cricklade Street

☎ 01285 656900

9-5.30

⌂Bottled: Minchews range

Delicatessen selling a comprehensive range of Minchews cyders and perries.

DOWNEND (BRISTOL)

 CIDER PUB

sells more cider than beer!

White Swan

70 North Street

☎ 0117 975 4154

11-11; 12-4, 7-10.30 Sun

⌂**Bulmers West Country, Inch's Stonehouse; Taunton Traditional**

Popular, traditional cider house with a convivial atmosphere, in which cider outsells beer roughly 6 to 1. Sells ten to twelve 11 gallon casks of Taunton Traditional per week alone, as well as 30-40 cases of Taunton Natch. One large main bar, a pool room, and a small enclosed outside seating area. The brass pipe on the gents urinal is kept well polished – always the sign of a good pub! At the time of writing the new licensee was planning to serve food.

GLOUCESTER

Black Swan

68-70 Southgate Street

☎ 01452 523642

11-11; 11-10.30 Sun

⌂**Westons Bounds Brand**

Town centre free house and hotel, with a good real ale range.

Imperial

Northgate Street

☎ 01452 539918

11-11; 12-10.30 Sun

⌂**Thatchers Traditional Dry**

Small town centre pub with a listed tiled exterior, selling as much cider as beer.

New Inn Hotel

Northgate Street

☎ 01452 522177

11-11; 11-10.30 Sun

⌂**Thatchers Cheddar Valley**

14th century coaching inn, with a courtyard surrounded by three bars and a restaurant. The first floor gallery leads to the accommodation. Between 6 and 10 real ales.

HAYDENS ELM

House in the Tree

(Just off the A40, west of Cheltenham)

☎ 01272 511493

11-11; 12-10.30 Sun

⌂**Bulmers Traditional, West Country, Inch's Harvest Dry;**

guest cider varies

Two-bar, thatched rural pub with a large beer garden. Cider festival early each summer.

◖ ◗

KINGSWOOD (BRISTOL)

 CIDER PUB

sells more cider than beer!

Essex Arms

237 Two Mile Hill Road,
☎ 0117 967 4161

12(11 Sat)-11; 12-10.30 Sun

⌣Moles Black Rat; Taunton Traditional

A traditional cider freehouse, built in 1732, with only two landladies in the last 70 years. The best selling cider is in bottles – Taunton Natch – and the customers drink their way through 60 cases a week. The Taunton Traditional is on handpump, but don't miss the Black Rat which is in a polycask behind the bar. There's a pool room at the back, and darts and crib teams play in the single bar at the front. The paved garden has a collection of caged birds. A Kingswood "institution", worth seeking out.

~~REAL ALE~~

(**Try also**: Kings Head (No real cider, but a great cider pub!))

NEWNHAM

Railway Inn

Station Road
☎ 01594 516317

11-11; 11-10.30 Sun

⌣Bulmers Traditional; Thatchers Cheddar Valley

Traditional village centre pub with a restaurant. Previously a cider house, and still sells as much cider as beer.

◖ ◗

PUCKLECHURCH

 CIDER PUB

sells more cider than beer!

Star Inn

37 Castle Street
☎ 0117 937 2391

11-11; 12-10.30 Sun

⌣Taunton Traditional; Thatchers Cheddar Valley, Traditional

Busy, welcoming pub, very much the centre of the local village life. The pub is L-shaped, and one corner is given over to diners who enjoy wholesome and good value food. Lots of cider sold, with the Cheddar Valley "Red" being a particular local favourite.

◖ ◗

STAPLE HILL

Humpers

26 Soundwell Road

☎ *0117 956 5525*

12-2, 5-10.30; (may open all day summer weekends)

⌢**Draught: Rich's Farmhouse Dry, Medium; Thatchers Cheddar Valley, Traditional**

Great off-licence selling competitively-priced traditional ciders and real ales. Sells 50 gallons of cider a week, and licensee Michelle will try to obtain any cider that customers request. Good Beer Guide listed for the past nine years.

TAYNTON

Taynton Farm Shop

☎ 01452 790220

9-6, 7 days a week

⌢**Draught: Thatchers Traditional Medium**

Bottled: Gregg's Pit; Gwatkins

Farm shop in a former cider mill, whose old press is now the shop's water feature! A comprehensive cider and perry selection is offered, as well as bottle-conditioned ales, Charles Martell's local cheeses, fruit wines, veg, honey, fruit, dairy produce, pies and cakes. Separate tea room. Notice the Taynton Squash perry pear tree on the village green outside.

WINTERBOURNE DOWN

Cross Hands

Down Road (Harcombe Hill junction)

☎ 01454 850077

12(11 Sat)-11; 12-10.30 Sun

⌢**Taunton Traditional; Thatchers Cheddar Valley**

Friendly, traditional village local with a large L-shaped bar and a small rear room. Large garden, children welcome. Five real ales, but beer only just outsells cider! Live music Fridays.

Photographs

Michael Buck, licensee of the Apple Tree, Bedminster, Bristol.
Photo: Dave Matthews

Orchard Inn, Bristol.
Photo: Dave Matthews

HAMPSHIRE

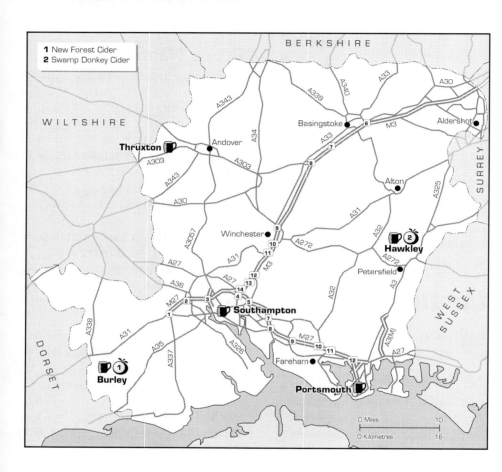

1 New Forest Cider
2 Swamp Donkey Cider

Hampshire Producers

NEW FOREST CIDER

Littlemead, Pound Lane, Burley, Ringwood, Hants, BH24 4ED.

☎ 01425 403589

Email newforestcider@msn.com

Although not in traditional cider country, Barry Topp's New Forest Cider company has a reputation for fine cider that extends well beyond the boundaries of Hampshire. Historically the village had its own cider-maker during the early part of the 20th Century, so when Barry started making cider

HEREFORDSHIRE

Herefordshire Producers

BROOME FARM CIDER

Broome Farm Perry

Medium Dry
Peterstow Perry

Broome Farm, Peterstow, Ross-on-Wye. HR9 6QG.
Tel. 01989 562824

75cl ℮   Alc.6% Vol
Best Before Dec 2000, Consume within 3 days of opening.
Store in cool, dark place. Best served chilled.

Broome Farm, Peterstow, Ross-on-Wye, Herefordshire, HR9 6QG.
☎ 01989 562824/769556

A visit to Broome Farm's cool cider cellar, to sample and buy Mike Johnson's excellent tradition-al farmhouse ciders, is one of life's great pleasures. If you're lucky he'll have some of his exquisite perry left (only limited quantities pro-duced), and if you ask he'll show you the stand of young perry trees which he has planted for the future. A recent innovation has been to bottle both the cider and the perry, carbonated versions courtesy of Hindlip College, and still versions put into wine bottles at the Three Choirs Vineyard. They're selling well due in no small part to the labels – some of the

most attractive in Britain – designed by Mike's wife.

Ciders
Draught:
Dry Cider, 6-7% abv (1 or 2 litre containers, or BYO)
Perry, 6-7% abv (1 or 2 litre con-tainers, or BYO)
Bottled:
Dry Cider, 6-7% abv (750ml bot-tles, filtered)
Perry, 6-7% abv (750ml bottles, filtered)
(Also available: 750ml bottles of Medium Dry Cider and Perry, 100% juice but carbonated and pasteurised)
Annual Production
1500 gallons
Visitors
Welcome
Directions
Turn off the A49 at Peterstow, follow the sign down a lane.
Sales
From the cellar at any reasonable time.

Also available: Bed & Breakfast, cream teas (summer only).

Outlets

Orchard, Hive & Vine, Leominster, Herefordshire.

Awards

Many awards, including:

1989: 1st in Cider Class, Hereford Cider Museum.

1999: 1st in Perry Class, Hereford Cider Museum (2nd and 3rd in Dry Cider Class)

BULMERS

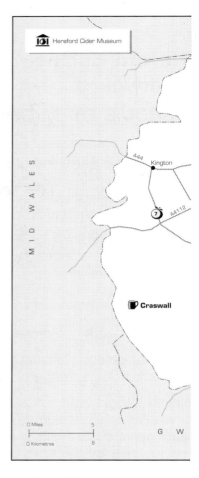

H P Bulmer Ltd, The Cider Mills, Plough Lane, Hereford, HR4 OLE.

☎ 01432 352000

Email enquiries@bulmer.com

Web site www.bulmer.com

With an annual production in the region of 55 million gallons, Bulmers is the world's largest cider maker, and enjoys a share of nearly 60% of the UK market.

Bulmers began in 1887 when Percy Bulmer first pressed apples

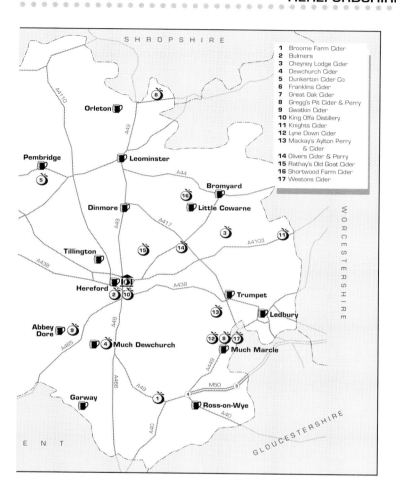

in his father's orchard. The following year he rented a warehouse in Maylord Street, Hereford and produced 4 000 gallons. Years of acquisitions and investment have allowed the company to grow from these modest beginnings to become the giant of the cider world. Most of its output today is industrial cider – cider which has been made using sugar and water, then pasteurised and carbonated – and includes such world-famous brands as Strongbow (currently the 11th biggest selling alcoholic long drink in the UK), Scrumpy Jack and Woodpecker.

Nevertheless, traditional cider is still an important part of Bulmers business, and their range was expanded in 1996 following the acquisition and then closure of Inch's of Devon. Bulmers traditional ciders are well worth trying, but most of the range can only be found in the south west of Britain. However, the medium version of Bulmers Traditional achieves UK-wide distribution, and is often the only oasis for 'Real Cider' in areas that are otherwise cider deserts.

Ciders

Bulmers Traditional, Medium or Dry, 4.9% abv (5 and 11 gallon casks).

Bulmers West Country, 5.5% abv (11 gallon casks).

Inch's Harvest Scrumpy, 8% abv (5 gallon casks).

Inch's Stonehouse Traditional, 6% abv (5 gallon casks).

(Also available: Many, including Strongbow, Scrumpy Jack, Woodpecker, White Lightning)

Annual Production

55 million gallons.

Visitors

Welcome. Tours of the cider mills that include tastings can be booked with Linda Torres on 01432 352000.

Sales

The company shop is open to visiting groups only.

Outlets

Widely available in pubs throughout the UK.

Wholesalers: most wholesalers stock Bulmers traditional ciders,

and at the time of writing Bulmers has just bought the 'Beer Seller' distribution chain.

CHEYNEY LODGE CIDER

Cheyney Lodge, Bishops Frome, Herefordshire.

☎ 01531 640159

A day job in the trade marketing department at Bulmers doesn't stop Mike Henney from running a small cider business at home in his spare time. He makes small amounts of traditional dry cider using local fruit, all of which is pressed, fermented and matured at Cheyney Lodge. Bishops Frome Cider is a blend of apple varieties, and according to Mike "the Foxwhelp in it makes it very distinctive." I would agree, and his most recent addition – Cheyney Lodge Cider – is an imaginative blend of a bitter-sweet cider apple (Dabinett) with an acidic cooker (Bramley).

Ciders

Bishops Frome Herefordshire Dry, 6-7% abv (2 litre corked glass jar)

Cheyney Lodge Dabinett and Bramley, 6% abv (37.5cl corked wine bottles)

Annual Production

1500 gallons.

Outlets

• Hop Pocket Wine Co, Bishops Frome, Herefordshire.

• Dickinsons Wine, Bridge St,

Hereford.
• Orchard, Hive & Vine, Leominster, Herefordshire.

Awards

1999. Joint 2nd , Dry Cider, Hereford Cider Museum.

1998. 1st, Dry Cider, Hereford Cider Museum.

DEWCHURCH CIDER

Hill Farm, Much Dewchurch, Hereford, HR2 8DG.

☎ 01981 540286

Robin Haig and his family started making their flavoursome cider and perry on a small scale in 1990. They use their own Kingston Black, Yarlington Mill, Dabinett, Stoke Red and Ashton Brown Jersey apples to produce a tasty blend and occasional single variety ciders. Robin no longer buys in perry pears, so until his young perry pear trees are mature enough to produce a viable crop, Dewchurch Perry will remain as only a tasty memory.

Dewchurch Dry and Sweet Cider is also available still and filtered, bottled at the Three Choirs Vineyard.

Cider

Dry Cider 7% abv

Sweet Cider 7% abv

(available in 5 litre and $2^{1}/_{2}$ litre plastic containers and 75cl glass bottles)

Plus a range of single varietal ciders, subject to availability.

(Also available: a Sparkling Medium Cider, 6.3% abv, in 75cl bottles.)

Annual Production

600 gallons

Visitors

Welcome

Directions

Heading South on the A49 out of Hereford, turn right onto the A466, then immediately right into a lane. The farm is $^{1}/_{2}$ a mile on the left. OS map reference 494326.

Sales

Farm gate sales, most days 9am – 5pm.

Outlets

Black Swan, Much Dewchurch, Hereford.

Awards

2nd Prize at the 'Big Apple' Cider and Perry Trials, Herefordshire, 1992 & 1997.

DUNKERTONS CIDER CO.

Luntley, Pembridge, Leominster, Herefordshire, HR6 9ED.

☎ 01544 388653

Web site www.kc3.co.uk/business/dunker.html

Ivor and Susie Dunkerton left TV production and theatre administration, respectively, to found Dunkertons Cider in 1981. They were one of the first in the new wave of cider revivalists, and the very first to start bottling single varietal ciders, an idea that has since inspired a number of others. In 1988 they became fully organic, and in doing so found a niche in which they excelled. As a result, the easiest way to find their bottled ciders and perries today is to visit almost any health food/organic shop in Britain. Their draught ciders and perries are also well worth trying, and can be sampled at Dunkerton's 'Cider House', an excellent gourmet restaurant that was opened in 1994, in a reconstructed 400 year-old barn.

Cider

Draught: Traditional Dry Cider, Medium Dry Cider, Medium Sweet Cider, Sweet Cider (all 7% abv)

Bottled: Improved Kingston Black Cider, (8% abv, 75cl). Court Royal Cider (8% abv, 75cl or 1 litre). Perry (8% abv, 75cl).

(Both the Breakwells Seedling and the Premium Organic Cider are filtered and pasteurised)

Annual Production

20 000 gallons

Visitors

Welcome. Tours available.

Directions

Travelling West along the A44 from Leominster, turn left at the New Inn. Carry on for one mile, and Dunkertons is on the left. Otherwise follow the brown signs.

Sales

Shop open 10am – 6pm, Mon – Sat all year.

Non-cider items on sale: cider house cakes.

Outlets

• All health food/organic shops throughout Britain. Good delicatessens.

• Selfridges, London.

• The Beer Shop, London N1.

• York Beer Shop.

Awards

Numerous, including:

Organic Food Awards 1999, Best Cider.

Best Cider, 1st Herefordshire

CAMRA Cider Festival.
CAMRA National Cider and Perry Championships 1998 and 2000 – Best Perry.

FRANKLINS CIDER

The Cliffs, Little Hereford, Near Ludlow, Shropshire, SY8 4LW.
☎ 01584 810488

Father and son team Jim and Lincoln Franklin make award-winning ciders and perries from their 8 acres of orchards on the banks of the River Teme, in the most northerly stretch of Herefordshire. The orchard was planted in 1974/75, and crops 60-100 tons per year. Apple varieties such as Dabinett, Yarlington Mill, Foxwhelp and Kingston Black are fermented using natural yeasts, then sold as either Dry, Medium or Sweet Cider. Franklins Dry Perry is one of the best I have ever tasted – very fruity, mellow and rounded – and was deservedly named overall champion at the Hereford Cider Museum's 1995 competition.

Visitors to Franklins shop at Little Cliffs can sample before buying, and can also choose from a range of local produce which includes a number of bottled beers from micro-breweries. However, levels of cider and perry production, as well as the shop's opening hours, may be scaled down from the 2000/2001 season onwards, as Jim approaches retirement age. Please ring ahead to avoid disappointment.

Ciders

Ciders: Dry, Medium and Sweet, 6.5-7% abv

Perries: Medium-Dry and Medium-Sweet, 6% abv

(All available in 75cl bottles; 1 litre, 2 litre, 3 litre, 5 litre and 5 gallon containers)

Annual Production

6000 gallons

Visitors

Welcome. Tours can be booked.

Sales

Shop open 9am to 6pm, Monday to Saturday.

Also on sale: Honey, wine, bees wax, apples, pottery, preserves and bottled beers.

Awards

Franklins have picked up many awards over the years, most notably:

1995 Hereford Museum of Cider, 1st Perry and Overall Champion.

GREAT OAK CIDER

Great Oak Cider and Apple Company, Roughmoor, Eardisley, Hereford, HR3 6PR.

☎ 01544 327400

Brian Jones, former Chairman of the Three Counties Cider and Perry Association, is one of cider's most respected veterans. These days his company is limited to contract pressing and sales of juice straight from the press, but he always makes the house vat available to guests and visitors for tastings.

Visitors
Welcome.

Directions
Take the A438 Hereford to Brecon road, turn north onto the A4111 to Eardisley. Turn right at the New Strand public house, after ¹/₂ a mile look for the 3rd house on the left after the 30mph sign.

Awards
Much Marcle Show 1999, 1st Dry Cider.

GREGG'S PIT CIDER & PERRY

Gregg's Pit, Much Marcle, Herefordshire, HR8 2NL.

☎ 01531 660687

James Marsden bought Gregg's Pit in 1992 and the title deeds showed that the cottage and 1.4 acre traditional orchard had been present since 1785. He immediately began to restore the orchard which had suffered from years of neglect, and started to identify the many varieties of eating, cooking, cider and perry fruit trees within it. James visited Bill George, the former owner of Gregg's Pit who was then blind, and took with him a plan of the orchard. "It was an amazing meeting," says James, "we walked through the orchard in Bill's mind and he was able to name several of the trees we hadn't then identified."

Today James is a small scale producer of craft cider and perry. He specialises in perry, made from fruit grown at Gregg's Pit and in a neighbour's adjacent orchards. Several single variety perries are usually available, and the range includes a blended perry made from the Gregg's Pit pear (whose trees are only found in and around Much Marcle) and other traditional varieties.

Ciders
Gregg's Pit Cider, 6% abv
Gregg's Pit Perry, 5.6-6.4% abv
(Draught in 2 litre containers or sterile filtered in 75cl bottles)

Annual Production
200-300 gallons.

Visitors
Welcome, by appointment only. Tours available.

Directions
Turn right off the Dymock Road

B4024 at the edge of the village of Much Marcle, up an unmade track for 400m to Gregg's Pit.
OS map reference: SO 663324

Sales

Farm gate sales by appointment only.

Outlets

• Marches Little Beer Shoppe, 2/4 Old Street, Ludlow, Shropshire (Tel: 01584 878999)
• Orchard, Hive & Vine, Leominster, Herefordshire (Tel: 01568 611232)
• Taynton Farm Shop, Taynton, Glos (Tel: 01452 790220).
Wholesaler: Jon Hallam (Tel: 0117 9660221).

Awards

'The Big Apple' Cider and Perry Trials, 1st Prize 1996, 1998 and 2000 (Best perry)
The Cider Museum, Hereford, Cider and Perry Competition 1st Prize 1996 (Best perry).

GWATKIN CIDER

Moorhampton Park Farm, Abbey Dore, Herefordshire, HR2 0AL.

☎ 01981 550258

Denis Gwatkin restarted cider-making at Moorhampton Park Farm in 1992 after a gap of some 50 years. Today he describes Gwatkin Cider as "a small firm that likes traditional ways". His traditional ways include using only cider fruit, maturing all of his cider and perry in oak casks, and never adding chemicals or carbonation of any kind. Dedication to traditional methods always pays off, and Denis has been rewarded with a whole host of awards, including CAMRA's National Champion Cidermaker of the Year in 1995. Denis specialises in single-varietal ciders and perries, and is one of the few cider makers to produce a Yarlington Mill cider, as well as perries made from Thorn, Oldfield, and Malvern Hills.

Cider

Ciders: Dry, Medium, Sweet, Yarlington Mill.
Perries: Thorn, Oldfield, Malvern Hills.
(All Gwatkin ciders and perries are available unfiltered in 5, 1 and $^1/_2$ gallon containers; or filtered in 75cl bottles)
The range of single-varietal ciders and perries changes from year to year.

Annual Production

1500 gallons

Visitors

Welcome

Directions

In the Golden Valley between Hereford and Abergavenny.

Sales

Farm gate sales 9am to 5pm.

Outlets

• Orchard, Hive and Vine (off-licence), Leominster.

• Neville Arms, Abbey Dore (and other pubs in the Golden Valley).

Wholesaler: Wye Valley Brewery (Tel 01432 342546)

Awards

CAMRA National Cider and Perry Championships – Gold 1995, Silver 1999. Stockport Beer Festival: Cider 1993, 1994, 1999; Perry 1992, 1998.

'Big Apple' Cider Trials: 2nd and 3rd in 1995.

Hereford Cider Museum: Best Presented Bottled Product 2000.

KING OFFA DISTILLERY

HEREFORD
CIDER BRANDY

5
years old
from
THE KING OFFA DISTILLERY
HEREFORD

40% vol   10 cl

Cider Museum, 21 Ryelands Street, Hereford, HR4 OLW.

☎ 01432 354207

Operated by, and part of, the Hereford Cider Museum, visitors can watch the distilling process through a viewing window. The cider brandy is made in an old calvados still brought back from Normandy. Some is blended with cider to produce a liqueur, some is blended with apple juice to produce an aperitif, and the remainder is sold in its natural form. All three are available from the museum shop.

Distilled Products

Hereford Cider Brandy, 40% abv.
Hereford Cider Liqueur, 25% abv.
Hereford Apple Aperitif, 18% abv.

Directions

To find the museum from the city centre, take the A438 Brecon Road and turn left at Sainsburys. OS map reference: GR 503399 (sheet 149).

Sales

Shop open: Jan-March, Tues-Sun, 11am-3pm.

April-Oct, daily, 10am-5.30pm.
Nov-Dec, daily, 11am-3pm.

Also on sale: books, gifts, tableware, goblets & decanters etc, all on a cider/apple theme.

Outlets

For details please ring 01432 354207.

KNIGHTS CIDER

Knights Cider Ltd, Crumpton Oaks Farm, Storridge, Nr. Malvern, Worcs, WR13 5HP.
☎ 01684 574594

Now a medium-sized regional cidermaker, Keith Knight planted his first apple trees in 1973 and made his first ciders in 1979. His planting programme has now yielded 200 acres of orchards. Visitors can sample Keith's cold filtered ciders in his farm shop, and walkers can follow a path from the shop, through the orchards and over the county border to the Worcestershire Way. Keith has always been a champion of traditional cider made from English apples, and his cidermaking efforts have been rewarded with regular prizes at the Hereford

Cider Museum competition.

Ciders

Knights Cider (Dry, Medium or Sweet), 6% abv.

Visitors

Welcome.

Directions

Turn off the A4103 onto the B4219 at Storridge. The farm is 400 yards on the left.

Map reference: 75.4 longitude, 78.5 latitude.

Sales

Shop open 10.30am to 5pm, Saturdays and Sundays.

Also on sale: Juices, cordials and small gifts.

Awards

Many prizes won at the Hereford Cider Museum competition, including:

1st, Medium Sweet Cider – 1993.
1st, Sweet Cider – 1993, 1997 & 1999.

LYNE DOWN CIDER

Lyne Down Farm, Much Marcle, Ledbury, Herefordshire, HR8 2NT.
☎ 01531 660691

HEREFORDSHIRE PRODUCERS

Award-winning, flavoursome, traditional ciders and perries are the hallmark of Lyne Down. Proprietor Jean Nowell has become famous for her perries, but she herself prefers to drink cider. As a result she kept a barrel of Kingston Black cider as her personal tipple, which became known as 'Mother's Special', and is today available in bottles.

Cider making at Lyne Down was revived in 1984 by Jean and her late husband Terry, and the equipment and methods used today are much as they once were in 1934. Jean attributes the house character of her ciders to both her use of strongly-flavoured sharp and bitter-sweet apple varieties, and to the unique strain of wild yeast that inhabits Lyne Down Farm. Draught ciders available usually include a Sweet, Medium, Dry and Very Dry. Jean's range of bottled ciders and perries changes from season to season.

Ciders

Draught Cider 7% abv, Draught Perry 7% abv (both available in 1 litre, 2 litre and 5 gallon plastic containers)

'Cidermakers Cider' 7.3% abv (a still, filtered cider in 75cl corked bottles)

(Carbonated bottled products available include 'Mother's Special' (a Kingston Black single varietal) and 'Pider' (a blend of pears and apples fermented together).

Annual Production

1500 gallons

Visitors

Welcome. Tours available during the cider-making season only (September to December)

Directions

Just off the A449, half way between Ross-on-Wye and Ledbury. Follow the 'Cider' signposts to Lyne Down.

Sales

Farmgate sales Easter to Christmas, during daylight hours, weekends and bank holidays. Other times by appointment.

Outlets

• Orchard, Hive & Vine (off-licence), Leominster.

• New Forest Cider, Burley, Hants.

Awards

Many, including: five-timer Best Perry at CAMRA's National Cider and Perry Championships, and various Perry of the Festival awards. Hereford Museum of Cider Overall Champion. In 1999, both Perry and Cider trophies at the 'Big Apple' Cider and Perry Trials at Putley, Herefordshire.

MACKAY'S AYLTON PERRY & CIDER

Aylton Perry

Made in Herefordshire
from local varieties
of perry pears.

7% A.B.V.   gall/litre
Glebe Farm, Aylton, Ledbury, Herefordshire,

Glebe Farm, Aylton, Ledbury, Herefordshire, HR8 2RQ.

☎ **01531 670121**

Janet Mackay was Secretary of the Three Counties Cider and Perry Association for many years, is a leading light in the 'Big Apple' organisation, and has formed her own company – 'Jus' – which produces a superb range of unfiltered single variety English apple juices. Cider and perry production therefore takes backstage somewhat, and of the small amounts produced most is for home consumption.

Glebe Farm is on the site of a rectory which had a cider house marked on the tithe map of 1841, and today is surrounded by the remnants of a perry orchard. Perry pears from two ancient trees in the orchard are used by Janet to produce her award-winning perry, and these are supplemented by fruit from Janet's perry

pear tree collection (20 varieties), planted between 10 and 12 years ago and now beginning to crop.

Ciders
Dry cider, 7.5% abv.
Perry, 7.5% abv.

Annual Production
Only a small amount that varies from year to year depending on the size of the harvest.

Visitors
Welcome informally, please telephone first.

Sales
Please telephone for availability.
Also on sale: Many single varieties of apple juice.

Outlets
The Yew Tree, Priors Frome, Herefordshire (Spring to Autumn).

Awards
'Big Apple' competition awards for perry.

OLIVERS CIDER AND PERRY

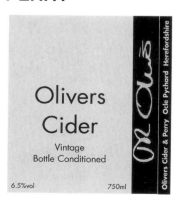

Olivers Cider
Vintage
Bottle Conditioned

6.5%vol   750ml

Olivers Cider & Perry Ocle Pychard Herefordshire

HEREFORDSHIRE PRODUCERS

Stanksbridge, Ocle Pychard, Herefordshire, HR1 3RE.

☎ 01432 820569

Email oliversciderandperry@theolivers.org.uk

Web site www.theolivers.org.uk

Founding his company in 1998, relative newcomer Tom Oliver produces his natural ciders and perries from unsprayed Herefordshire fruit. Tom sources the fruit from both his own orchard, and from orchards that are not commercially viable. He produces an interesting range of blended and single varietal ciders and perries, both on draught and in bottle.

Cider

Dry Cider, Medium Cider and Single Variety Ciders when available.

Dry Perry, Medium Sweet Perry and Single Variety Perries when available.

(Available on draught and/or sterile filtered in 750ml bottles)

Annual Production

500 gallons (increasing to 1500).

Sales

Wholesale only at present.

Outlets

• The Three Horseshoes, Little Cowarne, Herefordshire (Tel 01885 400276)

• Doodies Café Bar and Restaurant, St Owens St., Hereford (Tel 01432 269974)

• The Volunteer, Harold St.,

Hereford (Tel 01432 276189)

• Orchard, Hive & Vine (off-licence), Leominster (Tel 01568 611232)

Wholesaler: Richard Piggott at Winechooser in Brighton (Tel 01273 748672)

Awards

Second prize for medium/sweet perry at The Big Apple Cider and Perry Trials 2000.

RATHAYS OLD GOAT CIDER

RathayS Old Goat Cider

A blend of home grown apples including: Yarlington Mill, Tremlett's Bitter, Brown Thorn and Bulmer's Norman

Jenny Blackmore
Sutton St Nicholas, Hereford. HR1 3AY
Tel 01432-880936

Rathays, Sutton St. Nicholas, Hereford, HR1 3AY.

☎ 01432 880936

When Graham and Jenny Blackmore bought Rathays in 1996, it was as a smallholding with stables for their herd of pedigree angora goats. The two acre cider apple orchard was a bonus, but they soon set about exploring the possibilities of small-scale cider making. Just a few gallons of a clear, dry, traditional cider were made in both 1998 and 1999, but favourable feedback has persuaded them to step up production from the forthcoming 2000 harvest. Cider apple varieties used include Bulmers Norman, White Norman, Tremletts Bitter, Brown Thorn, Yarlington Mill, Foxwhelp and Vilberie.

The Blackmores see goat keeping as a natural partner to cider making. "It's a symbiotic relationship," says Graham, "the goats keep down the weeds and grass and fertilise the ground, and in return they scrump for whatever apples we don't use."

Cider
Old Goat Cider, 7-8% abv. (2 litre PET bottles).

Annual Production
48 gallons (1999).

Visitors
Welcome, but please ring first.

Sales
Farm gate sales, anytime but please ring first.

Also on sale: mohair fleece for hand spinners, blended mohair/wool/silk knitting yarn.

SHORTWOOD FARM CIDER

Shortwood Farm, Pencombe, Bromyard, Herefordshire.
☎ 01885 400205.

Shortwood Farm is one of Herefordshire's top family attractions, and Janet and David Legge allow visiting children to take part in a range of farm activities which include milking cows, collecting eggs, feeding calves and cuddling donkeys. For the adults, David's father Edward makes a fine drop of cider and perry. Visit Shortwood in the last two weeks of October and you'll be able to watch the cider being made, a spectacle that will include the rare treat of seeing a horse-powered circular stone mill, as used in days gone by.

Ciders
Cider.
Bramley Cider.
Organic Perry.
(All draught, unfiltered, available in 4 pint plastic containers).

Annual Production
Approx. 1000 gallons.

Visitors
Welcome. Tours available.

Directions

Shortwood Farm is signposted off the A417, north of Hereford.

Sales

The farm, which includes the farm shop, is open April to October, 11am onwards.

Shortwood is an organic farm, and also sells its own organic meat, vegetables and eggs.

WESTONS CIDER

H Weston & Sons Ltd, The Bounds, Much Marcle, Ledbury, Herefordshire, HR8 2NQ.

☎ 01531 660233

Email tradition@westons-cider.co.uk

Web site www.westons-cider.co.uk

A highly respected and award-winning regional cider maker, Westons remain an independent family business. They produce a comprehensive range of ciders and perries which are widely available throughout both the off- and on-licensed trade. In 1999 they achieved an unprecedented double – Westons Old Rosie won CAMRA's National Cider Gold Award and their Herefordshire County Perry clinched the Perry equivalent.

After buying 'The Bounds' in 1878, Henry Weston continued the farm's tradition of making cider for the resident family and for the workforce. In 1880 he decided to make cider for a living, and Westons has gone from strength to strength ever since. Today, cidermaking at The Bounds involves a mixture of tradition and technology, allowing the company to maintain flavour and quality despite the large volume of cider produced. Visitors to The Bounds can take a tour of the Cider Mill, visit the shop, or sample some of the draught ciders and perries whilst enjoying a meal in the excellent Scrumpy House Restaurant (tel: 01531 660626).

Ciders

Unfiltered:

Bounds Brand Scrumpy, 4.8% abv (22 & 50 litre polycasks).

Traditional Scrumpy, 6% abv (22 & 50 litre polycasks).

Old Rosie Scrumpy, 7.3% abv (1.7 litre glass jars, 22 & 50 litre polycasks).

In Bottle Conditioned Cider, 6% abv (500ml glass bottles).

Scrumpy Cider, 7.5% abv (1.7 litre glass jars).

Filtered:

Herefordshire County Perry, 4.5% abv (1.7 litre glass jars, 22 litre polycasks).

1st Quality, 5% abv (1.7 litre glass jars, 22 & 50 litre poly-casks).

Special Vintage, 7.3% abv (1.7 litre glass jars, 22 litre poly-casks).

(Also available: The Stowford Press range, an Organic Cider, the Oak Conditioned range, and new products such as a low-alcohol Organic Spritzer).

Annual Production

1 million gallons.

Visitors

Welcome. Public tours of the Cider Mill are on Monday, Wednesday and Friday at 2.30pm.

Private tours can be arranged by contacting the Tours Organiser on 01531 660233.

Directions

Travelling on the A449 from Ledbury, turn right at the cross roads with the B4024 in Much Marcle. Westons is 3/4 mile on your right.

Sales

Shop open Monday to Friday 9.30am to 4.30pm, Saturday 10am to 1pm.

Also on sale: selection of Westons and cider merchandise – books, clothing, memorabilia, collectables.

Outlets

Westons is readily available throughout Britain in pubs, off-licences (Oddbins always carry a good selection) and supermarkets (Sainsbury, Tesco, Waitrose and Safeway amongst others).

Wholesalers: many local and regional wholesalers, and Beer Seller nationally.

Awards

A great many, including:

CAMRA National Cider & Perry Championships 1999: Gold Award Cider – Old Rosie.

Gold Award Perry – Herefordshire County Perry. CAMRA National Cider & Perry Championships 1996: Gold Award Perry – Herefordshire County Perry.

Herefordshire Outlets

ABBEY DORE

Neville Arms

☎ 01981 240319

12-3, 7-11(10.30 Sun)

⌒Gwatkins Cider, Perry

This country pub is right opposite historic Abbey Dore, and close to the Abbey Court Gardens, in Herefordshire's Golden Valley. Phat is played on Saturday night, or try your hand at llama trekking! (contact the pub for details). Bed and Breakfast is available, and there is a campsite nearby. Disabled access to the restaurant.

BROMYARD

Bay Horse

21 High Street

☎ 01885 482600

11-3, 5.30-11; 12-3.30, 7-10.30 Sun

⌒Bulmers Traditional (summer)

The Bay Horse has its own 'Rhythm and Booze' festival each summer, and a folk club once a month on Fridays. No food Sunday evenings.

CRASWALL

 CIDER PUB

sells more cider than beer!

Bulls Head

On a minor road south-east of Hay-on-Wye. OS 278360

☎ 01981 510616

11-11; 12-4 Sun (closed Sunday evening)

⌒Westons 1st Quality, Old Rosie, Perry; local guest cider (summer)

The highest pub in Herefordshire. Isolated to say the least, it is nevertheless sought out by locals, walkers and tourists alike for its fine cider, ales and good food. Bought in 1997 by the current licencees, theirs is a classic example of how to take a failing rural pub and make it profitable without destroying its character. The rustic old bar with its serving hatches is much as it has always been, and the new restaurant offers excellent meals cooked to order with local ingredients – they even bake their own bread. Lovely garden with superb views. The Bulls Head hosts the "Crasfest" at the end of July, with marquee, bands, barbeque and mini cider/beer festival.

DINMORE

Green Acres

(On the A49 between Hereford and Leominster)

☎ 01568 797045

9-5.30, Tues-Sat

⏚**Bottled: Dunkertons; Franklins; Westons**

Organic farm shop that sells its own meat and vegetables, as well as ice-cream, jams, honey and fruit wines. Organic cider apples from their own orchard are supplied to Dunkertons and Bulmers.

GARWAY

 CIDER PUB

sells more cider than beer!

Moon

☎ 01600 750270

7-11; 12-2.30, 7-11 Fri/Sat; 12-2.30, 7-10.30 Sun

⏚**Bulmers Traditional**

Country pub on the Three Castles walking route. The pub sign is supported in an old cider mill and the fence has been fashioned from the horse-drawn tram lines that used to run past the pub up to Pontrilas. Caravan and campsite plus Bed & Breakfast at the pub. Cricket in the summer. Legend has it that there are fairies on the common...

A Local Story

Jones was the blacksmith at Garway and used to drink at the Moon. One night when he was drunk he took a £5 wager that he could shoe Dennis's (Dennis Gwatkin's great great grandad) donkey that grazed Garway Common. Now donkeys don't wear shoes so everyone in the pub pitches into the pot, thinking Jones would lose the wager. The next morning the donkey was still happily grazing the common – but wearing two pairs of blacksmith Jones' old boots!
(As told to Fiona Mac)

HEREFORD

Barrels

69 St Owens Street

☎ 01432 274968

11-11; 12-10.30 Sun

⏚**Bulmers Traditional; local guests (May onwards)**

Home of the Wye Valley Brewery, this classic town pub is popular with all ages, from students to pensioners. Can become loud and busy on and around the weekends. Barrels Beer Festival is held on August Bank Holiday weekend, and has an extensive local cider bar. Occasional live music once a month on a Saturday night.

 CIDER PUB

sells more cider than beer!

Brewers Arms

Eign Road

☎ 01432 273746

12-11; 12-10.30 Sun

⌒Bulmers Traditional; Westons Bounds Brand

A no-frills, traditional two-bar locals cider house. Lots of games played – phat, quoits, darts and a playstation. Mainly male clientele, good atmosphere, keyring collection over the bar.

~~NO REAL ALE~~

Buckingham Inn

141 Whitecross Road

☎ 01432 276087

4.30[12 Sat]-11; 12-10.30 Sun

⌒Bulmers Traditional

Two-bar estate pub with a classic

1950s interior. Vinyl 45s juke box in the bar, quoits played. Won a local floral display prize in 1999.

Horse & Groom

Eign Street

☎ 01432 355026

11-11; 12-10.30 Sun

⌒Bulmers Traditional

Working mens local opposite Moorfields Eye Hospital. Parts of the pub date from the 14th to the 17th centuries. Traditional cider served only in the bar. Sunday lunch sessions (with cabaret from the band *and* the local crowd) are legendary.

◁ ▶ ~~NO REAL ALE~~

A Local Story

The pub ghost sits in the Horse & Groom's lounge during the full moon. He is a one-legged surgeon who used to perform amputations in the stables before the days of hospitals. Some of his more unfortunate patients may be buried in the pub carpark – it was once a graveyard!

(As told to Fiona Mac.)

Imperial

Widemarsh Street

☎ 01432 273646

10-11; 12-10.30 Sun

⌒"Brew 11" (10am to 12 noon only); Westons Old Rosie

The front bar is packed from 10am with local cider drinkers (characters one and all) keen to get in the first "Brew 11" of the day. The pub has an interesting local history to be found in Ron Shoesmith's book *Pubs of Hereford* (Logaston Press). Cider in the front bar only. Restaurant.

~~NO REAL ALE~~

Victory

88 St Owens Street

☎ 01432 274998

11-11; 12-10.30 Sun

⌀**Bulmers Traditional**

The pub's interior is decked out as a sailing galleon with a lively locals bar at the front and a quieter area at the back, with a crow's nest and balcony. Also home to Hereford's newest brewery "Spinning Dog" named after the mad pub dog Polly. Lunches on Sundays only, and don't miss the huge "Workman's Tea" served 5-7pm every day. Interesting range of real ales.

⌀ ▶

CIDER PUB

sells more cider than beer!

Volunteer

21 Harold Street

☎ 01432 276189

11-11; 12-10.30 Sun

⌀**Bulmers Traditional; (all year) Westons Old Rosie, Perry; local guest ciders (summer only)**

Lively, contemporary local community pub and Hereford's premier cider outlet. Cider festival in the summer. Over 150 bottled ciders and perries available through the year. Folk club second Wednesday of the month, jazz brunch Sundays in the summer. Carrom, chess and skittles played. Home-cooked food using local ingredients available until 5pm – braille menu, allergy aware, lots of veggie options.

⌀

LEDBURY

Prince of Wales

Church Lane

☎ 01531 632250

11-3, 7-11; 12-3, 7-10.30 Sun

⌀**Bulmers Traditional**

Oak beamed inn, set in a picturesque cobbled lane near to Ledbury's historic church. Two bars with cosy alcoves give a comfortable mix of traditional and modern styles. The local Morris side meet in the pub after practice sessions. Summer folk and poetry festivals.

⌀

Royal Oak

The Southend

☎ 01531 632110

11-11; 12-10.30 Sun

🍎Westons Old Rosie (summer only)

A hotel whose rear section was built as a cider house in 1420. Cider only sold in the hotel bar.

🍺 ▶

Try Also: Brewery Inn, Bye Street (Westons)

LEOMINSTER

Chequers

Etnam Street

☎ 01568 612473

11-11; 12-10.30 Sun

🍎Bulmers Traditional

14th century coaching inn with wooden beams and flagstone floors. The building is a cruck house, built from oak and wattle. An elephant once got wedged between the pub and the adjacent stables (honest). An outlet for the local SP Sporting Ales.

🍺 ▶

Orchard, Hive & Vine

6 The Buttercross

☎ 01568 611232

Email sales@ohv.wyenet.co.uk

Web site www.orchard-hive-and-vine.co.uk

9-5.30, Mon-Sat

🍎Draught: Cider or perry varies (June to September)

Bottled: Cheyney Lodge; Broome Farm; Dewchurch; Dunkertons; Franklins; Gregg's Pit; Gwatkin; Lyne Down; Minchews; Westons

Excellent, switched-on, specialist off-licence. The emphasis is on local produce, but customers come from far and wide. The cider range varies continuously, but at any one time there are usually 30 different bottled ciders and 15 different bottled perries. New for 2000, a draught cider or perry, changing each week during June to September, can be taken away in 2 or 3 litre plastic containers. There are some 90 bottled beers, with strong representations from both local and Belgian brewers. Plans are afoot to sell draught ale during the winter. Other products include a range of some 30 English and Welsh wines, a dozen country wines and liqueurs, and a range of meads including Geoff Morris' (the owner) Meads of Mercia. There's a range of local honey, and in the summer customers can buy the local organic ice-cream. The shop web site is well worth a look, with photos of many of the bottles of cider and perry. Secured on-line shopping is available, with a case of cider delivered to your door in a matter of days. Well worth a visit.

LITTLE COWARNE

Three Horseshoes

☎ 01885 400276

11-3, 6.30-11; 12-3, 7-10.30 Sun

Westons Perry (demijohns, summer only)

Modern pub with en-suite accommodation and campsite. Family friendly, it makes a good stop after Shortwood Farm. Home-cooked Herefordshire specialities using local ingredients. The menu always features dishes cooked with local cider and perry from Shortwoods/Olivers; for example Cider and Onion Soup, Rabbit in Cider, Pheasant in Perry.

MUCH DEWCHURCH

Black Swan

☎ 01981 540295

12-3, 5.30-11; 12-3, 7-10.30 Sun

Dewchurch

Unspoilt, multi-roomed, 14th century inn with open fires in the winter. Excellent home-cooked food using local ingredients. Has its own library. Meeting place for the local Microlight Club and Harness Society.

MUCH MARCLE

Scrumpy House (at Westons)

The Bounds

☎ 01531 660626

11-3, Mon-Fri; 12-3 Sat; 12-4 Sun; 7pm-late Wed-Sat

Draught: Westons 1st Quality, Herefordshire Country Perry, Old Rosie, Special Vintage
Bottled: Westons range

Showpiece bar and restaurant at Westons cider mill. Converted from a 17th century cow barn to give a décor of stone walls and floor, oak beams, and a full window frontage with patio area. The lovely food features Westons ciders – ham braised in cider, steak pie with Old Rosie, roast pork served with an apple and perry sauce, pears poached in perry, sausages made with Stowford Press and apples – and the restaurant is the only outlet for Grandma Weston's chutney. Of course there's the full range of Westons draught and bottled products, as well as a real ale from the local Woodhampton brewery.

Slip Tavern

Watery Lane

☎ 01531 660246

11.30-2.30, 6.30-11; 12-2.30, 7-10.30 Sun

⌂Westons Old Rosie (bottles)

Set in the midst of Westons orchards. Named after the landslip of 1575 ('The Wonder') when Marcle Hill removed itself overnight burying a church and a herd of cattle. Good food, beautiful garden.

ORLETON

Boot Inn

(Just off the B4362, west of Woofferton)

☎ 01568 780228

12-2.30(3 Sat), 6-11; 12-3, 7-10.30 Sun; closed Monday lunchtime.

⌂Franklins (summer only)

Half-timbered friendly local opposite the village post office. Multi-roomed. Campsite nearby, large carpark. Parties welcome but please ring first. An outlet for Hobsons Ales.

PEMBRIDGE

Cider House Restaurant

At Dunkertons Cider

☎ 01544 388161

10-5, Mon-Sat; (closed Jan/Feb)

⌂Draught: Dunkertons Dry, Medium-Dry, Medium-Sweet, Sweet, Perry (occasional); guest cider (occasional)

Bottled: Dunkertons range

Suzie Dunkerton's lovely restaurant is in a 400 year old reconstructed barn, on the premises of Dunkertons cider mill. Opened in 1994, it seats 60-80, has a terrace overlooking meadows, a log fire in winter, and can be hired for parties and functions in the evenings and on Sundays. The food is really quite superb, and cider is used in most dishes, with a little added to the majority of stocks, sauces and preserves. The bread is home-baked and there is a selection of locally-made cheeses. Disabled access.

ROSS-ON-WYE

Drop Inn

Station Street

☎ 01989 563256

6-11; 11-11 Fri/Sat; 12-10.30 Sun

⌁Bulmers Traditional

An original 1960s illuminated sign marks this basic one-bar local, popular with rugby players. Food on Fridays and Saturdays only.

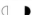 ~~REAL ALE~~

Horse & Jockey

9-10 New Street

☎ 01989 768180

11-11; 12-10.30 Sun

⌁Bulmers Traditional

Back-street community pub also used by tourists. Darts, pool and crib players. Pub interior traditional and unaffected by brewery refurbishment.

⌁ ▶

Prince of Wales

Walford Road

☎ 01989 562517

12-3, 6.30-11; 12-3, 7-10.30 Sun

⌁Bulmers Traditional

Large, modern family pub which is at the centre of its community's activities. The Royal British Legion, some deep sea fishermen, a

Divers Club and Ross Town Football Club all meet here. Skittle alley and pub games popular. Beer garden and children's playground.

⌁ ▶

Stag

5 Henry Street

☎ 01989 562893

10-11; 12-10.30 Sun

⌁Bulmers Traditional

A traditional two-roomed pub, very much a locals' bar. "Just like your own front room". Very friendly and full of characters. Handy head-cushion above the Gents' urinals.

TILLINGTON

Bell

Tillington Road

☎ 01432 760395

11-3, 6-11; 11-11 Sat; 12-5, 6-10.30 Sun

⌁Bulmers Traditional

Village local with a lively public bar

and separate restaurant and patio area. The bar serves "Farmers" – a local cider when available – which the locals like to follow with a 'chaser' of Stowford Press or Strongbow! Plans to replace Bulmers Traditional with a different traditional cider. Good food made from local ingredients. Garden with trees for children to climb.

TRUMPET

Trumpet Inn

☎ 01531 670277

11.30-2.30, 6-11; 12-2.30, 6-10.30 Sun

↻Draught: Westons Old Rosie (summer); local perry (as available)
Glass jars: Westons Perry (summer), Special Vintage

Timber-framed roadside inn recently made open-plan and renovated to modern standards. Clientele mostly interested in the good food. Camping and caravan site beside the pub. The owner may be making his own cider in 2000.

Other Places of Cider Interest in Herefordshire

Big Apple Association

By Janet Mackay, Chairman

The first Big Apple event was held in the Autumn of 1989 as a contribution by the seven parishes of the Marcle Ridge area of Herefordshire to the Year of Food and Farming. It was based on the traditional industry of the parishes involved which was apple growing, both dessert, culinary and cider.

The event was held over three weekends and based in different parishes each time. There were displays of fruit, tastings of cider, talks about fruit and growing, walks around orchards, cycle rides around lanes, and apple teas.

From this beginning the event has grown and evolved and changed but remained true to its concept of bringing people into this area to enjoy the fruit and to learn about orchards and apples. Within the first two years a national tourism award was won and then a European prize, fourth place in the "Village que j'aime" award. As this was a major prize the Big Apple took on a slightly more formal structure as an association and has continued as such since 1991.

Big Apple Cider and Perry Trial winners:

Year	Cider	Perry
1992	John George	Franklins
1993	Minchews Real Cyder	Richard White
1994	Hartlands Cider	Ted Jones
1995	Hindlip Cider	Minchews Real Cyder
1996	Gregg's Pitt	Hindlip Cider
1997	Lyne Down Cider	Hindlip Cider
1998	Gregg's Pitt	Hindlip Cider
1999	Lyne Down Cider	Lyne Down Cider
2000	John George	Gregg's Pitt

Presently there are events twice a year. The first is in the Springtime over the May Day Bank Holiday weekend. It is based in Putley centering around a cider competition and cider tastings. There are guided walks through orchards, demonstrations of rural crafts and apple teas as well as plenty of cider. In the neighbouring parish of Aylton there is a flower festival. The second event is held in October near Apple Day. It is based in Much Marcle with displays and tastings of fruit. As well as dessert and culinary fruit there is a display of cider apples and perry pears. There are cidermaking demonstrations and Westons is open with factory tours. An important activity of this weekend is our "enthusiasts' day" when people can book to come along and try their hand at cidermaking from picking up the fruit to going home with some juice to ferment. On both weekends there are walks, talks and teas.

For further information or to subscribe to the mailing list please contact the secretary Mrs. Jackie Denman, 01531 670 544

Cider Museum

21 Ryelands Street, Hereford,
HR4 0LW.

☎ 01432 354207

Museum housed in buildings that were once part of the original Bulmers factory, now an independent charitable trust adjacent to Bulmer's cider works. The story of traditional cider making is told through displays and exhibits. Antique equipment includes presses and mills, there's a cooper's workshop, and visitors can see the famous "Herefordshire Pomonas" – books illustrating many cider apples and perry pears grown through the ages. In the basement are Bulmers original Champagne Cellars, and many of the bottles and much of the equipment remains in place. Throughout the year the museum hosts a varied programme of events, including an annual Cider & Perry Competition (see below) each May, and a Cidermaking Weekend with cider-making demonstrations at around Apple Day, October 21st. The gift shop sells Cider Brandy from the museum's own King Offa Distillery. Well worth a visit!

Open

April-October, 7 days a week, 10am-5.30pm.

November-March, Tuesday-Sunday, 11am-3pm.

Results of the Museum's Cider and Perry Competition:

(* = Overall Champion)

Year	Dry Cider	Med Sweet	Sweet	Perry	Best-Presented Bottle
1991	Broome Farm*	Westons	Norbury's	Norbury's	-
1993	Gwatkin	Knights	Knights	John George*	-
1995	Hindlip	Minchews	Norbury's	Franklin's*	-
1996	Knights	Knights*	Westons	Gregg's Pitt	-
1997	Minchews	Lyne Down*	Knights	Minchews	-
1998	Cheyney Lodge	Hindlip*	Westons	C.Jackson	-
1999	Hecks	Minchews*	Knights	Broome Farm	-
2000	Veryan*	Hindlip	Hindlip	Archie Miles	Gwatkin

Herefordshire Cider Route

A full-colour fold-out map, showing a route around Herefordshire that visits eight cider makers plus the Orchard, Hive & Vine off-licence. Lots of information about Herefordshire cider, the history of cider, the cider making process, etc.

To obtain your copy, please contact:

Herefordshire Tourism

PO Box 44, Leominster, HR6 8ZD.

Tel: 01432 260621 Fax: 01432 260620

Email: tourism@herefordshire.gov.uk

Web site: www.herefordshire-shropshire.org.uk

Photographs

Oak barrels in the cider cellar at Broome Farm.

Photo: Dave Matthews

Dennis Gwatkin at Putley 2000.

Photo: Dave Matthews

Lyne Down Farm, Herefordshire.

Photo: Dave Matthews

Angora goats under the apple blossom at Rathays.

Photo: Rathays Old Goat Cider

H Weston & Sons Ltd sign.

Photo: Dave Matthews

Nevelle Arms, Abbey Dore.

Photo: Dave Matthews

Geoff Morris and his cider selection at Orchard, Hive & Vine, Leominster.

Photo: Dave Matthews

The Slip Tavern sign, Much Marcle.

Photo: Dave Matthews

The Stag, Ross-on-Wye.

Photo: Dave Matthews

Putley Village Hall, home of the Big Apple's 'Cider & Perry Trials'

Photo: Dave Matthews

HERTFORDSHIRE

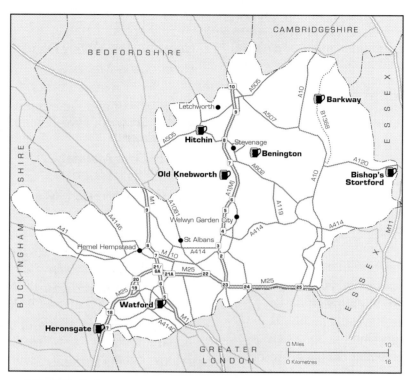

Hertfordshire Outlets

BARKWAY

Tally Ho

London Road

☎ 01763 848389

11.30-3, 5.30-11; 12-3, 6-11 Sat; 12-3, 7.30-10.30 Sun

🖰Addlestones

Former Greene King pub, now a pleasantly refurbished free house. Good quality food from a varied menu.

◖ ▶

BENINGTON

Lordship Arms

42 Whempstead Road

☎ 01438 869665

12-3, 6-11; 12-3, 6-10.30 Sun

↪**Cider varies**

Friendly, well-run country pub. Free house with a good range of real ale – 7 or 8 on at any one time – twice local CAMRA Pub of the Year. The licensee is passionate about his ale and cider and they are always well kept. Good home cooked food, the curry on Wednesday night is particularly recommended! A fairly remote pub but worth seeking out.

BISHOPS STORTFORD

Half Moon

31 North Street

11-11; 12-3, 7-10.30 Sun

↪Westons Old Rosie

A two-bar pub split between three levels. The five guest ales include a mild.

◖

HERONSGATE

Land of Liberty, Peace & Plenty

Long Lane (about 900m from M25 junction 17)

☎ 01923 282226

12-11; 12-3, 7-10.30 (12-10.30 summer) Sun

↪Thatchers Medium Dry

Isolated country pub. The cider is not obvious, tucked away in the cellar, so you'll need to ask for it. Six real ales and up to six draught Belgian beers. Evening food only by prior arrangement (24 hours notice).

HITCHIN

Sunrunner

Bancroft

☎ 01462 440717

12-11; 12-10.30 Sun

↪Westons Old Rosie

Friendly and popular high-street pub with a large and ever-changing range of real ales (over 200 each year). Hosts occasional festivals which feature extra cider/perry as well as ales. Live music on Wednesday evenings.

◖

OLD KNEBWORTH

Lytton Arms

Park Lane, OS 229202

☎ 01438 812312

11-3, 5-11; 11-11 Sat; 12-10.30 Sun

○Cider range varies

Large 19th century free-house overlooking Knebworth Park. Has a well-deserved reputation for its excellent and ever-changing range of real ales and ciders/perries. Always at least one cider, more often two, sometimes more. Up to a dozen real ales at any one time, has sold over 2600 different ones in the last ten years. Wide range of Belgian bottled beers and malt whiskies. Frequent beer festivals throughout the year. Bar skittles, shove ha'penny and dominoes all played. Well worth a visit.

◖ ◗

WATFORD

Hogwash

83 The Parade, High Street

☎ 01923 244369

11-11; 12-10.30 Sun

○Inch's Stonehouse; Biddendens

Hogshead pub situated in a parade close to Watford's nightclub, the building was originally a shop. The only outlet for Real Cider in Watford.

◖ ◗

Photograph

Lytton Arms, Old Knebworth.

Photo: Paul Gunningham

ISLE OF WIGHT

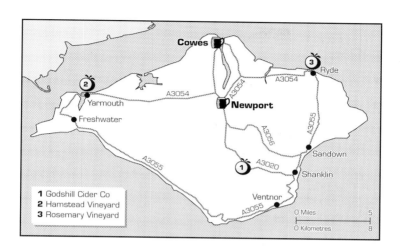

1 Godshill Cider Co
2 Hamstead Vineyard
3 Rosemary Vineyard

Isle of Wight Producers

GODSHILL CIDER CO.

The Cider Barn, High Street, Godshill, Isle of Wight.

The Brewery, Ventnor, Isle of Wight.

☎ 01983 840680

Founded in 1980 at The Cider Barn, with 100 apple trees and a wooden twin screw press (now defunct). The company has grown in size, so Peter Cramp has recently moved production away from the Cider Barn shop to the Ventnor Brewery.

Cider
Farmhouse Cider (bone dry, filtered), 6% abv (1, 2 & 5 litre containers).
(Also available: Rumpy Pumpy Scrumpy, 6% abv; Farmhouse Scrumpy, 6% abv.)
Annual Production
6000 gallons.
Visitors
Welcome at The Cider Barn shop only.
Directions
The Cider Barn shop is at the centre of Godshill village.
Sales
Cider Barn shop open 10am to 6pm, 7 days a week.
Also on sale: other local products.

Outlets

• Sainsburys, Newport, IOW.
English Farm Cider Centre, Firle, Lewes, Sussex.
• Wavells Fine Foods, The Square, Yarmouth, IOW.

HAMSTEAD VINEYARD

Homemead, Hamstead Road, Yarmouth, Isle of Wight, PO41 OYB.

☎ 01983 760463

Hamstead Vineyard was founded in 1976, and owner Terry Munt started to plant his cider orchard in 1984 to supplement sales of his white wine.

Cider

Yarmouth Cider, 6.5% abv (5 and 25 litre containers)

Annual Production

400 gallons

Outlets

• Wavells, Yarmouth, IOW.
• Benidicts, Newport, IOW.
• Buddle Inn, Niton, IOW.

ROSEMARY VINEYARD

Rosemary Lane, Ashey Road, Ryde, Isle of Wight.

☎ 01983 811084

Fax 01983 812899

Although primarily a vineyard producing red and white wines, cider production has risen to an annual output of 3000 gallons, all of it bottled and available either at the vineyard or from various outlets throughout the island. Rosemary Cider is filtered before bottling, whereas Rosemary Fermented Cider is produced using the champagne method.

Cider

Rosemary Cider, 7% abv (25cl and 75cl glass bottles)
Rosemary Fermented Cider, 10% abv (75cl glass bottles)

Annual Production

3000 gallons

Visitors

Welcome. Free entry and tastings, tours available.

Sales

Vineyard shop open 10-5 Mon-Sat, all year. 11-4 Sundays, summer only.

Non-cider items on sale: Wines (red and white), juices.

Outlets

70 various outlets in the IOW.

Isle of Wight Outlets

COWES

Kingston Arms

176 Newport Road

☎ 01983 293393

11-3, 6-11; 11-11 Fri, Sat & Mon; 12-4, 7-10.30 Sun

⌂Bulmers Traditional Medium

Large, friendly, regulars local that welcomes CAMRA members. The only outlet on the Island for Bulmers Traditional. Bed & Breakfast available.

◖ ▶

NEWPORT

Prince of Wales

36 South Street

☎ 01983 525026

11-11; 12-4, 7-10.30 Sun

⌂Inch's Stonehouse

Lovely old-fashioned town local; a mock-Tudor building.

◖

CAMRA QUIZ BOOK

by Jeff Evans

128 pages   Price: £3.99

Fun and games for beer fans, and their relations. Use this book to quiz your mates on real ale and CAMRA history. Great for fund-raising quiz events and for catching up on the campaign.

Use the following code to order this book from your bookshop:
ISBN 1-85249-127-2

Order directly with your credit card on 01727 867201.

KEGBUSTER CARTOON BOOK

by Bill Tidy

72 pages, including colour cartoons
Price: £4.99

A classic, hilarious, collection of cartoons from well-known funny man and cartoonist extraordinaire Bill Tidy. The perfect gift for the beer lover in your life!

Use the following code to order this book from your bookshop:
ISBN 1-85249-134-5.

Order directly with your credit card on 01727 867201.

KENT

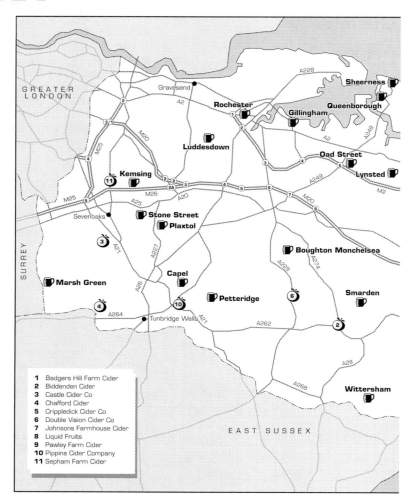

1 Badgers Hill Farm Cider
2 Biddenden Cider
3 Castle Cider Co
4 Chafford Cider
5 Crippledick Cider Co
6 Double Vision Cider Co
7 Johnsons Farmhouse Cider
8 Liquid Fruits
9 Pawley Farm Cider
10 Pippins Cider Company
11 Sepham Farm Cider

Kent Producers

BADGERS HILL FARM CIDER

Badgers Hill Farm, Newcut Road, Chilham, Canterbury, Kent, CT4 8BW.

☎ 01227 730573

Originally known as Pippin Cider, the company was founded by Bruce deCourcy in 1983, and moved to Badgers Hill Farm in 1987. The cider is made primarily from Cox's Orange Pippins (hence the original name of the company),

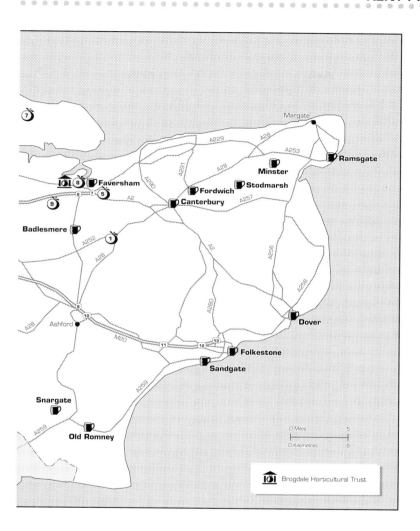

Margate
A229
A28
A253
A291
A28
Ramsgate
Minster
Faversham
Stodmarsh
A290
Fordwich
A2
Canterbury
A257
Badlesmere
A252
A28
A2
A256
A260
A258
A28
Ashford
Dover
M20
Folkestone
Sandgate
Snargate
A259
A259
Old Romney

0 Miles   5
0 Kilometres   8

Brogdale Horticultural Trust

but also uses the juice from Bramleys, and from a range of other eating apple varieties. The cider is fermented and matured in oak barrels, and in the early nineties Bruce started to experiment with turning his old, used barrels into water butts, furniture and dog kennels. Today Badgers Hill Farm is a fully-fledged Wooden Barrel Merchant, and part of this business is supplying barrels for home-brew cider makers. Less cider is made these days, but a visit to the farm, with its freely roaming animals, is still a most enjoyable experience.

Cider
Badgers Hill Farm Cider, 8% abv (¹/₂ gallon plastic containers, or customers can bring their own)

Annual Production
Less than 1500 gallons.

Visitors
Welcome.

Directions
On the A252 at Chilham.

Sales
Shop open 7 days, 10am-5pm, March-Oct; weekends Nov-Dec; closed Christmas Eve-Feb.

Also on sale: comprehensive range of pickled foods, cakes, wooden barrel products.

Awards
Kent CAMRA's Best Cider 1999.

BIDDENDEN CIDER

Biddenden Vineyards Ltd, Little Whatmans, Biddenden, Ashford, Kent, TN27 8DH.

☎ 01580 291726

A nationwide distribution of their draught ciders via wholesalers has helped Biddenden become one of the UK's largest regional producers. The vineyard diversified into cider production in 1978, and the advent of 'Cross Channel Shopping' has since spurred them on towards seeking new markets for their smooth and fruity draught ciders.

Ciders
Biddenden Strong Kentish Cider, 8% abv (2, 5 and 9 gallon containers)

Biddendens Bushels Cider, 6% abv (5 and 9 gallon containers)

(Also available:
Biddenden Monks Delight Mulling Cider, 7.5% abv, with spices and honey.

Biddenden Special Reserve Cider, 13% abv.)

Annual Production
1 million litres.

Visitors
Welcome. Tours available.

Directions
Situated 1¹/₂ miles outside the village of Biddenden, just off the A262 (Biddenden to Tenterden road).

Sales
Shop open: 10am to 5pm, Monday to Saturday.

11am to 5pm Sundays (closed Sundays in January & February)

Also available: wines, apple juice, quality preserves, honey, etc.

Outlets

Distributed nationwide via wholesalers (draught only).

A mail order service is offered for retail sales.

Wholesalers: The Beer Seller, Incider, Small Beer, East-West Ales.

Awards

Peterborough CAMRA Gold Award 1999.

Kent Award (more than once).

Portsmouth & District CAMRA Festival Award.

CAMRA National Cider and Perry Championships – Best Cider.

CASTLE CIDER CO.

Nestlewood, Wickhurst Road, Weald, Nr Sevenoaks, Kent, TN4 6LY.

☎ 01732 455977

Founded in 1987 by Tim and Richard Davies, and run since 1989 by Tim and Heidi Davies. They sell their 1500 gallons locally and direct to the public at craft fairs. In 1998 they won the Kent Cider of the Year Award.

Ciders

Chiddingstone Cider, 7.5% abv (5 or 9 gallon casks)

(Also available: Bottled Chiddingstone Cider as Bone Dry, Dry, Medium Dry and Medium Sweet.)

Annual Production

1500 gallons

Outlets

• English Farm Cider Centre, Firle, Lewes, Sussex (01323 811324)

• Crown Inn, Groombridge, Kent.

• Red House, Boughton Manchelsea

Awards

Kent Cider of the Year 1998.

CHAFFORD CIDER

Chafford Rise, Chafford Lane, Fordcombe, Tunbridge Wells, Kent, TN3 0SH.

☎ 01892 740437

Now in his 20th cidermaking year, Chris Ballenden uses a 2:1 blend of Bramleys and mixed eaters from his own orchard to produce his fine cider. The cider is matured for one to two years before being sold.

Ciders

Chafford Cider (5 gallon or 4 pint containers)

Annual Production

800 gallons

Visitors

By appointment only.

Outlets

• Chafford Arms, Fordcombe, Kent
• English Farm Cider Centre, Lewes, Sussex.

CRIPPLEDICK CIDER CO.

Bull Lane Garage, Bull Lane, Boughton, Faversham, Kent.

☎ 01227 751537

Kentish cider produced by P.B. Spillett and G. Clifford-Cox.

Cider

Crippledick Cider, 6% abv (75cl bottles and 15 litre wine-type boxes).

Annual Production

300 gallons.

Sales

Farm gate sales 9am to 5pm.

Outlets

• Three Horseshoes, Staplestreet Boughton. (Off-sales only.)
• Farming World, Boughton.
• The Dove, Dargate. (Off-sales only.)
• Macknade Farm Shop, Faversham.
• Mount Ephraim Gardens, Hernhill.

Awards

Canterbury Beer Festival: 'Cider of the Festival' 1997.

Brogdale Cider Festival: Joint 2nd 1997.

DOUBLE VISION CIDER COMPANY

Gunthorpe, Clapper Lane, Staplehurst, Tonbridge, Kent, TN12 0JT.

☎ 01580 891387

Ken Cramp started producing his unfiltered draught ciders as a hobby in 1984, and was joined in 1992 by Simon Barber. Double Vision Cider was officially born in 1995, and today is famous throughout Kent and East Sussex. With Ken now semi-retired, Simon does most of the work, and plans are afoot to bottle the cider and sell it further afield. The only Kent Perry maker.

Ciders

Double Vision Cider, Medium and Dry, 7.4% abv (2 litre jerry cans)
Double Vision Perry, 7.4% abv (2 litre jerry cans)

Annual Production

6000 gallons

Directions

One mile north of Staplehurst village.

Sales

Farm gate sales 10am to 6pm summer, 10am to 4.30pm winter, 7 days a week.

Also on sale: home-produced honey.

Outlets

• English Farm Cider Centre, Firle, East Sussex.

• The Bitter End (off-licence), Tonbridge Wells, Kent, & Bromley, Greater London.

• Red Lion, Snargate, Kent.

Man Of Kent, Rochester, Kent.

• Firemans Arms, Uckfield, E.Sussex.

• A.&R.Butchers, Robertsbridge, E.Sussex.

• The Cabin Restaurant, Dover, Kent.

Awards

Kent Cider & Perry Festival, Winner 1995 & 1996.

Catford Beer Festival, Cider of the Festival, 1997.

Kent Beer Festival, Overall Cider Winner, 1999.

JOHNSONS FARM-HOUSE CIDER

Cowstead Farm, Lower Road, Queenborough Road, Minster, Isle of Sheppey, near Kent, ME12 3RL.

☎ 0385 917395 (landline planned for 2000).

Cowstead Farm is a sheep farm with a small orchard of vintage cider apples. Paul Johnson started making cider as a hobby in 1995, and started selling in 1998. His increasing expertise was recognised at the 1999 Kent Cider & Perry Festival held at Brogdale Horticultural Trust with the award of a Silver Medal. Paul's cider is currently mainly 'Kentish' in style, but he has started to use 'real' cider apples and has plans to increase the production levels of tannic 'West Country' style ciders in the future. An increasing number of Island pubs are selling Johnsons unfiltered draught ciders, and, at the time of writing, Paul has plans to launch a bottle-fermented cider.

Ciders

Gobbledegook, 7.8% abv

Swampy, 7.8% abv

Loony Juice, 8.3% abv

(1 gallon demijohns, 3 gallon manucubes, 5 gallon polypins)

(Also available carbonated in 500ml bottles)

Annual Production

800 gallons

Visitors

By prior arrangement only.

Outlets

• Ship on Shore, Sheerness.

• Fiddlers Cat, Sheerness.

• Red Lion, Sheerness.

• Jolly Sailor, Sheerness.

• Trafalgar, Queenborough.

• Harty Ferry Inn, Harty.

• Plough and Harrow, Oade Street.

• Red Lion, Badlesmere.

Award

Silver Medal, Kent Cider of the Year 1999.

LIQUID FRUITS

Brogdale Horticultural Trust, Brogdale Road, Faversham, Kent, ME13 8XZ.

☎ 01795 535286

Email info@brogdale.org.uk

Web site www.brogdale.org.uk

Brogdale is home to the National Fruit Collection (see article under *Other Places of Cider Interest in Kent*), the largest collection of fruit trees and plants in the world, with over 2300 different varieties of apple alone, in 150 acres of orchards. 'Liquid Fruits' is Brogdale's marketing arm, and with the help of the presses at Biddenden Cider, Brogdale's apples are converted into single varietal apple juices and a filtered Brogdale Cider.

Cider

Brogdale Cider.

Annual Production

3000 gallons

Visitors

Welcome. Guided tours available.

Sales

Shop open 10am to 5pm.

Also on sale: apple juices, gift shop.

Outlet

Machnade Farm Shop, Faversham.

Award (for the Fruit Collection)

Pomona Awards 1998, Highly Commended.

PAWLEY FARM CIDER

Pawley Farm, Painters Forstal, Faversham, Kent, ME13 OEN.

☎ 01795 532043

At Pawley Farm they believe in doing things the old fashioned way. This means using their own apples (mainly Bramleys with some Coxs) and a recipe that has been hand-ed down through the family for over 200 years. It also means, that in common with most of Britain's best ciders, their cider is fermented in oak casks, is unpas-teurised and contains no chemical additives. Pawley Cider is matured in oak barrels for between 18 months and 2 years, and each year's vintage has its own unique character.

Cider

Pawley Farm Dry, Medium and Sweet Cider, 8.4% abv (On draught or in 1 litre plastic Bottles)

Annual Production

1000 gallons

Visitors

Welcome. Tours available.

Directions

Leave M2 at junction 6 – turn left to T junction A2 – turn left – first left Brogdale Road and proceed as signed Painters Forstal.

Sales

Farm gate sales, 8-late.

Outlets

• Shipwrights Arms, Faversham.
• Black Lion, Lynsted, Sittingbourne.

PIPPINS CIDER COMPANY

Pippins Farm, Pembury, Tunbridge Wells, Kent, TN2 4AB.

☎ 01892 824544

Pippins Cider started production in 1984, and today produces 500 gallons per year of filtered Vintage Cider.

Cider

Pippins Vintage Cider, 8% abv (1 litre bottles)

Annual Production

500 gallons

Directions

From the A21 take the A228. Follow signs for Hospice in the Weald. Pippins Farm opposite.

Sales

Farm shop open 10am to 5pm, mid-June to mid-October (closed Mondays). Other times by prior arrangement only.

SEPHAM FARM CIDER

Sepham Farm, Filston Lane, Otford, Kent, TN14 5JT.

☎ 01959 522774

Email chardnick@hotmail.com

Nick Chard started making cider 7 years ago, using a blend of Cox's and Bramleys. Most of his output is pasteurised and filtered into glass bottles, but smaller amounts of a natural, unfiltered version are produced for draught sales.

Cider

Sepham Cider, 7.5% abv (5 gallon polycasks)

(Also available:

Sepham Cider, filtered and pasteurised, in 750ml glass bottles)

Annual Production

900 gallons

Visitors

Welcome.

Directions

North-west of the village of Otford. Ask for directions either in Otford or Shoreham.

Sales

Shop open 9am-5pm, Tues-Sun.

Also on sale: Their own soft fruit range, their own apples, local eggs and honey.

Kent Outlets

BADLESMERE

Red Lion

Ashford Road

☎ 01233 740320

12-3, 6-11; 12-11 Fri/Sat; 12-10.30 Sun

👄**Johnson's Double Barrel or Gobbledegook**

Approximately half-way between Faversham and Ashford, this road-side pub offers Real Cider and Beer in a rural location. Live music Friday evenings. Camping available in pub grounds, by prior arrangement.

◖ ▶

BOUGHTON MONCHELSEA

Red House

Hermitage Lane, Wierton

☎ 01622 743986

Web site: www.the-redhouse.co.uk

12-3 (not Tues), 7-11; 12-11 Sat; 12-10.30 Sun

👄**Chiddingstone; Westons Old Rosie**

Friendly, traditional Kentish free-house with several drinking areas. A good selection of real ales, foreign bottled beers and fruit wines, as well as the two ciders. Large garden and campsite.

◖ ▶

CANTERBURY

Cherry Tree

10 Whitehorse Lane

☎ 01227 451266

11-11; 12-10.30 Sun

👄**Biddenden**

City centre pub catering for a large cross section of tourists, regulars and students. Claims to be the oldest in Canterbury (1372), and is on the site of a Roman building. Has connections with Charles Dickens, and a murder took place here in the 19th century!

◖

CAPEL

Dovecote

Alders Road

☎ 01892 835966

12-3(4 Sat), 6-11; 12-4, 7-10.30 Sun

👄**Chiddingstone**

Situated in a tiny hamlet on the back road between Tonbridge and Matfield. Cosy local with one long bar, bare brick walls and beamed ceilings. Interesting range of Real Ales all served on gravity, holder of the Cask Marque Award.

◖ ▶

DOVER

Mogul

Chapel Place

☎ 01304 205072

11-11; 12-10.30 Sun

🍎Thatchers

Turn of the century traditional two-bar local with friendly ambiance, overlooking the town centre and harbour. Old brewery posters and photos of Dover & Imperial India adorn the wall. Beer range has an emphasis on local brews. Food limited to Sunday lunches only.

FAVERSHAM

Shipwrights Arms

Hollowshore, OS 017636

☎ 01795 590088

11-11; 12-10.30 Sun; (12-3, 6-11 Mon-Fri Oct-March)

🍎Pawley Farm (April-Sep)

A lovely outpost for Real Cider and Ale. Located at the confluence of two creeks it offers superb views to the Swale estuary. No food Mondays or Tuesdays.

FOLKESTONE

Wetherspoons

Old Baptist Church, Rendezvous Street

☎ 01303 251154

10-11; 12-10.30 Sun

🍎Addlestones

18th century converted church retaining many original features including stained glass windows, organ pipes and a hand-painted ceiling.

FORDWICH

Fordwich Arms

King Street

☎ 01227 710444

11-11; 12-3, 7-10.30 Sun

🍎Theobolds

Fordwich is Britain's smallest town and this charming pub is opposite the tiny timber-framed town hall. The cider may not be on display, please ask the bar staff!

GILLINGHAM

Will Adams

73 Saxton Street

☎ 01634 575902

7-11; 12-3,7-11 Sat; 12-4, 7-10.30 Sun

🍎Cider varies

Single bar town house whose interior walls depict the life of Will Adams. Has a strong local following and a friendly welcome for visitors. Food on Saturday lunchtimes only.

KEMSING

Rising Sun

Cotmans Ash Lane, Woodlands,
OS 563599

☎ 01959 522683

11-3, 6-11; 12-3, 7-10.30 Sun

🍎Cider varies (May-Sep)

Isolated hill-top pub in pleasant
countryside. Step back in time to
the main bar, which is a converted
hunting lodge. Five varying and
interesting Real Ales. Popular with
hikers throughout the year, and
families in the summer months.
Camping available behind the pub.
Excellent quality home-cooked food.

◖ ◗

LUDDESDOWN

Cock

Henley Street

☎ 01474 814208

12-11; 12-10.30 Sun

🍎Cider range varies

Highly recommended two-bar genuine free house, with a convivial
atmosphere. Normally two ciders
on offer, but up to four may be
available. Large selection of real
ales. May be approached by a
3/4 mile footpath over the fields
from Sole Street station.

◖

LYNSTED

Black Lion

The Street

☎ 01795 521229

11-3, 6-11; 12-3, 7-10.30 Sun

🍎Pawley Farm

The Black Lion can be found in the
pretty village of Lynsted a few
miles south of Teynham. The Real
Cider (and three ales) all come
from small local producers.

 ◖ ◗

MARSH GREEN

Wheatsheaf

Marsh Green Road (B2028)

☎ 01732 864091

*11-11; 12-3, 7-10.30 Sun (12-
10.30 summer Sun)*

🍎Biddenden

Delightful, spacious country pub
with many drinking areas and
much pine wood-work. Old photographs adorn the walls. Large
range of real ales, excellent home-
cooked food. Family room, garden.

 ◖ ◗

MINSTER (THANET)

New Inn

2 Tothill Street

☎ 01843 821294

11.30-3, 5-11; 11.30-11

Fri/Sat; 12-10.30 Sun

🍶**Cider varies**

Attractive one-bar village local, warm and friendly. Rustic brass and stained glass 'Cobbs' windows. Large beer garden with aviary and children's adventure playground. Great food in generous proportions. No meals Mondays or Sunday evenings.

◖ ▶

OAD STREET
Plough & Harrow
☎ 01795 843351

11-11; 12-10.30 Sun

🍶**Johnson's**

Opposite the Oad Street Craft Centre, the Plough & Harrow offers local cider and a good selection of beers at very reasonable prices.

◖

OLD ROMNEY
Rose & Crown
Swamp Road
☎ 01797 367500

11.30-11; 12-10.30 Sun

🍶**Biddenden**

Friendly village pub with lovely views of the Marsh. Excellent, good value, home-cooked meals. Bed & Breakfast available all year.

◖ ▶

PETTERIDGE
Hopbine
Petteridge Lane, OS 668413
☎ 01892 722561

12(11 Sat)-2.30, 6-11; 12-3, 7-10.30 Sun

🍶**Westons Old Rosie**

Attractive, unspoilt, brick and weather-boarded pub built into the side of a hill. L-shaped bar divided by a fireplace. No meals Wednesdays.

◖ ▶

PLAXTOL
Golding Hop
Sheet Hill, OS 600547
☎ 01732 882150

11-3, 6(5.30 Fri)-11; 11-11 Sat; 12-4, 7-10.30 Sun

🍶**Westons Special Vintage; house cider; guests**

A 15th century gem, tucked away in a valley north of the village. Choose from four whitewashed rooms on different levels, two with open fires. Ciders and real ales all on gravity. Large garden. Camping and caravan space by prior arrangement. Good value pub food with vegetarian options.

◖ ▶

QUEENBOROUGH

Trafalgar

10-13 Rushenden Road

☎ 01795 663365

11-11; 12-10.30 Sun

⌾**Johnson's Swampy or Gobbledegook**

Club, hotel and restaurant. Immediate membership (you just have to sign in) for visiting drinkers. Decorated throughout with nautical memorabilia. Accommodation, live music every other Saturday.

◖ ▶

RAMSGATE

Artillery Arms

36 West Cliff Road

☎ 01843 853282

12-11; 12-10.30 Sun

⌾**Cider varies**

Superb, unpretentious Victorian pub with attractive leaded glass bow windows. A beer lover's paradise with its ever-changing roster of beers. Thanet CAMRA Pub of the Year 1999.

ROCHESTER

Man of Kent

6-8 John Street

☎ 01634 818771

12-11; 12-10.30 Sun

⌾**2 Kent ciders; Double Vision Perry**

Back-street pub with rare original tiled frontage. Normally two Kent ciders and Double Vision Perry (the only perry made in Kent), plus beers from most Kent micro-breweries. Also sells Kent wines, draught and bottled German beers.

SANDGATE

Ship

65 Sandgate High Street

☎ 01303 248525

11-11; 12-10.30 Sun

⌾**Biddenden**

Haunted two-bar seaside pub. Superb, good value home cooking.

◖ ▶

SHEERNESS

Fiddlers Cat

1 High Street

☎ 01795 581450

11-11; 12-10.30 Sun

⌾**Johnson's Swampy or Gobbledegook**

A fun pub just outside Sheerness Railway Station. Ask for the cider if you do not see the poster. The local headquarters of the Rock and Roll Looney Party. Something going on most evenings.

Jolly Sailor

16 West Lane, Blue Town

☎ 01795 585090

11-11; 12-10.30 Sun

⌁**Johnson's Sheppey Hog or Gobbledegook**

A hard-to-find pub in Blue Town, the most historic part of Sheerness. Cider sales have taken off since the pub re-opened after a period of closure.

◖ ◗

Ship on Shore

155 Marine Parade

☎ 01795 662880

12-2.30(2 winter), 7-11; 12-4, 7-10.30 Sun

⌁**Johnson's Sheep Dip or Gobbledegook**

A free house on the outskirts of Sheerness, this pub offers a log fire in the winter and a large beer garden in the summer. Noted for its very unusual grotto. Separate restaurant in the conservatory. Ask for the cider if you do not see the poster/sign.

◖ ◗

SMARDEN

Bell

Bell Lane

☎ 01233 770283

11.30-3, 6-11; 12-11 Sat; 12-

10.30 Sun

⌁**Cider varies**

Large, 17th century, tile-hung, country pub. Impressive interior with low beams and open fires in winter. Large secluded garden. Classic car meetings held second Sunday lunchtime each month.

◖ ◗

SNARGATE

Red Lion ☆

(On the B2080)

☎ 01797 344648

11-3, 7-11; 12-3, 7-10.30 Sun

⌁**Double Vision**

Beautiful pub dating from 1540 and run, with love and devotion, by the same family since 1911. On CAMRA's National Inventory for Outstanding Pub Interiors, and Highly Commended in the National Pub of the Year award 1999.

STODMARSH

Red Lion

☎ 01227 721339

11-11; 12-10.30 Sun

⌁**Draught: Theobolds**
Bottled: Biddenden Dry, Monks Delight

Friendly country pub off the beaten track, about 15 minutes drive from Canterbury. Well worth the drive if just for the warm welcome and good range of beer and cider! Food available at all times.

STONE STREET

Padwell Arms

Stone Street Road

OS 569551

☎ 01732 761532

12-3, 6-11; 12-3, 7-10.30 Sun

🍎2 ciders (summer only)

Oldish, dimly-lit pub opposite an orchard. Good selection of Real Ales, a former Kent CAMRA Pub of the Year. Convenient for Ightham Mote (National Trust).

◖

WITTERSHAM

Swan

1 Swan Street

☎ 01797 270913

11-11; 12-10.30 Sun

🍎Double Vision

Friendly local in the centre of the village, originally an old drover's pub. No food Tuesdays.

Other Places of Cider Interest in Kent

Brogdale Horticultural Trust

by Simone Stolton

The Brogdale Horticultural trust, a registered charity, was formed in 1990. A 148 acre farm, it houses one of the largest temperate fruit collections in the world, with over 2000 varieties of apples, 500 varieties of pears, not to mention the plums, cherries, gooseberries and much more besides.

Brogdale is a living, growing museum of the history and development of British fruit. With an experienced team working on research and development, Brogdale has a vast knowledge and experience on which to draw. Continuing to evaluate new fruit varieties for the professional grower and to provide a resource centre for the general public.

Guided tours of the orchards take place throughout the day during the spring and summer seasons. Knowledgeable guides accompany visitors to the most interesting and attractive parts of the orchards that are a visual and fragrant delight in blossom time.

Workshops and day courses take place throughout the year on such diverse subjects as pruning and grafting and organic fruit production. Details of these and other courses can be obtained from ringing the number below.

Special events are arranged throughout the year – kicking off with the 'Spring Bonanza' in March through to the ever-popular Brogdale 'Cider and Perry Festival'. Hundreds of people visit the festival over the weekend and the interest it generates in all things cider makes it a truly unique event and one that is growing steadily in popularity.

Of course Brogdale produces her own special Cider and apple juice varieties and is in an unrivalled position for knowing which apple makes for the best. Pressed at Biddenden Vineyard using their excellent Boran Belt Press from Austria the juice produced is of the highest quality. Clear, distinct and fresh.

Brogdale also has her own plant centre stocking a good supply of budwood & graftwood and a shop that stocks everything from books on horticulture to wellington boots! A cup of tea or something more substantial can be obtained from the delightful 'Pippins' restaurant.

Brogdale needs and deserves the support of all involved in fruit farming – to help maintain a truly unique wealth of fruit varieties.

To experience Brogdale in full bloom – either blossom or apple time – is to experience the very richness and diversity of British fruit farming and is well worth a visit...

For information on opening times please contact:

The Brogdale Horticultural Trust, Brogdale Road, Faversham, Kent., ME13 8XZ

Or phone: 01795 535286

Photographs

Friends of Brogdale display (opposite) and shop (above).

Photo: Simon Stolton

LANCASHIRE

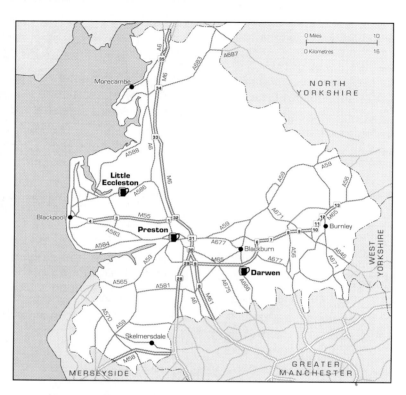

Lancashire Outlets

DARWEN

Punch Hotel

25 Chapels (¹/₂ mile from town centre)

☎ 01254 702510

12-11; 12-10.30 Sun

🍏1 unfiltered cider (usually Thatchers); 1 filtered cider (usually Saxon)

Large multi-roomed games pub with over twenty pub teams. Friendly locals. The pub opens when the first customer of the day rings the bell.

LITTLE ECCLESTON

Cartford Hotel

Cartford Lane

☎ 01995 670166

12-3, 6.30-11 (7-11 winter); 12-10.30 Sun

Cider varies

Riverside country free house, that acts as the Hart Brewery tap. West Pennines CAMRA Pub of the Year three times since 1990. Seven constantly-changing Real Ales, including two from Hart.

PRESTON
Flax & Firkin at the Corn Exchange

Lune Street
☎ 01772 880046

11.30-11; 12-10.30 Sun

Addlestones

One large open-plan bar with a relaxed atmosphere. Customers are a good mix of locals and students.

Hogshead (Moss Cottage)

99 Fylde Road
☎ 01772 252870

11-11; 12-10.30 Sun

Cider varies

A former doctor's surgery with various sections listed, this fine ale house opened in 1995 and is close to the university. A local CAMRA award winner, it has up to 13 guest ales, its own CAMRA noticeboard, and an annual cider and perry festival.

New Britannia

6 Heatley Street
☎ 01772 253424

11-3(4 Sat), 7-11; 7-10.30 Sun

Saxon Gold Digger

Small one-roomed pub with a separate games area, popular with students. Has been in the same family for many years – the licence recently passed from father to daughter.

Old Dog and Partridge

44 Friargate
☎ 01772 252217

11-2.30(3 Sat), 6-11; 12-3, 6.30-10.30 Sun

Cider varies

Town centre pub popular with bikers and other customers.

Real Ale Shop

47 Lovat Road (off the A6, to the north of the town)
☎ 01772 201591

11-2, 5-10; 12-2, 6-10 Sun

Draught: **Thatchers**
Bottled: **Various ciders**

Splendid off-licence with varying range of bottled ciders and beers available, including foreign beers. Draught Thatchers is good value. Situated in an area of terraced housing, so can be hard to find. Fancy dress hire upstairs.

LEICESTERSHIRE

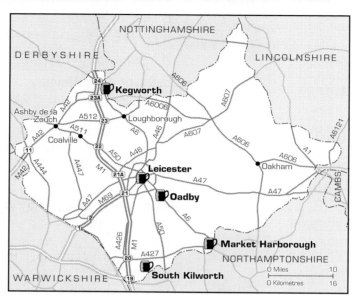

Leicestershire Outlets

KEGWORTH

Red Lion

24 High Street

☎ 01509 672466

11-11; 12-10.30 Sun

🍺Westons Old Rosie

Good, traditional local, now an independent free house. Four rooms with simple décor. The Old Rosie can occasionally be replaced with another cider. Dog friendly, no food Sundays.

◖ ◗

LEICESTER

Ale Wagon

14 Rutland Street

☎ 0116 2623330

11-11; 12-10.30 Sun

🍺Westons In Bottle Conditioned

Hoskins & Oldfield Brewery's full range is available on rotation at this pleasant city boozer. Close to the railway station.

Flynn's

171 Knighton Church Road, Knighton

☎ 0116 270 6331

9am-10pm; 10-10 Sun

Draught: Saxon Gold Digger, Diamond Lil

Corner-shop deli/bakery with Real Ales and Real Ciders to take home.

Last Plantagenet

107 Granby Street

☎ 0116 2555492

11-11; 12-10.30 Sun

Addlestones

Wetherspoon outlet close to the railway station. No smoking area. Guest ales, occasional beer festivals.

◐ ◑

Leicester Gateway

52 Gateway Street

☎ 0116 2557319

11-11; 12-10.30 Sun

Westons ciders (range varies)

Former hosiery mill thoughtfully converted by the Tynemill pub group. Five guest ales include a mild, and there's a good range of continental draught and bottled beers. Close to both the football and rugby grounds. No smoking area, good disabled access.

◐ ◑

Leicester Wholefood Co-op

Unit 3, Freehold Street

☎ 0116 2512525

9.30-6; 9.30-7 Fri; 9.30-5.30 Sat; closed Sun

Bottled: Dunkertons range

Shop selling wholefood and organic produce, including wine and bottled beers.

Vaults

1 Wellington Street

☎ 0116 2555506

5-11; 12-11 Fri/Sat; 12-3, 7-10.30 Sun

Draught: Saxon Gold Digger, Platinum Blond; Westons Old Rosie
Bottled: Westons In Bottle Conditioned

Atmospheric cellar bar specialising in guest beers (seven at any one time) from independent brewers. Regular live folk and blues sessions. Food limited to cobs and sandwiches.

MARKET HARBOROUGH

Sugar Loaf

18 High Street

☎ 01858 469231

11-11; 12-10.30 Sun

Addlestones

Pleasant town centre Wetherspoons. Guest beers and occasional beer festivals.

◐ ◑

OADBY

Cow & Plough

Stoughton Farm Park, Gartree Road

☎ 0116 2720852

5pm-9pm Mon- Sun

⌁**Saxon Platinum Blond; Westons Old Rosie**

Converted barn on the Farmworld Leisure Park, crammed with breweriana, and much loved by locals and cider/beer lovers alike. Interesting range of real ales. Family room, snug and no-smoking areas. Disabled access.

SOUTH KILWORTH

Chevelswarde Organic Growers

Chevel House, The Belt, OS 612821

☎ 01858 575309

9-6

⌁**Dunkertons bottled range**

Organic farm shop. Chevelswarde Organic Dry and Medium-Dry White Wine available. Hard to find, The Belt is a rough road off the North Kilworth Road.

LINCOLNSHIRE

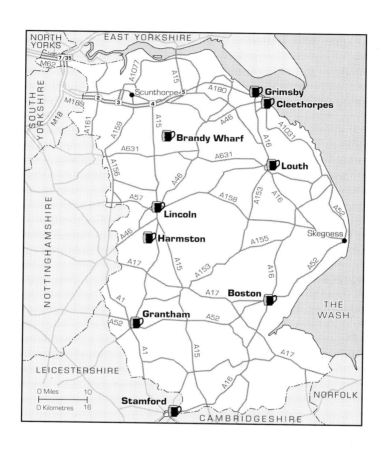

Lincolnshire Outlets

BOSTON

Eagle

144 West Street

☎ 01205 361116

*11-2.30, 5-11; 11-11 Fri/Sat;
12-10.30 Sun*

🍏**Biddendens**

Town-centre Tynemill pub, recently
refurbished, opposite the railway
station. Excellent real ale range.
No children under 14 allowed.

BRANDY WHARF

 ## CIDER HOUSE

national treasure – sells draught cider but no draught beer

Brandy Wharf Cider

Signposted off the A15

☎ 01652 678364

12-3, 7-11; 12-3, 7-10.30 Sun; (closed Christmas/New Year; Mon lunchtimes Dec-Easter)

⌒Saxon (Easter-Oct); Westons Bounds Brand, Old Rosie, Special Vintage, Traditional Scrumpy; guest ciders (occasional)

One of Britain's classic cider destinations, Brandy Wharf's Cider Tavern sells a fantastic range of 60 different ciders (both draught and bottled). Inspired by a visit to the Blue Bell Cider House at Hockley Heath, Birmingham, licensees Ian and Gillian Horsley started to emphasise cider in the Tavern, and finally removed beer for good at Christmas 1986. The Cider Tavern is on the banks of the River Ancholme, and customers enjoy its views on fine days from the garden, or can sit in the "Apple Foundry" bar or the "Cider Boutique" lounge. There's also a small cider museum, and a 180 tree orchard, in which events such as Wassailing and Tree Dressing are held. Bar meals include Scrumpy Cider Sausage, but no lunches on Tuesdays. This unique

Cider Centre offers proof, if any were needed, that cider can survive and prosper outside its traditional homeland – so long as it is promoted with knowledge and enthusiasm. Well worth a visit.

⌒ ▶ ~~REAL ALE~~

CLEETHORPES

Small Beer

199 Grimsby Road

☎ 01472 699234

10.30-10.30; 12-3, 6-10.30 Sun

⌒Bottled: Biddendens Dry, Sweet; Thatchers Medium; Westons Old Rosie

Street corner specialist beer off-licence. Two changing draught Real Ales, large selection of bottled beers. Two or five gallon poly-casks of cider can be ordered.

GRANTHAM

Hogshead

8 Market Place

☎ 01476 571660

11-11; 12-10.30 Sun

⌒Biddenden Medium

A Hogshead Ale House opened in January 1999. Good atmosphere and food. Has always got one real cider on handpump, as well as between 7 and 9 ales. Customers are encouraged to 'try before you buy'. Popular with the local CAMRA branch.

⌒ ▶

GRIMSBY

Tap & Spile

Haven Mill, Garth Lane
☎ 01472 357493

12-4, 7-11; 12-11 Fri/Sat; 12-4, 7-10.30 Sun

🍎**Cider varies**

Friendly local in an old Victorian flour mill, overlooking the river. 8 varying guest ales. Music at week-ends, quizzes Mondays and Thursdays.

Yarborough Hotel

29 Bethlehem Street
☎ 01472 368283

11-11; 12-10.30 Sun

🍎**Addlestones**

Spacious ground floor of a Victorian hotel, beautifully refur-bished by JD Wetherspoons.
◖ ◗

HARMSTON

Thorold Arms

High Street
☎ 01522 720358

11-3, 7-11; 12-3, 7-10.30 Sun

🍎**Biddenden (April to December)**

An outlet for the local Duffield Brewery ales. The cider may vary.
◖ ◗

LINCOLN

Golden Eagle

21 High Street
☎ 01522 521058

11-3, 5-11; 11-11 Fri/Sat; 12-10.30 Sun

🍎**Westons Old Rosie**

Friendly two-bar pub, handy for the football ground. Interesting range of Real Ales. Cider may vary.

Jolly Brewer

27 Broadgate
☎ 01522 528533

11-11; 12-10.30 Sun

🍎**Bulmers Traditional**

Art-deco style pub with several dis-tinctive drinking areas. Occasional guest cider in a 5 gallon polycask. 4 changing guest ales.
◖

Tap & Spile

21 Hungate
☎ 01522 534015

11-11; 12-10.30 Sun

🍎**Westons Old Rosie**

Town centre back street local with a varied clientele. Four changing Real Ales, non smoking area.
◖

Victoria

6 Union Road

☎ 01522 536048

11-11; 12-10.30 Sun

Biddenden Dry

Two-roomed pub in the shadow of the castle, with up to 7 guest beers, always including a mild. Ask for the Real Cider (which may vary), as it's hidden away in the cellar.

◖ ▶

LOUTH

Louth Wholefood Co-op

7-9 Little Eastgate

☎ 01507 602411

9-5 Mon-Sat

⌃Dunkertons bottled range

Wholefood shop near to St James Church (the tallest parish church spire in the country).

STAMFORD

Green Man

29 Scotgate

☎ 01780 753598

11-11; 12-10.30 Sun

Cider range varies

Split-level L-shaped one bar free house with a friendly atmosphere, just to the north of the town centre. The cider range normally numbers two ciders and one perry. Beer and cider/perry festivals in May and in the autumn. Good selection of Real Ales.

◖

Room at the Inn 2nd edition

by Jill Adam
324 pages   Price: £8.99

This second edition of the hugely popular Room at the Inn is your guide to quality overnight accommodation with a decent selection of real ale for good measure. The guide has been completely resurveyed and researched from scratch by the grass roots experts of the Campaign for Real Ale. Each entry in the guide gives local directions, contact details, opening times, type and extent of accommodation, list of beers, meal types and times, easy to understand price guide and snippets about local attractions and the sometimes centuries-old tales associated with your resting place.

Use the following code to order this book from your bookshop: ISBN 1-85249-150-7 Order directly with your credit card on 01727 867201.

GREATER LONDON

Greater London Producers

HACKNEY CIDER

Located in Hackney, London. Please use email for contact.

Email   hackneycider@hackney-cider.co.uk

Web site   www.hackneycider.co.uk

Graham Peters began making cider in 1998, and uses cider apples imported into London from the Devon/Somerset border. Commercial sales are due, at the time of writing, to begin during 2000, and the plan is to eventually relocate to south-west England.

Cider

Hackney Cider, 7.5% abv (bottle-fermented in various sized bottles or still in 15 litre Manucubes).

Sales

Direct sales only, via email and website.

THREE COUNTIES CIDER

16 Broadwater Gardens, Harefield, Middlesex, UB9 6AL.

☎ 01895 824268 / 01895 822058

Richard Ives and Michael Jones have been making small quantities of cider in a quiet Harefield suburb for some 12 years now. They scour the small orchards and private gardens of Buckinghamshire, Middlesex and Hertfordshire to source a variety of apples that lend their ciders a variety of flavours.

Cider

St.Marys, 7%+ abv (on draught or in 1 and 5 gallon plastic containers)

Annual Production

700 gallons

Sales

From private house at all times.

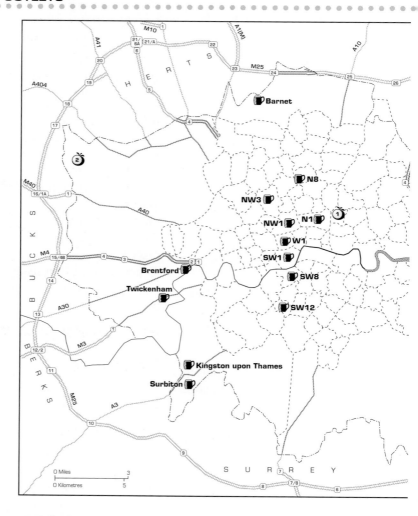

Greater London Outlets

North London

N1: HOXTON

Beer Shop

14 Pitfield Street
☎ 020 7739 3701
Web site
www.pitfieldbeershop.co.uk
11-7; 10-4 Sat; (closed Sun)

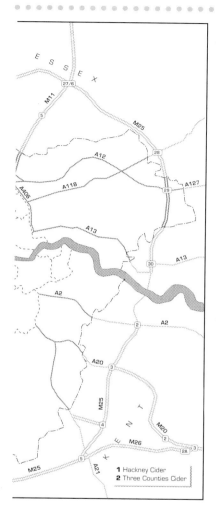

1 Hackney Cider
2 Three Counties Cider

⌂Draught: Cider varies

Bottled: Biddenden; Dunkertons; Lambourn Valley

Famous off-licence, opened in 1982. Large range of British and foreign bottled beers, plus a selection of real ales on draught that includes offerings from their own

brewery (Pitfield). Also sells cider-making equipment and home-brewing ingredients.

Wenlock Arms

26 Wenlock Road

☎ 020 7608 3406

12-11; 12-10.30 Sun

⌂**Cider varies**

Classic back-street single bar pub, the former Wenlock Brewery Tap. Taken over in 1994 by two long-standing CAMRA members, who now offer a changing range of at least six ales, plus either a cider or a perry. Jazz Sunday lunchtimes. Food limited to pasties and sandwiches.

N8: CROUCH END

Hogshead

33-35 Crouch End Hill

☎ 020 8348 3057

11-11; 12-10.30 Sun

⌂**Inch's Stonehouse**

Large pub converted from a funeral parlour, with 14 real ales (7 regular and 7 guest ales). Cider festival in the autumn.

BARNET

Albion

74 Union Street

☎ 020 8441 2841

11-11; 12-10.30 Sun

⌂**Addlestones**

Archetypal back-street pub retaining an outdoor Gent's toilet. One bar serves two interconnected drinking areas. One of the best pubs in the area, friendly local atmosphere. Cider sells well, several locals drink nothing else. Unusual pub games played.

◖

North-West London

NW1: CAMDEN TOWN

Fresh & Wild

49 Parkway

☎ 020 7428 7575

8am-9.30pm Mon-Sun

⌂**Bottled: Crones range; Dunkertons Organic**

One of a chain of five London-based organic supermarkets/health food stores. Unique and innovative food and drink range. Hot food from deli available. Juice bar.

Sauce Organic Diner

214 Camden High Street

☎ 020 7482 0777

12-11; 12-4 Sun

⌂**Bottled: Dunkertons Organic**

Bright and comfortable bar and restaurant, serving modern English food. Organic cider, wine, champagne and beer.

◖

NW1: EUSTON

Head of Steam

1 Eversholt Street

☎ 020 7383 3359

11-11; 12-10.30 Sun

⌂**Biddenden**

Railway-themed pub at the front of Euston station. Nine changing real ales, local CAMRA Pub of the Year 1999.

◖

NW3: HAMPSTEAD

Duke of Hamilton

23-25 New End

☎ 020 7794 0258

11-11; 12-10.30 Sun

⌂**Biddenden**

200 year old family-run pub. Local CAMRA Pub of the Year 1997. Cellar bar available for hire.

◖

South-West London

SW1: PIMLICO

Chimes Cider Wine Bar & Restaurant

26 Churton Street

☎ 0171 821 7456

12-3, 5.30-11, 7 days a week

⌣**Draught: Biddenden Dry; Westons Bounds Brand, Herefordshire Country Perry, Old Rosie**

Bottled: Biddenden Sweet; Dunkertons Medium-Dry

A cider-themed wine bar and restaurant first established in 1983. The cider bar at the front has country-style fittings – wooden floor, old church pews – and the bright eating area at the back serves traditional English food, often cooked with cider. Dishes include West Country Cider Cod and Haddock, and all the sauces are made with cider. The house cider, "Chimes Traditional", is Westons Bounds Brand in disguise.

◖ ◗

SW8: SOUTH LAMBERT

Priory Arms

83 Lansdowne Way

☎ 020 7622 1884

11-11; 12-10.30 Sun

⌣**Thatchers**

Single-bar free house, regular winner of the SW London CAMRA Pub of the Year Award.

◖

SW12: BALHAM

Moon Under Water

194 Balham High Road

☎ 020 8673 0535

11-11; 12-10.30 Sun

⌣**Addlestones**

A good down-to-earth pub with efficient service. An extremely busy Wetherspoons outlet.

◖ ◗

KINGSTON UPON THAMES

Canbury Arms

49 Canbury Park Road

☎ 0208 288 1882

11-11; 12-10.30 Sun

⌣**Cider varies**

Community pub with varied clientele. Live music at weekends. Cider changes weekly, annual cider festivals.

Druids Head

2-3 Market Place

☎ 0208 546 0723

11-11; 12-10.30 Sun

⌣**Biddenden**

Hogshead which has been extended from the original historic pub into the adjoining premises. Two floors, lots of wood.

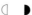 ◖ ◗

Kings Tun

153 Clarence Street

☎ 0208 547 3827

11-11; 12-10.30 Sun

Addlestones

Large Wetherspoons with the usual facilities. Trade moves from shoppers at lunchtimes to a younger crowd in the evening.

◖ ❯

SURBITON

Cap in Hand

374 Hook Rise North

☎ 0208 397 3790

11-11; 12-10.30 Sun

Addlestones

A Wetherspoons pub that is very much a local. Unusually, the building was a pub prior to Wetherspoons ownership.

◖ ❯

West London

W1: MAYFAIR

Hogshead

11/16 Dering Street

☎ 020 7629 0531

11-11; 12-11 Sat; closed Sun

Inch's Stonehouse; occasional guest cider

A pub near the junction of Oxford Street and New Bond Street, popular with both office staff and shoppers.

◖ ❯

BRENTFORD

Magpie & Crown

128 High Street

☎ 020 8560 5658

11-11; 12-10.30 Sun

Cider varies

Mock-Tudor high street pub, noted for its varying ale selection. Local CAMRA Pub of the Year 1999, good foreign bottled beer selection.

TWICKENHAM

Eel Pie

9/11 Church Street

☎ 020 8891 1717

11-11; 12-10.30 Sun

Inch's Stonehouse

Traditional pub in an historic street. The famous Eel Pie Thames island is nearby. Lunches weekends only.

GREATER MANCHESTER

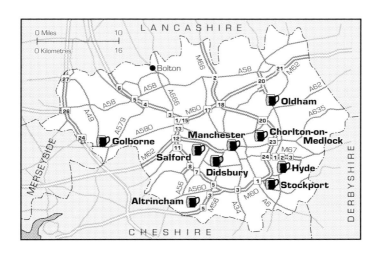

ALTRINCHAM

Old Market Tavern

Old Market Place

☎ 0161 927 7062

12-11; 12-10.30 Sun

⌂**Cider range varies**

Originally a 19th century coaching inn, part of the building was used as a town hall. Up to four ciders available, varying beer range, selection of Belgian beers.

◖

CHORLTON-ON-MEDLOCK

Hogshead

421-423 Oxford Road

☎ 0161 273 1490

11-11; 12-11 Sat; 12-10.30 Sun

⌂**Inch's**

Busy two-floored Hogshead pub housed in a new building. Customers from both the hospital and the universities.

◖ ▶

DIDSBURY

Carringtons

688/690 Wilmslow Road

☎ 0161 446 2546

9.30am-11pm; 12-10 Sun

⌂Bottled: Dunkertons range; Thatchers range

Enterprising independent off licence. Large range of British and foreign bottled beers in addition to the cider and perry.

GOLBORNE

Railway

131 High Street

☎ 01942 728202

12-11; 11-11 Sat; 12-10.30 Sun

⌂Saxon

A good locals' pub, and the only free house in the area. The landlady, Sarah, brews and sells her own beer ("Sarah's Hop House") on the premises. Has a beer club. Live music on Friday nights.

HYDE

Sportsman Inn

57 Mottram Road

☎ 0161 368 5000

11-11; 12-10.30 Sun

⌂Cider varies

Superb community local, a real social centre with keen sports teams and a full size snooker table upstairs. The cider and (many) real ale selection is always an interesting one, and the Sportsman has been CAMRA's Regional Pub of the Year in both 1998 and 1999. Extensive vegetarian and vegan menu.

◖ ◗

MANCHESTER

Bar Fringe

8 Swan Street

☎ 0161 835 3815

12-11; 12-10.30 Sun

⌂Knights Sweet (can vary)

The former White Bear rescued from closure, popular with rock music lovers. A 'brown bar' in the Belgian style, bizarrely decorated, watch out for the motorcycle and the rats! Heated beer garden.

◖

Beer House

6 Angel Street

☎ 0161 839 7019

11.30-11; 12-10.30 Sun

⌂Westons Traditional Scrumpy; guest cider

Manchester's premier free house; two drinking areas downstairs plus additional space on the first floor. Usually bustling with dedicated drinkers and office types alike. The beer range varies, always 12 different ales on, plus a wide range of German and Belgian bottled beers. Frequent beer festivals. Bar billiards table. Evening meals Thusdays and Fridays only.

◖ ▶

Hogshead

64-66 High Street
☎ 0161 832 4824

12-11; 12-10.30 Sun

⌒Cider range varies

Large, open-plan pub with wooden floorboards and several distinct drinking areas. The cider available rotates between Biddendens, Inch's Stonehouse, Moles Black Rat and Westons Old Rosie. Occasional cider festivals. The beer range includes six guest ales. Home-made chillied pickled eggs a speciality.

◖ ▶

Lass o'Gowrie

36 Charles Street
☎ 0161 273 6932

11.30- 11; 12-10.30 Sun

⌒Inch's Stonehouse

A turn-of-the-century public house with fine exterior tiling. Formerly a Chesters house, now run as a Hogshead by Whitbread who have added a small brewery. Gas lighting throughout, popular with the local BBC studios. Ale range includes a selection of house-brewed beers.

◖

On The 8th Day

107-111 Oxford Road
☎ 0161 273 1850

9.30-5.30; closed Sun

⌒Bottled: Dunkertons range

Long-established co-operative veggie/wholefood shop with adjoining café. Bottles can be purchased in the shop and taken through to the café.

◖ ▶

Pot of Beer

36 New Mount Street
☎ 0161 834 8579

12-11; closed Sun

⌒Mole's Black Rat

Small two-roomed free house in a maze of back streets. Polish food a speciality.

◖ ▶

OLDHAM

Ashton Arms

26-30 Clegg Street
☎ 0161 284 2070

12-11; 7-10.30 Sundays and winter

⌒Cider varies

Town centre pub, refurbished by micro-brewery.

SALFORD

Crescent

18/20 Crescent

☎ 0161 736 5600

11.30-11; 12-10.30 Sun

Thatchers; guest cider/perry

Famous free house with a three-roomed rambling interior, plus a separate "festival vault" where regular beer festivals and an annual cider festival are held. Beer range includes six guest ales plus a guest mild. Good value and inventive food from many ethnic origins. Function room.

◖ ▶

King's Arms

11 Bloom Street

☎ 0161 832 0167

12-11; 12-7 Sun

Pitching Green Medium Organic Perry

Large free house near the Bridgewater micro-brewery. Live music is a feature most evenings.

◖ ▶

STOCKPORT

Railway

1 Avenue Street

☎ 0161 429 6062

11-11; 12-10.30 Sun

⌣**Cider varies**

A flagship alehouse belonging to the Porter Brewery, with continually rotating fine real ciders.

◖

MERSEYSIDE

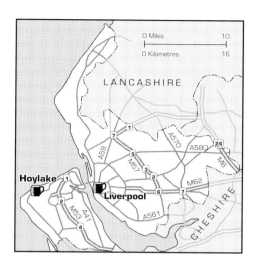

Merseyside Outlets

HOYLAKE

Hoylake Lights

52 Market Street

☎ 0151 632 1209

11-11; 12-10.30 Sun

Addlestones

Wetherspoons pub in Hoylake centre, formerly a shop. Local events and people in pictures on the walls. One of the first pubs in the area to receive the Cask Marque Award.

◖ ▶

LIVERPOOL

Baltic Fleet

33A Wapping

☎ 0151 709 3116

11.30-11; 12-10.30 Sun

Saxon range

Opposite the Albert Dock, so has a nautical theme. A pub that has its place in local history and is well known. Beers include some from Passageway, who brew the house beer 'Wapping Bitter'. Good food, kitchen closed Mondays.

◖ ▶

Cracke

13 Rice Street

☎ 0151 709 4171

11-11; 12-10.30 Sun

🍏Two varying ciders

Basic, multi-roomed pub with varied clientele. Good food.

Everyman

5-9 Hope Street

☎ 0151 709 477

12-2am; (closed Sundays)

🍏Bulmers Traditional

Beneath the Everyman Theatre. Good food in a candlelit environment. Late licence, beer range includes up to four guest ales. Trendy!

Ship & Mitre

133 Dale Street

☎ 0151 236 0859

11.30(12.30 Sat)-11; 2.30-10.30 Sun

🍏Cider range varies

Pub near the Moorfields and Lime Street stations with a gas-lit interior and art deco features. Up to ten ever-changing guest ales, oversized lined glasses, regular beer festivals. Two ciders on at any one time.

Swan Inn

86 Wood Street

☎ 0151 709 5281

11.30-11; 12-10.30 Sun

🍏Westons Old Rosie

Basic two-storey pub popular with bikers and students. Sunday breakfasts served until 5pm come highly recommended. Upper storey called "The Attic Bar" with separate entrance.

NORFOLK

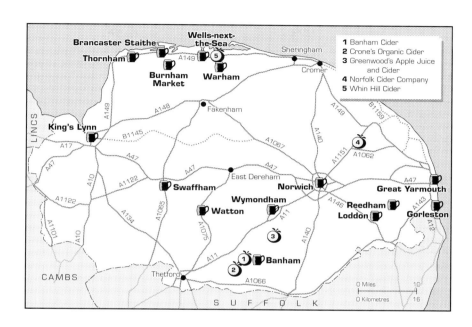

Map key:
1 Banham Cider
2 Crone's Organic Cider
3 Greenwood's Apple Juice and Cider
4 Norfolk Cider Company
5 Whin Hill Cider

Norfolk Producers

BANHAM CIDER

The Appleyard, Kenninghall Road, Banham, Norwich, NR16 2HB.
☎ 01953 888593

Web site www.cidershed.co.uk

Banham Cider is a small, independent company that has been producing fine cider for some ten years. Its traditional ciders are made from a blend of cider and culinary apples, and contain no additives or water whatsoever. The Banham Cider Shed is a fully licensed bar on site, and a visit to it is a must for all cider fans in the area.

Ciders
Russet (up to 7.5% abv)
Cox (up to 7.5% abv)
Strong Dry (up to 7.5% abv)
Rum Sweet (up to 7.5% abv)
Old Hardys Sweet (up to 7.5% abv)
Perry (occasional, up to 7.5% abv)
(All available in 1, 2, and 2¹/₂ litre plastic containers, and 5 gallon polykegs)
Annual Production
About 10 000 gallons

Visitors

Welcome. The cider making process may be viewed in season.

Directions

Banham Cider is opposite Banham Zoo. Follow the brown tourist signs for the zoo.

Sales

Shop open 12-6, 7 days a week.

Also on sale: apple juice

Outlets

Fat Cat, Norwich.

• Alexandra Tavern, Norwich.

• Ribs of Beef, Norwich.

• Rose, Norwich.

• Fat Cat, Ipswich.

Awards

Various awards at the Norwich Beer Festival, including Best Cider.

CRONE'S ORGANIC CIDER

Fairview, Fersfield Road,
Kenninghall, Norfolk, NR16 2DP.

☎ 01379 687687

Fax 01379 688323

Cabinet maker Robert Crone started making cider as a hobby in 1984, and Crones Organic Cider became a full-time business in 1989. The business has grown, and as well as producing 5000 gallons of flavoursome organic cider, Robert has diversified and now does a large range of organic apple juices.

Ciders

User Friendly, 6.2% abv.

Original, 7.5% abv.

Special Reserve, 7.5% abv.

Crone's Nouveau, 6.2% abv.

Annual Production

5000 gallons

Visitors

By appointment only.

Sales

Farm gate sales by appointment only.

Also on sale: organic cider vinegar and a large range of organic apple juices.

Outlets

Selected pubs in the Norfolk/Cambridgeshire/London area. For example:

• Take 5 (Cinema City, Norwich)

• Jug & Firkin (Cambridge)

• Freshlands (London)

Wholesalers:

- Suma Wholefoods, 01422 345513.
- Rainbow Wholefoods, 01603 630484.
- Infinity Wholefoods, 01273 424060.

Awards

Joint winner of the 1998 National Cider Awards.

GREENWOOD'S APPLE JUICE & CIDER

The Ashes, Carlton Rode, Norwich, NR16 1NN.

☎ **01603 403386**

boc@greenwoodsapple.freeserve.co.uk

In 1995, Chartered Insurer Trevor Greenwood decided to start a new career as an apple juice and cider maker, and today he and his family run a farm with 7 acres of their own orchards. Apple juice production forms the bulk of the business – they produce up to 12 varieties, unfiltered and with Vitamin C as the only additive – but, says Trevor, "we also dabble in the art of cider-making." The fruit used for cider making (mainly dessert apples) mostly comes from their own orchards, and the juice is fermented by the local Norfolk natural yeast. The finished product is an unfiltered, traditional Norfolk cider.

Cider

Greenwoods Orchard Dry, 8% abv. (Containers 75cl upwards.)

Annual Production

400 gallons

Visitors

Welcome. No formal tours, but visitors can see pressing in the apple season.

Directions

Situated on the B1113, 5 miles East of Banham Zoo. Second crossroads through New Buckenham.

Sales

Farm gate sales 7am to 7pm most days.

Also on sale: apples and apple juice.

Apple pressing service also available.

Awards

Norwich Beer Festival, Cider of the Festival 1998, Runner-up 1999.

NORFOLK CIDER COMPANY

Wroxham Barns, Tunstead Road, Hoveton, Norfolk, NR12 8QU.

☎ 01603 784876 (day) 01953 860533 (evening).

Email info@wroxham-barns.co.uk

Founded in 1987, the Norfolk Cider Company is now the county's longest established cider maker. Steven Fisher produces his fine 'Kingfisher Farm Cider' at Wroxham Barns rural craft centre, using antique Norfolk cider equipment. His 'Ingenio' apple mill dates from around 1870, and his nineteenth-century Norfolk box press does not have the stone base of its West Country counterparts, being made from wood due to the scarcity of Norfolk stone.

Ciders
Kingfisher Farm Cider, 7¹/₂% abv. (Dry, Medium Dry, Medium or Sweet)
(5 gallon barrel or 9 gallon keg)

Visitors
Welcome. Talks by appointment.

Directions
Signposted to Wroxham Barns from Wroxham Centre – 1¹/₂ miles.
OS map reference: Sheet 133, 305207.

Sales
Shop open 11am to 5pm.
Also on sale: apple-related products.

Outlets
• Kings Arms, Hall Rd, Norwich (Dry)
• Trafford Arms, Trafford St, Norwich (Dry)
• Rosary Tavern, Rosary Rd, Norwich (Medium)
Wholesaler: Wolf Brewery, tel 01953 457775 (distributes through much of the SE).

Awards
Norwich CAMRA Festival. Winner 1989, 1992 & 1993.
CAMRA's National Cider and Perry Championship – Runner-up 1990.

WHIN HILL CIDER LTD

The Stables, Stearman's Yard, Wells-next-the-Sea, Norfolk, NR23 1BW.
☎ 01328 711033
Email jfergus412@aol.com

Established in 1995, Jim Fergusson and Pete Lynn produce cider from their own orchards which are planted with traditional cider apple varieties such as Dabinett, Major and Browns Apple. 1999 saw the first worthwhile crops of these cider apples, and so for the first time Whin Hill Cider contains at least 50% cider fruit, with the remainder being dessert varieties in the traditional manner of the Eastern counties. Pete and Jim firmly believe that traditional methods produce the best ciders, so only pure Norfolk apple juice is used, and no sugar, water, yeast or artificial sweeteners are added.

Adjacent to the cider works in Stearman's Yard is their new cider shop. Here customers can enjoy free tastings of cider and apple juice, and can relax with a drink in the courtyard outside.

Whin Hill Cider delivers locally at no extra charge.

Cider

Draught: Dry 6% abv, Medium 5% abv, Sweet 4% abv. (Filtered, 5 litre flagons)

Bottled: Dry 6% abv, Medium 5% abv, Sweet 4% abv. (Filtered, still, 750ml bottles)

Bottle fermented: Dry 6% abv. (750ml bottles)

(Also available: Dry, Medium and Sweet sparkling ciders)

Annual Production

1500 gallons

Visitors

Welcome during shop hours.

Directions

On main car park in Wells, adjacent to Ark Royal pub.

Sales

Shop open: Fri-Sun, 11-5.30 (summer). Sat-Sun, 11-5.30 (spring & autumn).

Other periods please ring.

Non-cider items on sale: apple juice, cider vinegar, Iceni beers.

Awards

Best Cider, Norwich Beer Festival 1996.

Photographs

Bottle of Crone's Special Reserve Organic.

Photo: Dave Matthews

Traditional dress in front of the Apple Shop.

Photo: S Fisher, The Norfolk Cider Company

Norfolk Outlets

BANHAM

 CIDER PUB

sells more cider than beer!

Banham Cider Shed

The Appleyard, Kenninghall Road

☎ 01953 888593

Web site www.cidershed.co.uk

12-7.30; 11-11 Fri/Sat; (closed Sun)

🍎**Banham range**

Opened in 1996, this fully licensed pub shares premises with the Banham Cider Works and Shop. Banham's Farmhouse Cider is served from the bar, and the rest of the Banham draught range can be poured in the shop and brought through to the pub on request. Draught Adnams and Czech Budweiser are also offered, but overall more cider is sold. Live music Sunday lunchtimes and Friday nights. No hot food, but ploughmans made with Real Cheese available at all times. Food nights once a month.

BRANCASTER STAITHE

Jolly Sailors

Main Road

☎ 01485 210314

11-11; 12-10.30 Sun

🍎Kingfisher (Easter to Sept)

Traditional pub offering a friendly welcome. Situated near the harbour in a pretty coastal village.

◖ ◗

BURNHAM MARKET

Hoste Arms

The Green

☎ 01328 738777

11-11; 12-10.30 Sun

🍎**Whin Hill (Easter, Whitsun and Summer)**

17th century coaching inn, now with smart accommodation and restaurant. The old bar still welcomes locals and visitors.

◖ ◗

GORLESTON

Dock Tavern

Dock Tavern Lane

☎ 01493 442255

12-11; 12-10.30 Sun

🍎Kingfisher Medium/Dry

Old-fashioned quayside tavern. 6 to 10 varying real ales. Weekend entertainment includes traditional bands.

GREAT YARMOUTH

Red Herring

24/25 Havelock Road

☎ 01493 853384

11.30-3, 6-11; 12-4, 7-10.30 Sun

⌒**Theobolds Dry**

A Victorian pub by the town wall, a friendly community local. Popular for its Real Ale choice.

◖ ◗

KINGS LYNN

Ouse Amateur Sailing Club

Ferry Lane (off King Street)

☎ 01553 772239

11.30-4, 7-11; 11.30-11 Fri; 12-4, 8.30-10.30 Sun

⌒**Weston Old Rosie**

Popular, cosy, local club with a verandah overlooking the river. The sailing club dates back to 1881. CAMRA National Club of the Year 1999. Show CAMRA membership or this guide for entry. Batemans ales plus four guest beers.

◖

LODDON

Swan

Church Plain

☎ 01508 520239

10.30-11; 12-10.30 Sun

⌒**Addlestones**

Town centre pub with a separate restaurant and a no-smoking area.

◖ ◗

NORWICH

Alexandra Tavern

16 Stafford Street

☎ 01603 627772

11-11; 12-10.30 Sun

⌒**Banham**

Street-corner local much frequented by every type of customer. Traditional central bar with two adjoining rooms.

Billy Bluelight

27 Hall Road

☎ 01603 623768

11-11; 12-10.30 Sun

⌒**Banham; Biddenden; Westons Old Rosie**

Spartan yet warm and cosy single-bar pub divided by wooden partitions. Norfolk brewer Woodforde's flagship pub, named after a local Victorian character. Petanque played.

◖ ◗

Fat Cat

49 West End Street

☎ 01603 624364

12(11 Sat)-11; 12-10.30 Sun

⌣Banham Rum Cask, Dry Red; seasonal guests

Corner local famed far and wide for its Real Ale choice. CAMRA Pub of the Year 1998.

Kings Arms

22 Hall Road

☎ 01603 766361

11-11; 12-10.30 Sun

⌣Kingfisher Dry

A proper old-fashioned 18th century city centre pub. Real ale range includes 12 guests, East Anglia CAMRA Pub of the Year 1999. Bring your own food. Plates and cutlery provided!

Rosary Tavern

Rosary Road

☎ 01603 666287

11.30-11.30; 12-10.30 Sun

⌣Kingfisher Medium

A proper city pub housed in a Victorian building. Five changing guest ales.

◖

Take 5

Suckling Hall, St Andrews Street

☎ 01603 763099

10.30-11; 6-10.30 Sun

⌣Crones Organic

Café bar in a restored medieval hall, part of a cinema complex. Open to non-cinema goers, good food always on offer.

◖ ◗

Trafford Arms

61 Grove Road

☎ 01603 628466

Web site www.traffordarms.co.uk

11-11; 12-10.30 Sun

⌣Addlestones; Kingfisher

Friendly street-corner local, former Norwich CAMRA Pub of the Year. Popular with locals, students, businessmen and shoppers. Large and changing ale range includes house beers brewed by Woodfordes.

◖

White Lion

73 Oak Street

☎ 01603 620630

11-11; 12-10.30 Sun

⌣Kingfisher Medium/Dry

Historic city centre pub with live music once or twice a week. 'Proper' food with four local and three guest Real Ales.

◖ ◗

REEDHAM

Railway Tavern

17 The Havaker

☎ 01493 700340

11-3, 6-11; 11-11 Sat; 12-10.30 Sun

⌂Kingfisher Dry, Sweet (summer)

Friendly, listed, Victorian free house. Has its own brewery, the Humpty Dumpty Brewery, on site. Sells a wide variety of ales and has achieved the Cask Marque Award for cask ale quality. Cider available during the summer months or at one of the pub's beer festivals.

◖ ◗

SWAFFHAM

Norfolk Hero

48 Station Road

☎ 01760 723923

12-11; 12-4, 7-10.30 Sun

⌂Banham or Kingfisher (Easter to Sept)

Small two-bar local. Function room, real fire in the public bar.

◖ ◗

THORNHAM

Lifeboat

Ship Lane

☎ 01485 512236

11-11; 12-10.30 Sun

⌂Westons Old Rosie

Large and busy pub on the edge of the saltmarsh. The conservatory is light and airy during the day, and two open fires and two woodburners welcome customers on cold evenings.

◖ ◗

WARHAM

Three Horseshoes ☆

Bridge Street

☎ 01328 710547

11.30-2.30, 6-11; 12-2.30, 6-10.30 Sun

⌂Whin Hill (Easter to Sept)

Village pub with an electric Pianola. Accommodation available.

◖ ◗

WATTON

Breckland Wines

80 High Street

☎ 01953 881592

9-9 Mon- Sun

⌂Bottled: Whin Hill Cider

Well-stocked off licence with a wide range of bottled beers. Plans to extend the cider range.

WELLS-NEXT-THE-SEA

The Stables

Stearmans Yard

☎ 01328 711033

Easter-Oct, Sun 11-5.30; End July-Mid Sept, Fri/Sat/Sun 11-5.30; other times by appointment.

👄Whin Hill range

An off licence with a cider on licence! Tables and chairs in the courtyard outside Whin Hill's cider mill and shop allow customers to sit and sample the fine ciders.

WYMONDHAM

Feathers

13 Town Green

☎ 01953 605675

11-2.30, 7-11; 12-2.30, 7-10.30 Sun

👄Bottled: Eddie's Dry

An old town-centre pub with a good atmosphere and many interesting agricultural artefacts on the walls.

HOME BREWING

by Graham Wheeler
240 pages   Price: £8.99
Recently redesigned to make it even easier to use, this is the classic first book for all home-brewers. While being truly comprehensive, Home Brewing also manages to be a practical guide which can be followed step by step as you try your first brews. Plenty of recipes for beginners and hints and tips from the world's most revered home brewer.
Use the following code to order this book from your bookshop: ISBN 1-85249-137-X

BREW YOUR OWN REAL ALE AT HOME

by Graham Wheeler and Roger Protz
194 pages   Price: £8.99
This book contains recipes which allow you to replicate some famous cask-conditioned beers or to customise brews to your own particular taste. Use the following code to order this book from your bookshop: ISBN 1-85249-138-8

BREW CLASSIC EUROPEAN BEERS AT HOME

by Graham Wheeler and Roger Protz
196 pages   Price: £8.99
Learn how to brew superb pale ales, milds, porters, stouts, Pilsners, Alt, Kolsch, Trappist, wheat beers, sour beers, even the astonishing fruit lambics of Belgium.
Use the following code to order this book from your bookshop: ISBN 1-85249-117-5

Order directly with your credit card on 01727 867201.

NORTHAMPTONSHIRE

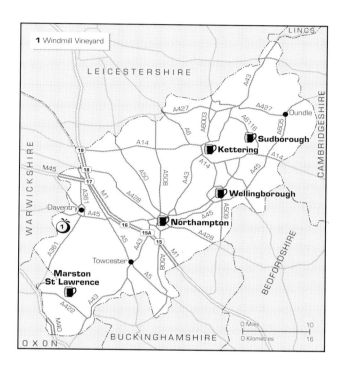

1 Windmill Vineyard

LINCS
LEICESTERSHIRE
CAMBRIDGESHIRE
WARWICKSHIRE
Oundle
Sudborough
Kettering
Wellingborough
Daventry
Northampton
Towcester
BEDFORDSHIRE
Marston
St Lawrence
OXON
BUCKINGHAMSHIRE

0 Miles 10
0 Kilometres 16

Northamptonshire Producers

WINDMILL VINEYARD

Windmill Hill Farm, Hellidon, Daventry, Northamptonshire, NN11 6HZ.

☎ 01327 262023

Doreen and Thomas Hillier-Bird planted their vineyard and orchard in 1978, and it was opened to the public for guided tours and tastings in 1995. Today they produce an enterprising range of ciders and perries, selling all they can produce from the vineyard shop. Wild crab apples are blended with their own apples to provide some tannin for a fuller-bodied flavour. They are also one of the few producers of 'cyser', an ancient drink that the Hillier-Birds make by fermenting apple juice with honey from their own colonies.

The Windmill tower is used for tastings of ciders and wines, with customers enjoying views over six counties.

Ciders

Unfiltered:

Scrumpy Apple, 8.5% abv.

Filtered:

Millers Fancy, 7.5% abv.

Fancy Oaked, 7.5% abv.

Windmill Perry, 8.5% abv.

(All available in .75, 1 and 1.5 litre containers. Larger containers available if notice given.)

(Also available:

Windmill Pyeder, a blend of apple and pear juice.

Pippin Cyser, apple juice fermented with honey.)

Annual Production

1000 litres

Visitors

Welcome. Tours available.

Directions

5 miles South of Daventry, signposted from the A361 and the A425.

OS map reference: 58N 52W.

Sales

Shop open 12 noon to 6pm, Wednesday to Sunday.

Also on sale: grape wine, country wines, grape and cider vinegars, mead.

Northamptonshire Outlets

KETTERING

Earl of Dalkeith

13-15 Dalkeith Place

☎ 01536 312589

11-11; 12-10.30 Sun

⌣**Addlestones**

Former shop, now a spacious, air-conditioned Wetherspoons pub. No-smoking seating area upstairs.

Old Market Inn

Market Place

☎ 01536 513999

11-11; 12-10.30 Sun

⌣**Sheppy's Medium (occasional)**

A six-roomed hotel with a restaurant and a bar offering 8 real ales and 110 malt whiskies. The accommodation is 4-star equivalent. The restaurant offers a full à la carte menu in the evenings, and outside catering/bars can be provided. The cider is on sale whenever the licensee can get down to Somerset!

Shire Horse

18 Newland Street

☎ 01536 519078

11-11; 12-10.30 Sun

Bulmers Traditional Medium

Family-run, open-plan free house. Occasional guest ciders from Biddendens or Lyne Down. Pub games include pool, pinball and Northamptonshire skittles.

MARSTON ST LAWRENCE

Marston Inn

☎ 01295 711906

12-2.30(3 Sat), 7-11; 12-3, 7-10.30 Sun; (closed Mon lunch)

Westons Old Rosie (summer)

Popular, end-of-row, stone-built Hook Norton pub. Aunt Sally played Thursday nights in the summer, dominoes and quiz teams in the winter. Home cooked food not available Mondays or Sunday evenings. Campers and caravaners welcome to stay in the back field.

◖ ◗

NORTHAMPTON

Hogshead

15-17 The Drapery

☎ 01604 635445

11-11; 12-10.30 Sun

Cider range varies

One of the Hogshead chain, refurbished May 2000. Up to five ciders available from polykegs on the back bar, typically from Biddendens, Bulmers and Westons. Free tasters available. Up to nine real ales, with 20p off each pint for card-carrying CAMRA members. A tasting event is held each month, and a micro-brewery beer festival each April.

◖ ◗

Malt Shovel Tavern

121 Bridge Street (opposite Carlsberg brewery)

☎ 01604 234212

11.30-3, 5-11; 12-4, 7-10.30 Sun

Rich's

Single-roomed pub, decorated with breweriana. Up to 13 real ales, twice-yearly beer festivals, regular themed beer weekends. Local CAMRA Pub of the Year 1997, 1998 and 1999. Licensee & Morning Advertiser's "Cask Ale Pub of Great Britain 1999", runner-up 1998 and 2000. Good range of continental draught and bottled beers.

◖ ◗

SUDBOROUGH

Vane Arms

High Street

☎ 01832 733223

11.30-2.30(not Mon), 5.30(6 Sat)-11; 12-3, 7-10.30 Sun

Saxon Diamond Lil; guest cider

Popular village free house, with nine varying real ales. Two Belgian fruit beers on tap. Games room in which pool, darts and Northamptonshire skittles can be played. The restaurant offers both an English and a Mexican menu in the evening.

◖ ◗

WELLINGBOROUGH

Red Well

16 Silver Street

☎ 01933 440845

10.30-11; 12-10.30 Sun

Addlestones

Wetherspoons shop conversion, in a building that was once the old town jail. Patio at the back, full disabled facilities.

◖ ◗

GOOD BOTTLED BEER GUIDE

by Jeff Evans
128 pages   Price: £8.99

When early nights and unfriendly traffic conspire to keep you at home, there's no risk these days of missing out on drinking a fine real ale. Britain's off-licences and supermarkets now stock bottle-conditioned ales – real ale in a bottle. The book describes the ingredients and history behind Britain's traditional bottled beer, and conjures up the tastes and smells.

Use the following code to order this book from your bookshop:
ISBN 1-85249-157-4.Order directly with your credit card on 01727 867201.

NORTHUMBERLAND

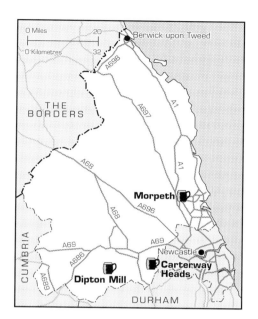

Northumberland Outlets

CARTERWAY HEADS

Manor House Inn

On the A68

☎ 01207 255268

11-3, 5.30-11; 12-3, 7-10.30 Sun

🍺 **Westons Old Rosie**

Isolated pub and restaurant on the Northumberland/Durham border affording excellent views over the Derwent reservoir. Has a reputa-

tion for excellent food with meals served in both the pub and restaurant – booking advisable. Accommodation available.

◖ ◗

DIPTON MILL

Dipton Mill Inn

Dipton Mill Road

☎ 01434 606577

12-2.30, 6-11; 12-4, 7-10.30 Sun

🍺 **Westons Old Rosie**

The Brewery Tap for the Hexhamshire Brewery, in a picturesque location just two miles from Hexham. Renowned for its good food and cheese specialities. Cider is often brought direct from the cellar – please ask if it's not visible.

◖ ◗

MORPETH

Tap & Spile

23 Manchester Street

01670 513894

12-2.30, 4.30-11; 12-11 Fri/Sat; 12-10.30 Sun

Westons Old Rosie

Small two-roomed traditional pub situated behind the bus station. A selection of six guest ales are available and the cider is brought up direct from the cellar.

◖

GOOD BEER GUIDE TO BELGIUM, HOLLAND AND LUXEMBOURG

by Tim Webb

286 pages   Price: £9.99

Discover the stunning range and variety of beers available in the Low Countries, our even nearer neighbours via Le Tunnel. Channel-hopping Tim Webb's latest edition – the third – of the guide offers even more bars in which an incredible array of beers can be enjoyed. There are maps, tasting notes, beer style guide and a beers index to complete the most comprehensive companion to drinking with your Belgian and Dutch hosts.

Use the following code to order this book from your bookshop: ISBN 1-85249-139-6

GOOD BEER GUIDE TO NORTHERN FRANCE

by Arthur Taylor

256 pages   Price: £7.99

Discover the excitement of the bars and cafes, the tranquillity of the village breweries which hold the secrets of generations of traditional brewing. Join the many festivals and cultural events such as the beer-refreshed second-hand market in Lille and the presentation of the Christmas ales. Find out where the best beer meets the best mussels and chips. Cuisine à la bière and more! Arthur Taylor is a leading authority on French beer and a member of Les Amis de la Bière, who have co-operated in the research for this book.

Use the following code to order this book from your bookshop: ISBN 1-85249-140-X

NOTTINGHAMSHIRE

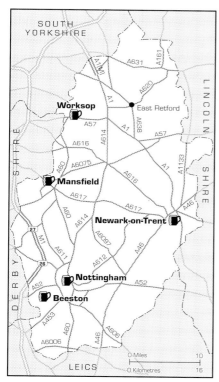

Nottinghamshire Outlets

BEESTON

Victoria Hotel

Dovecote Lane

☎ 0115 9254049

11-11; 12-10.30 Sun

🍎 **Cider varies**

Four-roomed Victorian architectur-

al gem, popular with all age groups. The varying range of around ten Real Ales always includes a mild. Regular live music.
◖

MANSFIELD

Bold Forester

Botany Avenue

☎ 01623 623970

11-11; 12-10.30 Sun

🍎 **Cider varies**

Large, new pub with 12 Real Ales and an annual beer festival. Live bands Sunday evenings.
◖

NEWARK-ON-TRENT

Fox & Crown

4-6 Appleton Gate

☎ 01636 605820

11-11; 12-10.30 Sun

🍎 **Biddenden**

Town centre pub that caters for cider and beer drinkers alike.
◖

NOTTINGHAM

Bunkers Hill Inn

36-38 Hockley

☎ 0115 910 0114

11-11; 12-10.30 Sun

⌀Westons Old Rosie

A family owned and run pub in former bank premises, next door to the new National Ice Centre. Up to ten guest beers with the emphasis on small and micro-brewers.

Forest Tavern /The Maze

257 Mansfield Road

☎ 0115 947 5650

4-11; 12-11 Sat; 12-10.30 Sun (Forest Tavern)

10pm-2am (The Maze)

⌀Cider varies

The Forest Tavern is a continental bar/pub at the front of the premises, with The Maze nightclub at the rear. Many draught ales including continental beers.
⌀ ◗

Langtrys

4 South Sherwood Street

☎ 0115 9472124

11-11; 12-10.30 Sun

⌀Inch's; Westons (summer)

Hogshead traditional ale house. Large range of Real Ales, customers can try free samples before buying. Curry quiz on Wednesdays.
⌀ ◗

Ye Olde Salutation Inn

Maid Marion Way

☎ 0115 958 9432

11-11; 12-10.30 Sun

⌀Inch's or Westons

One of Nottingham's three Hogsheads, originally dating from 1240. Features include a number of downstairs snugs, tours of the caves, and ghost tours on Saturdays!
⌀ ◗

WORKSOP

Mallard

Station Approach

Carlton Road

☎ 01909 530757

2-11; 12-11 Sat; 12-3 Sun

⌀Biddenden

The old refreshment room (a grade II listed building) on Worksop railway station. A cosy atmosphere and lots of interesting things to drink, including two ever-changing real ales, draught and bottled foreign beer, traditional English fruit wines, and, of course, real cider.

OXFORDSHIRE

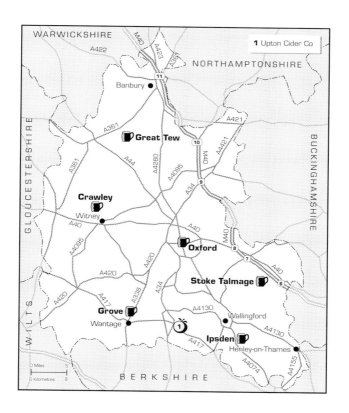

Oxfordshire Producers

UPTON CIDER CO.

Upton Fruit Farm, Upton, Didcot, Oxfordshire, OX11 9JE.

Cider has been made on the farm for some time, but the new owners, Mr and Mrs Fitchett, only arrived in February 1999. They plan to continue the cidermaking tradition (from selected cider apples), and also to produce freshly-pressed apple juice from single varieties of cooking and eating apples.

Cider

Real Farmhouse Cider, 7% abv (filtered, available in 2 and 4 pint containers).

Real Farm House Cider
STRONG MEDIUM
KEEP CHILLED
Made and bottled at Upton Fruit Farm, Upton
from selected Cider Apples.
2.2L Min. contents 1/2 Gall. ALC 7% vol.

Annual Production

1500 gallons.

Visitors

Welcome.

Directions

The fruit farm is at Upton on the A417, between Wantage and Goring.

OS map reference: SU517861.

Sales

Shop open between May and Christmas, Friday to Sunday, 12 noon to 5pm. Opening hours may be extended in the future.

Also on sale: apple juice, apples.

Oxfordshire Outlets

CRAWLEY

Crawley Inn

Foxburrow Lane

☎ 01993 708930

12-3, 7-11 (12-11 summer); 12-10.30 Sun

Thatchers Cheddar Valley

A true free house; natural and unconventional. A pub for all – regardless of age or species. Interesting range of real ales, often served by gravity.

GREAT TEW

Falkland Arms

Off B4022

☎ 01608 683653

11.30-2.30, 6-11; 12-3, 7-10.30 Sun; (open all day summer weekends)

Inch's Stonehouse

Traditional, one-bar rural gem in a picturesque village, featuring a flagstoned, beamed bar. Popular with tourists and locals alike. Accommodation available, evening meals 7-8pm Monday to Saturday.

GROVE

Volunteer

Station Road

☎ 01235 769557

11-11; 12-10.30 Sun

⌣Westons Old Rosie

Old rail station pub, now part of the Hook Norton estate. Beer festivals, large car park.
◖

IPSDEN

King William IV

Hailey, OS 643858

☎ 01491 681845

11-2.30, 6-11; 12-3, 7-10.30 Sun

⌣Bulmers Traditional Medium

Country pub in an idyllic setting with lovely views and Brakspear's ales. Close to the Ridgeway footpath.
◖ ◗

OXFORD

Wharf House

14 Butterwyke Place (at the junction of Thames St & Speedwell St)

☎ 01865 246752

11-3, 6.30-11; 11-11 Sat; 12-4, 7-10.30 Sun

⌣Cider and perry range varies

Oxford's only true free house, offering two varying ciders (one fairly mainstream, one unusual) plus a changing perry. Interesting range of real ales and Belgian beers. A down-to-earth boozer with a mixed clientele.

STOKE TALMAGE

Red Lion ☆

Off A40 at Tetsworth

☎ 01844 281343

6-11; 12-2.30 Fri/Sat; 12-3.30, 7-10.30 Sun

⌣Westons Old Rosie; other varying cider

A step back in time. A truly traditional country pub whose unspoilt interior is on CAMRA's National Inventory. Bar billiards and Aunt Sally. Closed Monday to Thursday lunchtimes.

SHROPSHIRE

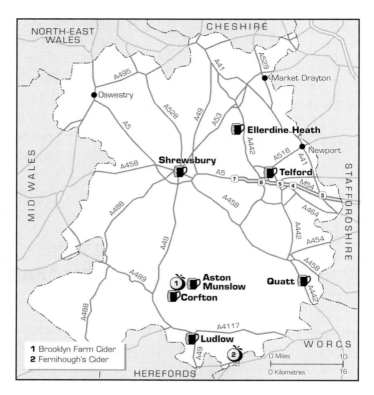

1 Brooklyn Farm Cider
2 Fernihough's Cider

Shropshire Producers

BROOKLYN FARM CIDER

The Swan Inn, Aston Munslow, Craven Arms, Shropshire, SY7 9ER.

☎ 01584 841415

Cider was originally made by the Williams family just for their own consumption, but in 1997 they bought an old cider press and started selling their unfiltered draught ciders firstly at the Swan Inn, and then at beer festivals.

Cider
Shout Clout Cider, 7.5% abv. (Available in 5 gallon containers or bring your own)
Production
1500 gallons.
Visitors
Welcome

Outlet

The Swan Inn, Aston Munslow, Craven Arms, Shropshire, SY7 9ER.

FERNIHOUGH'S CIDER

Fernihough's
Traditional Strong
Dry Cider

Ashdown, Tenbury Wells - Telephone: 01584 819632
1.5 Litre   KEEP IN A COOL PLACE   7.2% ABV
Once opened, consume within 3 days.

Ashdown, Worcester Road, Boraston, Tenbury Wells, Worcestershire, WR15 8LL.

☎ 01584 819632

Traditional, unfiltered ciders made by Carolyn Fernihough.

Ciders Strong Dry, 7.2% abv.
Strong Sweet, 7.2% abv.
Dry, 4% abv.
Sweet, 4% abv.
(All available in 1.5, 4.5 and 10 litre containers.)
Annual Production
1500 gallons
Sales
Farm gate sales 10am to 8pm, 7 days a week.
Awards
1st Prize at the Tenbury Show, each year since 1997.

Shropshire Outlets

ASTON MUNSLOW

Swan Inn

On the B4368 Bridgnorth to Craven Arms road.

☎ 01584 841415

11-11; 12-10.30 Sun

⌒Brooklyn Farm Shout

Warm and welcoming to all visitors, this pub is situated in the picturesque Corve Dale. Run by the wife and family of the owner of Brooklyn Farm Cider. Cider takeaways available to those customers who bring their own containers.

◖ ▶

CORFTON

Sun Inn

On the B4368 Bridgnorth to Craven Arms road.

☎ 01584 861239

11-2.30, 6-11; 12-3, 7-10.30 Sun

⌒Cider varies

Family-run 17th century inn set in the beautiful Corve Dale. A regular *Good Beer Guide* entrant, uses oversize glasses, brews its own beer. Holds a Children's Certificate and is a regular winner of awards for disabled facilities.

◖ ▶

ELLERDINE HEATH

Royal Oak

(Between A53 and A442)

☎ 01939 250300

12-3, 5-11; 11-11 Sat; 12-3, 7-10.30 Sun

🍏**Westons Old Rosie**

Real pub with real everything – food, staff, customers, as well as cider and beer. Known locally as the Tiddly Wink, it offers a lovely rural setting with a games room and very good value food (not served Tuesdays) and beer. Children's Certificate. Cider festival held each July.

◖ ◗

LUDLOW

Marches Little Beer Shop

2 Old Street

☎ 01584 878999

10.30ish-5.30, Wed-Sat; 2-5 Sun; (closed Mon/Tues)

🍏**Bottled: Cheyney Lodge; Dunkertons range; Franklins range; Hindlip range**

Independent off-licence, opened on May 1st 2000 by Georgina Harris, whose husband runs Marches Ales. Apart from the ciders and perries, the shop stocks a wide range of local and continental bottled beers, and English fruit wines.

All come with suggestions on the best food to match them with. Both the product range and opening hours are expected to evolve according to local demand.

QUATT

CIDER HOUSE
national treasure – sells draught cider but no draught beer

Cider House

Wootton Green

☎ 01746 780285

11.30-2.30, 7-10.30; 12-2, 7-10.15 Sun

🍏**Bulmers Traditional Dry, Medium**

Classic, popular cider house. Once a smallholding with orchards that made and sold its own cider, today it is one of only a handful of pubs that does not sell draught beer, offering instead a total of 13 draught and bottled ciders. Has a bar, snug and lounge (the "Orchard Room"), as well as outdoor seating and barbecues for the summer. The pub runs four mobile cider

bars, which can be hired for outdoor events. Burrow Hill Cider
Brandy on optic, cider take-outs
available. Well worth a visit!

REAL ALE

SHREWSBURY

Boat House

New Street,
Port Hill
☎ 01743 362965

11-11; 12-10.30 Sun

♻Inch's Stonehouse

Hogshead pub in a listed building
dating from the 1700s, whose
very large beer garden overlooks
the River Severn. The Inch's
Stonehouse is occasionally substi-
tuted with a guest cider, and
there's a cider festival each
August. Up to 8 real ales plus two
annual beer festivals.

TELFORD

Coalbrookdale Inn

12 Wellington Road,
Coalbrookdale
☎ 01952 433953

12-3, 6-11; 12-3, 7-10.30 Sun

♻Bulmers Traditional

Former CAMRA National Pub of
the Year. Not to be missed!

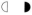

Cock Hotel

Holyhead Road, Wellington
☎ 01952 244954

*4-11; 12-11 Thur-Sat; 12-3, 7-
10.30 Sun*

♻Cider varies

18th century coaching inn, popular and convivial with up to six real
ales available in the Old Wrekin tap
bar, which links via a wood-pan-
elled reception area to a no-smoking lounge. Local CAMRA Pub of
the Year for 1998, 1999 and
2000. Bed & Breakfast available.

Crown Inn

Market Street, Oakengates
☎ 01952 610888

*12-3, 7-11; 12-11 Thur-Sat; 12-
3.30, 7-10.30 Sun*

♻Cider varies

Traditional market town pub with
three distinct drinking areas. Sells
250 to 300 Real Ales per annum,
and holds twice yearly beer festivals.

Photograph
The Cider House.

Photo: Brian & Kath Jervis

SOMERSET

Somerset Producers

AVALON VINEYARD

Avalon Vineyard, East Pennard, Shepton Mallet, Somerset, BA4 6UA.

☎ 01749 860393

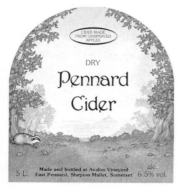

Hugh Tripp has been making his organic Pennard Cider, on a hand-turned twin-screw press with a straw cheese, since 1986. Chiefly available on draught, Hugh has plans at the time of writing to bottle his cider once again; let's hope that he uses the Traditional Method to produce the naturally-sparkling cider that he once made some years ago.

Cider

Pennard Cider, Dry, Medium or Sweet, all 6-7% abv. (5 litre or ¹/₂ gallon containers)

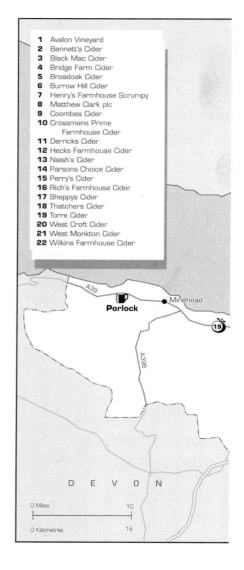

1. Avalon Vineyard
2. Bennett's Cider
3. Black Mac Cider
4. Bridge Farm Cider
5. Broadoak Cider
6. Burrow Hill Cider
7. Henry's Farmhouse Scrumpy
8. Matthew Clark plc
9. Coombes Cider
10. Crossmans Prime Farmhouse Cider
11. Derricks Cider
12. Hecks Farmhouse Cider
13. Naish's Cider
14. Parsons Choice Cider
15. Perry's Cider
16. Rich's Farmhouse Cider
17. Sheppys Cider
18. Thatchers Cider
19. Torre Cider
20. West Croft Cider
21. West Monkton Cider
22. Wilkins Farmhouse Cider

Annual Production

Less than 1500 gallons.

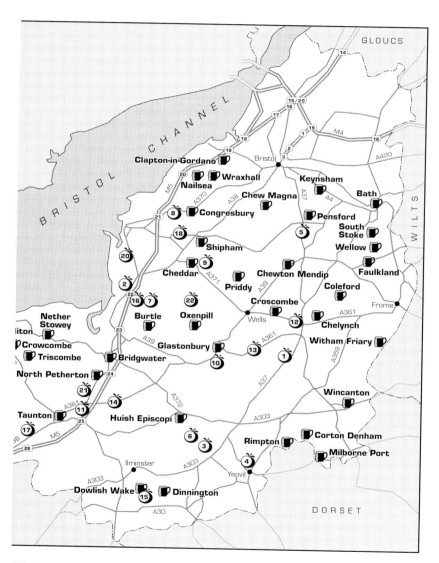

GLOUCS

14

BRISTOL CHANNEL

15/20
16
17
1
19
M4
18
18
A420

19
18
Clapton-in-Gordano
Bristol
3
2

20
Nailsea
Wraxhall
Keynsham
Bath
WILTS

M5
A38
A370
A38
Chew Magna
A37
A4

21
8
Congresbury
Pensford
South Stoke

18
Shipham
5
Wellow
Faulkland

20
9
Cheddar
A371
Chewton Mendip
Coleford

2
Priddy
A39
Croscombe
Frome
A361

22
16
7
22
Oxenpill
Wells
12
Chelynch

Burtle
A361

Nether Stowey
23
A39
Glastonbury
13
1
Witham Friary
A359

liton
Crowcombe
Bridgwater
10
A37

Triscombe

North Petherton
24
14
Wincanton

21
A372

A361
11
Huish Episcopi
A303

Taunton
25

17
M5

26
Ilminster
6
Rimpton
Corton Denham

3
Milborne Port

A303
4
Yeovil

A303
A303

A303

Dowlish Wake
15
Dinnington
Ilminster

A30
DORSET

Visitors
Welcome. Tours available.

Directions
5 miles South of Shepton Mallet on A37. Turn West at foot of

Wraxall Hill (opposite Queens Arms pub), proceed for $1^1/_2$ miles, look for sign on the right. OS map reference ST 588 374.

Sales

Vineyard shop, 10am-6pm.

Outlet

Nisa Heritage Fine Foods, High Street, Glastonbury.

BENNETT'S CIDER

V.V.G. & V.H.Bennett, Chestnut Farm, Edithmead, Highbridge, Somerset.

☎ 01278 785376

Viv Bennett suggests that: "Farmhouse cider has always been part of life on our dairy farm, I must be the fourth generation of cider makers here." The cider is chiefly made from their own apples, with a few bought in. Only one barrel is tapped at any one time, and the medium-dry, natural cider is sold to regular customers and visiting cider fans.

Viv's father, 80 years old at the time of writing, made cider for 70 years. When he gave up milking at the age of 60 he started entering his cider in local shows, and managed to pick up 150 prize cards in 15 years. Viv took over showing five years ago, and his ciders have managed to win the Champion Prize at both the Devon County and Royal Bath & West shows.

Cider

Dry-medium, 6.5% abv ($2^1/_2$ and

5 litre plastic containers, or bring your own).

(Sweet, filtered and champagne ciders produced for Shows, not for sale)

Annual Production

3000 to 3300 gallons.

Visitors

Please telephone ahead.

Directions

Leave the M5 at Junction 22 and head towards Burnham-on-Sea. After half a mile, Chestnut Farm is on the left.

Sales

Farm gate sales 10am to 5pm.

Outlets

English Farm Cider Centre, Lewes, Sussex.

Awards

Many prizes at Shows, including: Devon County Show: Champion Prize 1995, 1997, 1998. Royal Bath & West Show: Champion Prize 1995, 1998, 1999.

BLACK MAC CIDER

Pippin, The Orchards, Stembridge, Martock, Somerset, TA12 6BP.

☎ 01460 241736

Email john.mcgrouther@connect-2.co.uk

Black Mac is an interesting new craft cider company using ultra-traditional methods that include pressing the pomace through straw. John McGrouther's first year production (1999) was an experimental 400 gallons, using the 150-year-old press and mill that came from Bruce Bond's 'Black Toad Cider', Bruce having ceased production to concentrate on more artistic endeavours.

John has an orchard of 300 cider apple trees, from 3 to 30 years old, that have never been sprayed. Most of the varieties (Bulmers Norman, Dabinett, Michelin, Tremlett Bitter, Yarlington Mill, Vilberie, etc,) are blended to make 'Tail-ender', John's standard cider. He has also produced trial amounts of single variety Worcester Pearmain, Stembridge Cluster and Bulmers Norman ciders, as well as some ciders derived from pairs of apple varieties.

Cider

Tail-ender, 5.6% abv   (15 litre manucubes).

Annual Production

400 gallons in 1999.

Visitors

Welcome.

Directions

Stembridge is not on many maps, but is part of the parish of Kingsbury Episcopi. Go up the hill (west) from Kingsbury, turn left at the 'Rusty Axe' pub, go on for some 200 metres.

Pippin is on the left opposite the Junior School. Black Mac Cider is only half a mile from the renowned Burrow Hill Cider company.

OS map reference: ST 424 199.

Sales

Farm gate sales, please ring first. Also on sale: free range eggs, bedding plants and organic pumpkins.

Outlets

Under research at the time of writing, please ring for up-to-date information.

BRIDGE FARM CIDER

Bridge Farm, East Chinnock, Yeovil, Somerset, BA22 9EA.
☎ 01935 862387

Email   nigelstewart@lineone.net

Nigel Stewart started making cider in 1986 under the name of Sandford Cider in Dorset. He moved to Bridge Farm in 1990, and produces some very fine ciders that regularly win prizes at agricultural shows in the south west. Nigel uses only fresh juice from cider apples, all of which are either grown in his own orchards or harvested by himself locally. All of his ciders are unfiltered and fully traditional, but he is also currently experimenting with bottle fermented ciders.

Ciders

Bridge Farm Cider, (Dry, Medium or Sweet), 7% abv (2 or 4 litre containers).

Annual Production

3000 gallons.

Visitors

Welcome. Tours available.

Directions

East Chinnock is on the A30, south west of Yeovil. Bridge Farm is a short drive off the main road, passing beside a young orchard to arrive at the central yard, with its Cider Shed full of barrels, press, etc.

OS map reference: 494131, sheet 193.

Sales

Shop open May to September, 7 days a week, 10.30am to 6.30pm. The rest of the year, Friday and Saturday only, 10.30am to 6.30pm.

Also on sale: cider fruit cakes, apple juice.

Outlets

• East Chinnock Post Office (01935 862157)

• Mandeville Arms, Hardington Mandeville (01935 862418)

• White Post, Rimpton (01935 850717)

• Prince of Wales, Ham Hill (01935 822848)

Awards

Many 1st Prizes at local shows, including:

Devon Show, Champion Cider 1994 & 1996 (Reserve Champion 1987 & 1997).

Bath & West Show, Best Sparkling Cider 1994.

BROADOAK CIDER

Broadoak Cider Group, The Cider Mill, Clutton Hill Farm, Clutton, Somerset, BS39 5QQ.

☎ 01275 333154

Despite a relatively recent origin (the company was founded in 1984), Broadoak Cider is already one of Britains largest regional producers. They produce a comprehensive range of 'Premium' ciders – draught, kegged and bottled – as well as offering contract pressing and bottling.

Ciders

Unfiltered:

Broadoak Dry, Medium and Sweet, 5.5% abv.

Filtered:

Moonshine, both 8.4% and 7.5% abv.

Kingston Black, both 8.4% and 7.5% abv.

(Also available: Broadoak Strong Dry, Rustic Gold, Blackout, Red Oak, Mega White, Pheasant Plucker, Classic Gold.)

Annual Production

700 000 gallons

Sales

Shop open 7am to 6pm.

Awards

Moonshine Draught, Cider of the Festival, CAMRA Winterfest 1999.

Moonshine Draught, Cider of the Festival, Portsmouth Beer Festival, August 1999.

BURROW HILL CIDER

Pass Vale Farm, Burrow Hill, Kingsbury Episcopi, Martock, Somerset, TA12 5BU.

☎ 01460 240782

Web site www.ciderbrandy.co.uk

Burrow Hill Cider is one of Somerset's largest farm cider producers, and has perhaps Britain's most innovative range of cider-based products. Proprietor Julian Temperley has developed a reputation for being outspoken, and deserves respect for producing ciders (both draught and bottle-fermented) and cider brandies of the highest quality.

Cider has been made at Burrow Hill for at least 150 years, and Julian Temperley has been at the helm for the last 30. The unfiltered and beautifully balanced Burrow Hill Draught Cider is a blend of varieties ("Blending is the cider makers art", says Julian), and 40 varieties alone are grown in the 140 acres of orchards at Pass Vale Farm. Bitter-sharp apple varieties are used, namely Kingston Black and Stoke Red, for the two classy single-variety bottle fermented ciders.

Julian was granted a full cider distilling licence in 1989, the first in recorded history. His Somerset Cider Brandy Company now produces a range of distilled products, culminating in the release of a ten year-old cider brandy on 1st January 2000.

Ciders

Burrow Hill Draught Cider, 6.5% abv (available in a variety of containers)

Kingston Black Bottle Fermented Cider, 8% abv (75cl glass bottles)

Stoke Red Bottle Fermented Cider, 8% abv (75cl glass bottles)

Distilled Products

Eau-de-Vie, 40% abv (35cl and 5cl bottles)

Three Year Old Cider Brandy, 42% abv (70cl, 35cl and 5cl bottles)

Five Year Old Cider Brandy, 42% abv (70cl, 35cl and 5cl bottles)

Ten Year Old Cider Brandy, 42% abv (70cl and 5cl bottles)

Kingston Black Aperitif, 18% abv (50cl bottles)

Annual Production

80 000 to 100 000 gallons.

Visitors

Welcome. Tours available.

Sales

Shop open every day 8.30 to 5.30.

Outlets

Burrow Hill Draught Cider is on sale in a large number of local pubs, sometimes 'live' from wooden barrels, often in metal kegs.

Awards

Many awards. In 1984, for example, Burrow Hill Cider won competitions in Devon, Somerset and Hereford.

More recently, in 2000, Burrow Hill won the overall cider championship at the Devon County Show, and its bottle-fermented ciders won two gold medals in the West Country Food Awards.

COOMBES CIDER

Japonica Farm, Mark, Highbridge, Somerset, TA9 4QD.

☎ 01278 641265

Christopher Coombes is the third generation of a family which began cider making in 1919, and is still making cider today in the same traditional manner.

Visitors to Japonica Farm can sample the ciders and perry from black and gold-painted barrels in the shop, and further attractions are provided by a cider museum, a tea room and a children's play area.

Cider

Dry, Medium and Sweet Cider, all 6% abv.

Kingston Black Cider, Dry, 8.4% abv.

Perry, 7% abv.

(All in 2, $2^1/_2$ and 4 litre plastic containers; and 5 gallon polycasks.)

(Also available:

Bottled sparkling perry.)

Annual Production

15 000 gallons

Visitors

Welcome. Tours available.

Directions

On the B3139 Wells to Highbridge Road, 2½ miles from Junction 22 of the M5.

Sales

Shop open Monday-Saturday 9am-5.30pm.

Also on sale: Apple juice, cheeses, gifts.

CROSSMANS PRIME FARMHOUSE CIDER

Mayfield Farm, Hewish, Weston-Super-Mare, Somerset, BS24 6RQ.

☎ 01934 834921

Email
ben.crossman@ukonline.co.uk

Ben Crossman uses a wide range of Somerset cider apple varieties – including Harry Masters Jersey, Stembridge Jersey, Somerset Redstreak, Dabinett, Chisel Jersey and Yarlington Mill – to produce his traditional, unfiltered, farmhouse cider.

Cider

Dry, Medium or Sweet, all 6% abv (2½ litre jugs, 5 litre jerry cans, 20 litre manucubes and 5 gallon polykegs).

Annual Production

5-8000 gallons

Visitors

Welcome

Directions

Leave the M5 at Junction 21, take the A370 towards Bristol. After one mile you will find Mayfield Farm.

Sales

Farm gate sales 9am to 6pm Monday to Saturday, 9am to 1pm Sunday.

Also on sale: free-range eggs, vegetables in season.

Wholesalers: Jon Hallam, RCH Brewery, Crouch Vale Brewery.

DERRICKS CIDER

A.J.Derrick, Cheddar Valley Cheese Depot, The Gorge, Cheddar, BS27 3QE.

☎ 01934 743113

Deep in Cheddar Gorge, the Derrick family business was established in 1870 as a cheese retailer and wholesaler. Cider was introduced in 1975, and today the shop sells both cheese and cider to the many tourists who squeeze into the Gorge during the summer months.

Cider

Country Bumpkin, Dry or Sweet, 6.5% abv.

Tanglefoot, Medium, 6.5% abv.

(All available in 75cl glass bottles; 1, 2 and 4 litre plastic containers; and 1pint, 1, 2 and 4 litre stone bottles).

Annual Production

2000 gallons

Sales

Shop open 9am-5pm.

Also on sale: Cheeses, preserves, gifts, wines.

HECKS FARMHOUSE CIDER

9-11 Middle Leigh, Street, Somerset.

☎ 01458 442367

John Heck's family have made their award-winning traditional cider since 1896. The cider is a blend of apples from their own orchards and local farms, and it is fermented in wooden barrels and sold draught from the wood. They also produce ten varieties of farm-pressed 'Torside' apple juice, from their own dessert apples. Visitors can look around the small Cider Museum.

Cider

Cider 6.5% abv and Perry 6.5% abv. (Unfiltered in 5 gallon or 4 litre containers, or filtered in 75cl bottles)

(Also available:

An occasional Kingston Black single variety cider.)

Annual Production

8000 gallons

Visitors

Welcome. Tours available.

Sales

Farm shop open 9-6pm each week day.

Also on sale: 10 varieties of farm-pressed apple juice.

Outlets

Local shops in the Street and Glastonbury area.

Awards

Devon County Show, Champion Cup 1985, 1989, 1991.

Royal Bath & West Show, Champion Winners.

Mid Somerset Show, Champion Winners 1997.

HENRY'S FARMHOUSE SCRUMPY

Tanpits Cider Farm, Dyers Lane, Bathpool, Nr Taunton, Somerset, TA2 8BZ.

☎ 01823 270663

Mrs Dawn Pring combines cider-making with running a caravan and camping park at her Tanpits Cider Farm. The lucky campers and other visitors can wander around the farm to look at its antique machinery and cider equipment, say 'Hello' to the varied pets and animals, and sample the traditional unfiltered cider before buying.

Mrs Pring took over the farm from her Grandfather, who had started making cider at around 1912. The original press and mill are on display, and now a hydraulic press is used to squeeze juice from apples mostly grown on the farm.

Cider

Henry's Scrumpy, 6.5% abv (4 litre, $^1/_2$ gallon and 1 gallon containers).

Annual Production

Approximately 3000 gallons.

Visitors

Welcome.

Directions

Leave the M5 at Junction 25. Head towards Taunton, then follow the 'Caravan and Camping' signs on the Bridgwater main road.

Sales

Shop open 8.30am to 6pm, Monday to Saturday.

Also on sale: free range eggs, potatoes.

MATTHEW CLARK plc

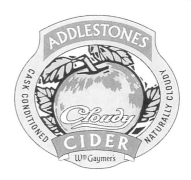

The Cider Mill, Kilver Street, Shepton Mallet, Somerset, BA4 5ND.

☎ 01749 334000

Web site www.mclark.co.uk

Along with H.P.Bulmer Ltd, Matthew Clark plc are one of the Big Two cider producers. Founded in 1810 as a wine company, Matthew Clark had no cider interests until it purchased both Taunton Cider and Coates-Gaymer in the 1990s. Their two cask-conditioned ciders are Taunton Traditional, found mainly in its south western homeland, and Addlestones, which has a national distribution. Of the two, Addlestones is the most astringent, being made from 100% cider apples.

Ciders
Addlestones, 5.2% abv.
Taunton Traditional, 5.2% abv.
(Also available: Dry Blackthorn, Gaymer's Olde English, K, Diamond White & Red C.)

Annual Production
43 million gallons.

Visitors
Organised trade parties, by appointment.

Directions
The company's cider mill is situat-ed at Shepton Mallet, Somerset, which is alongside the A37 some 20 miles south of Bristol. Visitor parking is signposted as is Reception.

OS map reference: ST 626436.

Outlets
(A great number of outlets, the following form a selection for Addlestones.)
• Eagle, South St, Eastbourne, Sussex.
• Cherub, Higher St, Dartmouth, Devon.
• Baccy Jar, Court Farm, Whitchurch, Bristol.
• Tut 'N' Shive, West Laithe Gate, Doncaster, S.Yorks.
• Apsley House, Auckland Rd West, Southsea, Portsmouth, Hants.
• Machine Man, Fieldside, Long Wittenham, Abingdon, Oxfordshire.
• Market Inn, The Square, Petersfield, Hampshire.
• Mill Tavern, Liphook Rd, Shottermill, Haslemere, Surrey.

Wholesalers
Addlestones: Carlsberg-Tetley, Matthew Clark Wholesale, Whitbread, Beerseller, various regionals.
Taunton Traditional: Ushers, Scottish Courage, Matthew Clark Wholesale, Bass, Carlsberg-Tetley, various regionals.
Matthew Clark Wholesale, Tel 01275 836100.

NAISH'S CIDER

Piltown Farm, West Pennard, Glastonbury, Somerset.

☎ 01749 890260

Pensioners Harold and Frank Naish are two of cider's great characters. Now both in their 70s, the brothers started making cider in 1937, on the beef farm where the Naish family has been making cider for 150 years. Fruit from their 6 orchards is milled, pressed and barrel-fermented in the traditional manner. The result is a fine, dry, unfiltered farmhouse cider. Some visiting tourists from Eastbourne, not used to farm cider, weren't so impressed though: "They said 'We don't like this, it's too dry and bitter'," Harold told me, "so I said 'Don't have two gallons then, just have the one'!"

Cider
Dry, 6% abv ($^1/_2$ gallon containers or bring your own).

Annual Production
1400 gallons

Sales
Harold and Frank currently have enough customers to sell all of their production to, and are therefore not looking for any new ones thankyou!

Outlets
English Farm Cider Centre, Lewes, Sussex.
Wholesaler: Jon Hallam.

Awards
1991 Newcastle-upon-Tyne Beer Festival: Cider of the Festival. 1996 Westmorland Beer Festival: Cider of the Festival.

PARSONS CHOICE CIDER

Parsonage Farm, West Lyng, Nr Taunton, Somerset.
Tel: 01823 490978

Parsonage Farm, West Lyng, Nr. Taunton, Somerset, TA3 5AP.

☎ 01823 490978

Jeanette and Phil Dolding have been making traditional cider on the Somerset Levels for ten years. They use a blend of cider apples such as Kingston Black, Crimson King and Bulmers Norman, all sourced from local orchards.

Cider
Parsons Choice (Dry, Medium or Sweet), 6% abv (2.2 or 4.4 litre containers).

Annual Production
4000 gallons.

Visitors

Welcome. Tours available by appointment.

Directions

Parsonage Farm is situated on the A361 road between East and West Lyng, about 7 miles north of Taunton.

Sales

Shop open 8am to 6pm, 7 days a week.

Also on sale: Vegetables, jams, honey, stone jars, mugs, candles (all locally produced).

PERRY'S CIDER

1.7 Litres **MEDIUM VINTAGE** 6% vol
Perry Bros • Dowlish Wake • Somerset

Perry's Cider Mills, Dowlish Wake, Ilminster, Somerset.

☎ 01460 52681

Perry's Cider is one of Somerset's most respected cider makers, and one of the most picturesque too, with cider being made in a six-teenth-century thatched barn. Founded in 1923 by Dowlish Wake's village blacksmith, it was taken over on his death in 1946 by his nephews Henry and Bert

Perry. Both brothers have since passed on, but the business remains in the family with Henry's wife and two sons.

Today Perry's produce an impressive range of traditional ciders, including rare examples of single varietal Somerset Redstreak and Morgan Sweet ciders. The draught Traditional and Vintage ciders can be sampled from the barrel in the shop before buying, and are blends of cider apple varieties that include Dabinett, Somerset Redstreak, Tremletts Bitter, Yarlington Mill and Kingston Black. The ciders are well received by the many tourists, who also have a cider museum and gift shop to choose from.

Ciders

Traditional (Dry, Medium Dry and Medium Sweet, all 6% abv, all available in 4 pint or 4 litre containers).

Vintage (Dry, Medium, Sweet, all 6% abv, all available in 4 pint or 4 litre containers).

(Also available: Redstreak Cider, Morgan Sweet Cider, Hogshead Scrumpy, Lightly carbonated 1 litre bottles of Traditional and Vintage Cider)

Visitors

Welcome. Tours available.

Directions

2 miles South of Ilminster, follow brown tourist cart signs.

Sales

Shop open Monday-Friday 9-5.30,

Saturday 9.30-4.30, Sunday 10-1. Also on sale: Apple juice, chutneys, jams, honey, garden tubs, gifts, etc.

Outlets

• New Inn, Dowlish Wake.
• County Stores, Taunton.
• Cott Farm, East Chinnock.
• Brimsmore Farm Shop, Brimsmore, Yeovil.
• Stewley Filling Station, Ashill, Somerset.

Awards

Prizes won in the past at both the Bath & West Show and the Devon & Exeter Show.

RICH'S FARMHOUSE CIDER

Mill Farm, Watchfield, Near Highfield, Somerset, TA9 4RD.
☎ 01278 783651

Gordon Rich started making farmhouse cider and supplying it to local pubs over 50 years ago. Today the business is being carried on by his daughter, and Rich's cider is supplied to pubs both locally and nationally. Only Somerset cider apples are used, and the result is a fully traditional unfiltered farmhouse cider, with a tasty balance of fruit and gentle sharpness. Rich's cider is matured in huge oak vats; the largest – named 'Gog' – holds 10 000 gallons, the second largest is a 6 000 gallon version – named after Adge Cutler of The Wurzels fame – and was bought from Coates.

Ciders

Rich's Farmhouse Cider (Sweet, Medium and Dry), all 6% abv.
(2, 2.5 and 4 litre containers, and stone jars)

Annual Production

50 000 gallons plus.

Visitors

Welcome. Tours available.

Directions

Only 2 miles from Junction 22, M5. On the B3139 opposite the Watchfield Inn.

SOMERSET PRODUCERS

Sales

Shop open 9am to 7pm Monday to Saturday, 10am to 7pm Sunday.

Also on sale: pottery, Somerset Royal cider brandy, apple juice and an interesting range of local cheeses.

Outlets

A large range of pubs and off-licences both locally and nationally. A selection:

• Cheddar Gorge Cheese Co., Cheddar Gorge.

• A J Derrick Cider Shop, Cheddar Gorge.

• Labour Club, Bridgwater.

• Railway Club, Taunton.

• Ritz Social Club, Burnham-on-Sea. Lamb & Fountain, Frome.

• Fox & Hounds, Warminster, Wilts.

• Seymour Arms, Frome.

• Rock House Inn, Dulverton.

• Egremont Hotel, Williton.

SHEPPYS CIDER

R.J.Sheppy & Son, Three Bridges, Bradford-on-Tone, Taunton, Somerset, TA4 1ER.

☎ 01823 461233

Sheppys are a traditional family-run farm cidermaking company, that has become one of Somerset's largest and most respected. The family started making cider over 200 years ago, and moved to the present site in 1918. Today, Sheppys cider farm is a major stopping point on the West Country tourist trail, and visitors can see cider being made from a viewing gallery, visit the Farm and Cider Museum (with a video of the cider maker's year), and sample before buying in the cider shop.

Groups of 20 or more who book ahead can enjoy a guided tour of the cellars and the 42 acres of orchards, where varieties such as Kingston Black, Yarlington Mill, Dabinett, Stoke Red and Tremlett's Bitter are grown.

Sheppys ciders are widely available, and over the years have accumulated over 200 awards, including two gold medals at the Brewers Exhibition.

Ciders

Sheppys Farmhouse Draught, 6% abv. (Dry, Medium or Sweet, all filtered)

(Available in $^1/_2$ gallon, 1 gallon, $2^1/_4$ gallon, 20 litre or 5 gallon containers)

Also available:

(All of the following bottled ciders are flash pasteurised, and all except Gold Medal Vintage are lightly carbonated)

Gold Medal Vintage, 8% abv. (Still. Dry, Medium or Sweet. 1 litre bottles)

Goldfinch, 7% abv. (Dry. 1 litre bottles)

Bullfinch, 7% abv. (Medium. 1 litre bottles)

Kingston Black, 7.2% abv. (500ml bottles)

Dabinett, 7.2% (500ml bottles)

Oakwood Special, 6.5%. (Medium dry. 330ml bottles)

Oakwood Draught, 6.5%. (Dry. 1.7 litre glass jar)

Annual Production
60 000 gallons

Visitors
Welcome. Guided tours are available for groups of 20 or more, please book ahead.

Directions
M5 Junction 26. Head for the A38, turn right onto the A38 towards Taunton. Sheppys is on your right after about 1 mile, 3¹/₂ miles away from Taunton.

Sales
Shop open 8.30-6.00 Mon-Sat,

12-2 Sunday.

Outlets
Many, including:
• Waitrose & Budgens (most stores)
• Braz (restaurant/bar), Taunton.
• County Stores, Taunton.
• Fermoys Garden Centre, Newton Abbot.
• Chatsworth Farm Shop.
Wholesalers: Vitis Wines (01295 251786). Mariposa (01963 32879).

Awards
Over 200, including 2 gold medals at the Brewers Exhibition, and 3 Gold Awards at the International Food Exhibition.

TAUNTON CIDER
(See Matthew Clark, Somerset)

THATCHERS CIDER

Thatchers Cider Co Ltd, Myrtle Farm, Sandford, Winscombe, Somerset, BS25 5RA.
☎ 01934 822862.

SOMERSET PRODUCERS

Email
martin@thatcherscider.co.uk

Web site
www.thatcherscider.co.uk

William John Thatcher started making cider at Myrtle Farm in 1904. Martin Thatcher is his great grandson, and today he presides over one of the five largest cidermakers in Britain. The introduction of state-of-the-art cider-making facilities have transformed Myrtle Farm, but traditional methods have not been forgotten. As a result Thatchers enjoy a good reputation amongst cider drinkers, and their fine traditional draught ciders are amongst some of the most widely distributed in the land. The Cheddar Valley brand, darker than the Thatchers Traditional, was acquired with the Cheddar Valley Cider Company in 1984.

Thatchers produce Black Rat Cider for Moles Brewery in Wiltshire.

Ciders

Thatchers Traditional (Sweet, Medium or Dry), 6% abv.

Cheddar Valley, 6% abv.

(2¹/₂ & 5 litre containers from the shop, 5 and 11 gallon kegs to the trade).

(A large range of other ciders are produced, all of which are artificially carbonated:

Big Apple, Bruscatio, Mendip Scrumpy, Millfield, Old Rascal, Premium Press, White Magic, and a range of single variety bottled ciders that includes Dabinett

and Somerset Redstreak.)

Annual Production
2 million gallons.

Visitors
Welcome.

Directions
Sandford is East of Weston-Super-Mare and the M5, on the A368. Myrtle Farm is west of the village centre.

Sales
Shop open 8.30am to 6pm, Monday to Saturday. 10am to 1pm Sunday.

Outlets
Too many to mention all of them here, but what follows is a selection:
• Cotham Porter Stores, Bristol.
• Cider Bar, Newton Abbot, Devon.
• Beehive, Bath.
• Star, Pucklechurch, near Bristol.
• Black Horse, Clapton-in-Gordano, near Portishead, Somerset.
• Butchers Arms, Yatton, Somerset.
• Uncle Toms Cabin, Wincanton, Somerset.
• Tuckers Grave, Faulkland, Somerset.
• Trout Tavern, Keynsham, Somerset.
• Kings Head, Kingswood, Bristol.
Wholesalers: Jon Hallam, East-West Ales, Crouch Vale Brewery, Ringwood Brewery.

Awards
West Country Food Awards: Bronze & Silver 1999.

TORRE CIDER

Torre Cider Farm, Washford,
Watchet, Somerset, TA23 OLA.
☎ 01984 640004

Email torre_cider@freenet.co.uk

Torre Cider Farm is a popular
tourist destination because of its
farmshop and tearoom, and above
all for its range of traditional farmhouse ciders. Only local apples are
used – varieties include Kingston
Black, Yarlington Mill, Dabinett,
Sweet Coppin, Somerset Red
Streak, and Harry Masters Jersey
– and the finished product is promoted at over 100 shows every
year by owners Jill and Steve
Gillman.

Ciders

Farmhouse Medium-Dry, 6¹/₂%
abv

Farmhouse Medium-Sweet, 6¹/₂
abv

Sheep Stagger (medium), 5% abv

Tornado (v.dry), 8.4% abv

(All available on draught, or in 1,
2 & 4 litre plastic jerry cans. The
1 litre bottled versions are filtered and pasteurised)

(Also available: Vintage Cider,
cask matured for one year, then
filtered and pasteurised in ¹/₄, ¹/₂,
& 1 litre flip-top glass bottles)

Annual Production

15 000 gallons

Visitors

Welcome, self-guided tours available.

Directions

Follow the brown tourist signs
from Washford on the A39.

Sales

Shop open 7 days a week, 9am to
6pm April to September, 10am to
4pm October to March.

Also on sale: Torre apple juice,
country wines, cheeses, preserves and pickles.

Outlets

• First Quench (Threshers) off-
licences, Somerset.

• Cheddar Gorge outlets,
Somerset.

• Roly's Fudge, Dunster, Somerset.

• Caravel, Lynmouth, Devon.

• St James Dairy, Ilfracombe,
Devon.

• Sanders Sheepskin Shop,
Barnstaple, Devon.

• Palmers Brewery, Bridport,
Dorset.

• Londis, Porlock, Somerset.

• Agricultural and County Shows
around the country.

WEST CROFT CIDER

West Croft Farm, Brent Knoll, Highbridge, Somerset, TA9 4BE.

☎ 01278 760762/760259

Email cider@burnham-on-sea.co.uk

John Harris, like his Grandfather before him, is a traditional cider maker. Although he only founded his company in 1992/93, West Croft's tasty, unfiltered ciders have won a whole clutch of awards, including Gold at CAMRA's National Cider and Perry Championships in 1996. His cider range includes Janet's Jungle Juice (using apples from his own small orchard), and single-variety specials such as a Morgan Sweet – an early-cropping variety whose cider is available between October and December.

Ciders

Dry Cider, 6% abv.

Medium Cider, 5^{1}/$_{2}$% abv.

Janets Jungle Juice (Medium or Dry), 6% abv.

Occasional Ciders:

Strong Dry, 7% abv.

Morgan Sweet, 7% abv.

Annual Production
7000 gallons

Visitors
Welcome. Tours available.

Directions
M5 Junction 22. A38 towards Bristol, 400 yards left into Brent Knoll, 1 mile (past Red Cow pub on the right), T-junction, right into farm opposite the post office.

Sales
Farm gate sales, 10am-7pm, 7 days a week. (Shut Sunday afternoons in the winter).

Outlet
Monkey Mix Cider Bar, Ben Johnson public house, Corporation Street, Birmingham. Wholesalers: Merrylegs; RCH brewery; and Rob Wilson.

Awards
Gold at CAMRA's National Cider and Perry Championships 1996, Bronze 1998 and 1999.

Hereford Cider Museum, 2nd Dry, 2nd Sweet, 1997. 3rd Sweet 1998.

Various 1st prizes at beer festivals, including Cardiff and Nottingham.

West Monkton Cider

West Monkton Cider Co. Ltd, 'Overton', West Monkton, Taunton, Somerset, TA2 8LS.

☎ 01823 412345.

A new company formed in 2000 by Gary Lane. An amalgamation of Lanes Cider (founded 1983) and

Kingston Vale Cider (founded 1995).

Ciders

Unfiltered:

Lanes Traditional Draught, 5.5% abv (2.5 & 4 litre jerry cans).

Kingston Red, 5.5% abv.

Golden Rutter, 6% abv (1 litre jerry cans).

Filtered:

Bonking Billy, 6% abv (550ml glass bottles, 1 litre jerry cans, 2 litre glass jars, 2.5 litre c/kegs).

(Also available: Scratch, 5.2% abv, in 1.13 litre glass flagons.)

Visitors

By prior arrangement only.

Sales

Farm gate sales by prior arrangement only, wholesale only – 5 gallon minimum.

Outlets

• **Rose & Crown, Nether Stowey, Somerset (Lanes Draught).**

• **Kings Arms, Fore Street, Seaton, Devon (Kingston Red Draught).**

• **Woolacombe Off Licence, Woolacombe, Devon (Bonking Billy).**

• **Wholesaler: Jolly's Drinks Group, Wellington, Somerset.**

WILKINS FARMHOUSE CIDER

Land's End Farm, Mudgley, Wedmore, Somerset, BS28 4TU.
☎ 01934 712385

Roger Wilkins is one of the best-known cider characters (amongst the many) in Somerset. He took over the family cider business – started by his Grandfather in 1917 – in 1966. A great promoter of traditional farm cider, he is keen to point out to city-dwellers: "What you've been drinking out of a bottle ain't never seen an apple!" Land's End is a working farm but Roger is kept busy with a continuous stream of locals and visitors who make the pilgrimage to his cider cellar, to buy his tasty, appley, still farm cider.

Ciders

Wilkins Dry, Medium and Sweet, 6.2% abv.

(Containers from 1 litre up to 5 gallons)

Annual Production

30 000 gallons

SOMERSET PRODUCERS

Visitors
Welcome. Tours available, but no big coaches please.

Directions
2¹/₂ miles south of Wedmore on the B3151. Left turn into Mudgley, ³/₄ of a mile to Land's End Farm.

Sales
Shop open 10am to 8pm.
Also on sale: Cheddar cheese, Stilton, pickles.

Outlets
A selection:
Bird in Hand, Westhay.
Railway Inn, Ashcott.
Country Man, Meare.
Riflemans Arms, Glastonbury.
New Inn, Wedmore.
Pack Horse, Mark.
Poachers Pocket, Cranmore.
Ring O' Bells, Moorlynch.
Burtle Inn, Burtle.
New Inn, Priddy.
Wholesaler: Jon Hallam, 0117 966 0221

Photographs
The Cider Cellar at Burrow Hill Cider. *Photo: Dave Matthews*

Apples arriving at Matthew Clark's Shepton Mallet plant. *Photo: Andrew Chamberlain Photography*

Barrel sign. Photo: *Dave Matthews*

This way please to Sheppy's. *Photo: Dave Matthews*

Somerset Outlets

BATH

 CIDER PUB

sells more cider than beer!

Bee Hive
3 Belvedere, Lansdowne
☎ 01225 420274

11-11; 12-10.30 Sun

⌀Thatchers Cheddar Valley, Traditional; Westons Old Rosie

Small, single-roomed traditional locals pub, set halfway up Lansdown Hill in a lovely Georgian terrace. Bath's only true cider pub.

BRIDGWATER

 CIDER PUB

sells more cider than beer!

Bristol & Exeter
135 St Johns Street
☎ 01278 423722

Opening hours vary

⌀Lanes or Perrys or Thatchers

Old pub close to the station, the last Real Pub in Bridgwater!

~~REAL ALE~~

BURTLE

Ye Olde Burtle Inn

Catlott Road

☎ 01278 722269

Web site
www.burtleinn.fsnet.co.uk

11-11; 12-10.30 Sun; (closed 4pm-6pm, Mon-Fri, winter)

🍎**Burtle Cider; Thatchers Cheddar Valley**

17th century inn that was once a cider house. Beamed ceilings and large log burning open fires. Specialises in locally-produced food, large selection of coffees.

◖ ◗

CHEDDAR

Bath Arms Hotel

Bath Street

☎ 01934 742425

11-11; 12-10.30 Sun

🍎**Thatchers Cheddar Valley (April to Oct)**

A village pub/hotel that was origi-nally a coaching inn called The George. A plaque in the lounge marks the occasion when King George VI had lunch at the hotel in 1941. Today the village bar offers Real Ales as well as cider, and the restaurant opens for breakfast at 8am. Local Cheddar cheese is used in the cooking, and the Bath Arms is one of only 52 pubs in the

UK to have been awarded Recommended Status by the British Cheese Board. Accommodation available.

◖ ◗

Cheddar Valley Cheese Depot

The Gorge

☎ 01934 743113

9-5

🍎**Bottled: Burrow Hill; Derricks Country Bumpkin Dry, Country Bumpkin Sweet, Tanglefoot; Torre**

Cheddar's oldest cheese and cider shop, in a prime position deep in Cheddar Gorge. Over 50 different country wines available.

Kings Head Inn

1 Silver Street

☎ 01934 742153

12-2.30, 5.30-11; 5.30-11 Mon; 12-11 Sat; 12-10.30 Sun

🍎**Thatchers Dry**

17th century thatched pub, with lounge and public bars, courtyard and large garden. A great base for rambling over the Mendips, walkers and their dogs always afforded a warm welcome. No lunches Mondays or Tuesdays.

◖ ~~REAL ALE~~

CHELYNCH

Poachers Pocket

$^1/_2$ mile north of A361 at Doulting

☎ 01749 880220

12-3, 6-11; 12-3, 7-10.30 Sun

↻**Addlestones; Wilkins**

Family-run 16th century rural free house, keeping up the traditions of a village pub. Flagstone floors, open fire, pub games. A Beer Festival is held every September, and a Cider Festival has now been introduced at Easter. Good value home-cooked food.

◖ ▶

CHEW MAGNA

Pony & Trap

New Town

☎ 01275 332627

12-3, 7-11; 12-3, 7-10.30 Sun

↻**Bulmers West Country**

200 year old village pub with a large garden.

◖ ▶

CHEWTON MENDIP

Chewton Cheese Dairy

Priory Farm

10-4.30

↻**Sheppy's Farmhouse Medium**

A working cheese dairy making traditional Farmhouse Cheddar. The farm shop and restaurant pro-

motes farmhouse cider as a good accompaniment to their cheese. The restaurant's food is made on the premises from local ingredients whenever possible.

◖

CLAPTON-IN-GOR-DANO

Black Horse

Clevedon Lane

☎ 01275 842105

11-3, 6-11; 11-11 Fri/Sat; 12-3, 7-10.30 Sun

↻**Bulmers West Country; Thatchers Dry**

Traditional 14th century pub with flagstone floors and large open fireplace. Formerly the village lock-up!

◖

COLEFORD

Kings Head

☎ 01373 812346

12-3, 6-11

↻**Bulmers Traditional Dry**

A pub built in 1742 that has customers of all ages. Lots of traditional pub games including shove ha'penny. Meeting place for both the fishing club and the carnival club. Food limited to rolls and pasties. Sells about the same amount of cider as beer.

~~REAL ALE~~

CONGRESBURY

Plough Inn

High Street

☎ 01934 832475

11-3, 5-11; 11-11 Sat; 12-4, 7-10.30 Sun

🍶Thatchers Cheddar Valley (occasional), Traditional

Locals pub with flagstone floors, known for its Real Ales. Smutty postcards in the gents!

CORTON DENHAM

Queens Arms

3 miles south of A303

☎ 01963 220317

12-2.30, 6.30-11; 11.30-2.30, 6-11 Fri/Sat & summer; 12-3, 7-10.30 Sun

🍶Thatchers Cheddar Valley, Traditional Medium (mostly April to Sept)

Excellent cider, beer and food.

CROSCOMBE

Bull Terrier

☎ 01749 343658

12-2.30, 7-11

🍶Thatchers Traditional Dry

15th century village pub first licensed in 1612. Good Real Ale range, no keg beers! Always a

wide choice on the menu for vegetarians. Bed & Breakfast available.

CROWCOMBE

Carew Arms ☆

High Street

☎ 01984 618631

11.30-3.30, 6-11

🍶Lanes; Thatchers

Historic building in the centre of the village, unspoilt by the passage of time.

DINNINGTON

Rose & Crown

Lower Street

☎ 01460 52397

11-3.30, 6-11; 11-11 Sat; 12-4, 7-10.30 Sun

🍶Burrow Hill

Traditional village pub, popularly known as 'The Docks'.

DOWLISH WAKE

New Inn

☎ 01460 52413

11-3, 6-11; 12-3, 7-10.30 Sun

🍶Perrys Medium Dry

Centuries-old pub in a picturesque village close to Perry's Cider Mill.

Two bars, family room, skittle alley and beer garden.

FAULKLAND

Tuckers Grave Inn

On A366, 1 mile east of village

☎ 01373 834230

11-3, 6-11; 12-3, 7-10.30 Sun

⌂Thatchers Cheddar Valley

Friendly, welcoming country pub whose unspoilt interior is on CAMRA's National Inventory. There is no bar, the stillage is set in a small bay window. Three small cosy rooms and a fine garden. Said to be the grave of Edward Tucker, who hung himself in the barn behind the pub in June 1747.

GLASTONBURY

Riflemans Arms

4 Chilkwell Street

☎ 01458 831023

12-2.30, 5-11; 12-11 Fri/Sat; 12-10.30 Sun

⌂Wilkins

Interesting old pub with an 'alternative' clientele. Near to the Tor and Abbey.

HUISH EPISCOPI

Rose & Crown (Eli's) ☆

☎ 01458 250494

11.30-2.30, 5.30-11; 11.30-11 Fri/Sat; 12-10.30 Sun

⌂Burrow Hill

Somerset's most famous cider house, though these days it sells more beer than cider. It's a traditional British inn with a thatched roof, pointed Gothic windows and stone-flagged floors. The Rose & Crown has been in the same family now for at least 5 generations, a period of over 130 years. It is known universally as "Eli's" after the present landlady's father, Eli Scott, who was licensee for 55 years. The landlady's grandfather, William Slade, was also licensee for 55 years before that. The Burrow Hill cider is poured directly from 6 gallon wooden barrels.

Eileen Pittard, landlady of the Rose & Crown, writes:

"In the old days we used to make our own cider – good apple orchards in this district – and when a child I would steal away to

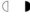

the cider-house and catch the golden liquid dripping through the straw. With my father, in the pony and trap, we visited farms to sample their cider with a view to augmenting supplies as the demand was great; cider being much cheaper than other alcohol and popular with the village folk. There are many stories, come and hear them!"

KEYNSHAM

 CIDER PUB

sells more cider than beer!

Trout Tavern

Temple Street

☎ 0117 986 2754

10-11; 12-4, 7-10.30 Sun

⌂Taunton Traditional; Thatchers Traditional

Two-bar locals pub on the main street, with a large, busy lounge and a smaller bar.

MILBORNE PORT

Queens Head

High Street

☎ 01963 250314

11-2.30, 7-11; 12-2.30, 7-11 Sat; 12-2.30, 7-10.30 Sun

⌂Westons 1st Quality

Welcoming village pub full of characters. Grade II listed building with

a friendly ghost. Good beer and food, accommodation available.

NAILSEA

Blue Flame Inn

West End

☎ 01275 856910

12-3(5 Sat), 6-11; 12-5, 7-10.30 Sun (12-10.30 Sun summer)

⌂Thatchers; guest cider

Free house over 200 years old, tucked away on country lanes between Clevedon and Nailsea. Open fires, huge garden, and barrels where they've always been – behind the bar. Food limited to rolls. "A real pub not a theme pub!"

NETHER STOWEY

Cottage Inn

Keenthorne

☎ 01278 732355

11-11; 12-10.30 Sun

⌂Coombes

Big, comfortable roadhouse, with a large function/family room.

NORTH PETHERTON

Globe Inn

High Street

☎ 01278 662999

11-11; 12-10.30 Sun

⌂Taunton Traditional; Thatchers

Small, cosy local.

OXENPILL

Countryman Inn

☎ 01458 860225

11-3, 6-11; 12-4, 7-10.30 Sun

⌂Wilkins

Village pub that was once an old scrumpy house. Good food includes a carvery for Sunday lunch.

PENSFORD

The Rising Sun

Church Street

☎ 01761 490402

11.30-3, 7-11; 11-11 Sat; 12-10.30 Sun

⌂Thatchers Dry

300-400 year old pub where Judge Jeffries is reputed to have once held court. The riverside garden contains an old mill. The homecooked food is not available Mondays or Sunday evenings. Function room.

PORLOCK

Ship

High Street

☎ 01643 862507

10.30-11; 12-11 Sun

⌂Perry's

13th century pub that was mentioned in Lorne Doone. As well as the draught Perry's Cider, bottles of Taunton Natch also sell well.

PRIDDY

New Inn

Priddy Green

☎ 01749 676465

11.30-2.30, 7-11; 12-2.30, 7-10.30 Sun

⌂Wilkins

15th century former farmhouse in Somerset's Mendip Hills. Log fire, flagged bar floor, conservatory, skittle alley. Good food, ales and cider.

RIMPTON

White Post

☎ 01935 850717

12-3, 6.30-11; 12-3, 7-10.30 Sun

⌂Bridge Farm

Free house straddling the Somerset/Dorset border. It's possible to drink in both counties.

SHIPHAM

Lillypool Café

Lillypool Farm, Shipham Hill

☎ 01934 743994

8am to 6pm

⌂**Burrow Hill**

Lillypool Farm, in the Mendip Hills, dates back to the 18th century, and has been a cider and cheese farm for around 100 years. The licensed café offers breakfasts and lunches. Ten acre camping site.

SOUTH STOKE

Packhorse Inn

South Stoke Lane

☎ 01225 832060

11-11; 12-10.30 Sun

⌂**Taunton Traditional; Thatchers Cheddar Valley**

Pub built in 1489 that sells as much cider as beer. Popular with both locals and tourists, well used by walkers. The original-beamed bar has an inglenook fireplace.

TAUNTON

GWR Staff Association Club

Upper Station Approach

☎ 01823 275048

11-2, 7-11; 11-11 Sat; 12-10.30 Sun

⌂**Rich's**

Great Western Railway social club next to the station. Visitors can be signed in by a member.

TRISCOMBE

Blue Ball

01984 618242

12-2.30, 7-11

⌂**Bollhayes**

A pub/restaurant that was once a quarryman's cottage.

WELLOW

Fox & Badger

Railway Lane

☎ 01225 832293

11-3.30, 6-11; 11-11 Sat; 12-10.30 Sun

⌂**Thatchers Cheddar Valley**

A 16th century village pub that boasts a bar, lounge, dining room, conservatory, courtyard and skittle alley.

WILLITON

Foresters Arms Hotel

55 Long Street

☎ 01984 632508

11-11; 12-10.30 Sun

⌂Rich's

Former 17th century coaching inn on the edge of the village, close to the railway station. Popular with locals and touring cricket teams. Interesting Real Ale range. Said to be haunted by the ghost of a 14 year old girl.

◖ ▶

WINCANTON

Uncle Toms Cabin

51 High Street

☎ 01963 32790

11-11; 12-10.30 Sun

⌂Heck's Perry; Thatchers Cheddar Valley, Traditional Dry

Picturesque thatched pub, selling roughly equal quantities of cider and beer. Customers of all ages can choose between the bar, lounge, snug and beer garden, as well as the upstairs pool and function rooms. Heck's Perry also sold in bottles.

WITHAM FRIARY

Seymour Arms ☆

☎ 01749 850742

11-2.30, 6-11; 12-3, 7-10.30 Sun

⌂Rich's Dry, Medium

Classic, traditional old village local, whose unchanged and unspoilt interior is on CAMRA's National Inventory. The Seymour Arms has been in the same family since 1943, and has a friendly, sociable atmosphere. Get served through the central hatch and drink in either of the stone flagged rooms or in the stand-up passageway. Cider outsells beer in the summer, when the large garden comes into its own.

WRAXALL

Old Barn

Bristol Road (next to Wraxall Manor)

☎ 01275 819011

11.30-3, 5-11; 11.30-11 Fri/Sat; 12-3, 7-10.30 Sun

⌂Thatchers

A Real Ale country pub in a c1600 old barn. The rustic bar and lounge have a log fire. Outside drinking area.

Other Places of Cider Interest in Somerset

Royal Bath & West Show

The Royal Bath & West of England Society, The Showground, Shepton Mallet, Somerset, BA4 6QN.

☎ 01749 822200

Email: general.office@bathandwest.co.uk

Web site: www.bathandwest.co.uk

The Royal Bath & West is one of many annual shows which holds a cider competition, but this one is set to become particularly prestigious. The Show is held at the end of May/start of June, and it's Cider and Orchard Area boasts presentations from cider makers of all sizes, has stands from nurseries selling cider apple trees, and has displays on many other cider and orchard-related subjects.

At the 2000 Show, the first ever

Gold Medal was awarded 'for a lifetime contribution to the cider and orchards of the West Country'. The inaugural recipient was Ray Williams, former Pomologist at the Long Ashton Research Station, and 'father' of modern orcharding practice. Ray's two particular orcharding successes have been the development of bush apple trees, and his work on pollination which greatly increased apple yields.

Also at the 2000 Show, Matthew Clark plc planted the UK's 2 millionth cider apple tree, a Somerset Redstreak, in the showground's permanent orchard.

Photographs

Rose & Crown, Huish Episcopi.
Photo: Mark Foot

Uncle Tom's Cabin.
Photo: Paul & Alison Matthews

BREWERY BREAKS

by Ted Bruning
64 pages   Price: £3.99

A handy pocket guide to brewery visitor centres and museums. Keep this in the car on your travels and you'll never be far from the living history of brewing. An ideal reference for CAMRA members, and others, wishing to organise a trip to one of Britain's best known breweries or a tasting at a local microbrewery.

Use the following code to order this book from your bookshop:
ISBN 1-1-85249-132-9. Order directly with your credit card on 01727 867201.

STAFFORDSHIRE

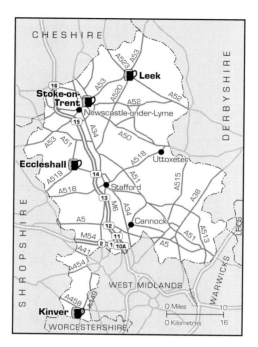

Staffordshire Outlets

ECCLESHALL

George Hotel

Castle Street

☎ 01785 850300

11-11; 12-10.30 Sun

👌Cider varies (May-Sept)

Home to the Eccleshall Brewery. Their first tied house, opened in 1995.

◖ ◗

KINVER

Cross

Church Hill

☎ 01384 872435

12-4, 7-11; 12-11 Fri/Sat; 12-3, 7-10.30 Sun

👌Rich's Medium

Friendly two-roomed local at the southern end of the High Street.

LEEK

Den Engel

23-25 St Edward Street

☎ 01538 373751

*7-11 Mon/Tue; 5-11 Wed/Thur;
12-3, 5-11 Fri; 12-3, 7-11 Sat;
12-3, 7-10.30 Sun*

🍎**Cider or perry varies**

Authentic Belgian bar with upstairs
restaurant. Large range of
draught and bottled beers.
Licensee is a partner in a beer
wholesaler offering a range of real
cider and perry.

Try Also:

Wilkes Head, St. Edward Street

STOKE-ON-TRENT

Blue Bell

25 Hardingswood, Kidsgrove

☎ 01782 744052

*7.30-11; 1-3.30, 7-11 Sat; 12-
3.30, 7.30(7 summer)-10.30
Sun*

🍎**Cider range varies (always one
Dry and one Medium)**

Genuine free house with a canalside location. Potteries CAMRA
Pub of the Year 1999, five rotating guest ales. No TV, juke box,
pool or bandits. The pub owner is
a partner of a beer wholesaler
which distributes real cider.

SUFFOLK

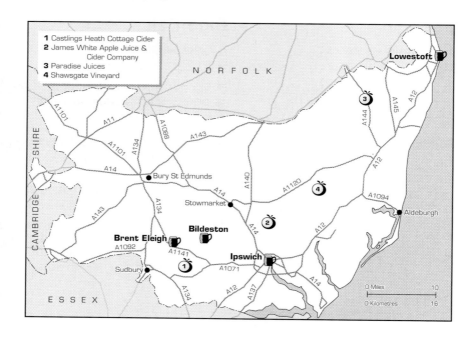

1 Castlings Heath Cottage Cider
2 James White Apple Juice &
  Cider Company
3 Paradise Juices
4 Shawsgate Vineyard

NORFOLK

Lowestoft

CAMBRIDGESHIRE

Bury St Edmunds

Stowmarket

Bildeston

Brent Eleigh

Sudbury

Ipswich

Aldeburgh

ESSEX

0 Miles   10
0 Kilometres   16

Suffolk Producers

CASTLINGS HEATH COTTAGE
Castlings Heath Cottage
Groton, Boxford, Suffolk
(01787) 210899

ORGANIC
CIDER

CASTLINGS HEATH COTTAGE CIDER

Castlings Heath Cottage, Groton, Sudbury, Suffolk.

☎ 01787 210899

John Norton is a traditional Suffolk cider maker, using organic apples and no additives whatsoever. The unfiltered cider is matured in oak hogsheads, and customers visiting Castlings Heath Cottage will have their cider drawn directly from the wood.

The main outlet for Castlings Heath Cottage Cider is the Brent Eleigh Cock at Lavenham, Suffolk's last remaining ale house.

Cider

Castlings Heath Cottage Cider, 7% abv.

Perry, 6% abv (occasional).

Strong, 8.5% abv.

(all available in a variety of containers)

Annual Production

1000 gallons

Visitors

Welcome. Tours available.

Directions

2 miles North of Boxford. OS map reference 596935/243036.

Sales

Farm gate sales. Please ring first. Non-cider items on sale: barrels and tubs.

Outlets

• Brent Eleigh Cock, Lavenham.

• White Horse, Edwardstone, Sudbury.

Awards

East Anglian Cider Of The Year 1997/98.

JAMES WHITE

James White Apple Juice & Cider Company, Whites Fruit Farm, Helmingham Road, Ashbocking, Ipswich, IP6 9JS.

☎ 01473 890111

Email info@jameswhite.co.uk

Web site: www.jameswhite.co.uk

Founded in 1989 from the ashes of the Suffolk Cider Company, which had been selling cider in the Suffolk/Norfolk area throughout the 1980s. Although cider-making is done in the traditional East Anglian manner with a blend of eating and cooking apples, it is now very much a secondary activity, and the company has found success with its range of premium non-alcoholic drinks.

Ciders

James White Strong & Dry, 7.5% abv. (Filtered. 75cl glass bottles or $2^1/_2$ litre plastic flagons)

James White Medium, 7.5% abv. (Filtered. $2^1/_2$ litre plastic flagons.)

Annual Production

25 000 litres (500 000 litres of apple juice).

Visitors

Visitors welcome to visit the farm shop, tours for pre-arranged groups only.

Directions

8 miles North of Ipswich on B1077 between Ashbocking and Helmingham.

Sales

Farm shop open 9am to 5pm Monday to Sunday.

Also on sale: James White apple juices, Spiced Ginger Aperitif and

Big Tom

Bloody Mary Mix. Full range of fruit and vegetables.

PARADISE JUICES

'The Cider Place' at Cherry Tree Farm, Ilketshall St. Lawrence, Near Beccles,

Suffolk.

☎ 01986 781353

'The Cider Place' is a friendly, family-run cider and apple juice farm on the Suffolk tourist trail. The cider is made from a blend of culinary and dessert Suffolk apples, using wooden grinding mills and wooden presses dating from 1864. All the cider is matured for at least two years in oak barrels before being released, and is neither pasteurised nor carbonated.

The freshly-pressed apple juices are pasteurised (to prevent them becoming cider!) and are available as four different single varieties.

The Coules family founded Paradise Juices when they bought Cherry Tree Farm in 1980, and today claim to have the only licenced converted calf house in Britain!

Cider

Scrumpy (extra dry), Dry, Medium and Sweet, all 6% abv. (available in 2 litre PET bottles only).

Annual Production

800 gallons (cider)

4000 gallons (apple juice)

Visitors

Welcome. Informal tours with free samples.

Directions

Midway between Bungay and Halesworth.

Sales

Farm shop open 9am-1pm and 2pm-6pm. Closed all day Wednesdays and Sunday mornings.

Other items on sale: 58 local jams, pickles, chutneys, honeys and fudges.

SHAWSGATE VINEYARD

Badingham Road, Framlingham, Suffolk, IP13 9HZ.

☎ 01728 724060

Email wines@shawsgate.co.uk

Shawsgate Vineyard was established in 1973. Cider is very much a sideline in comparison to its red and white wine production. On-line sales through a web site are planned at the time of writing.

Ciders

Shawsgate Cider, 7.5% abv. Shawsgate Apple Dessert Wine, 11.5% abv.

(Both filtered, and available in 75cl bottles.)

Annual Production

4000 litres.

Visitors

Welcome. Tours available, Easter to October.

Directions

Enter Framlingham from the Parham direction. Turn right onto the B1120, site entrance on the left after 1 mile (see vineyard signs).

Sales

Vineyard shop, 10.30am to 5pm.

Outlet

The Old Tea Shop, Wortham, Near Diss, Norfolk.

CELLARMANSHIP

by Ivor Clissold

144 pages   Price: £6.99

This book explains every aspect of running a good cellar and serving a great pint of real ale which does both pub and brewer proud. It's a must have book for all professionals in the drinks trade, for all those studying at college to join it, and for all those who need to tap a cask of real ale for a party or beer festival.

Use the following code to order this book from your bookshop: ISBN 1-85249-126-4.

Order directly with your credit card on 01727 867201.

Suffolk Outlets

BILDESTON

Kings Head

132 High Street (B1115)

☎ 01449 741434

11-3(not winter Mon-Thu), 5-11; 11-11 Sat(& winter Fri); 12-10.30 Sun

⌀Banham (Sept-May)

Brettvale Brewery stands behind this large village inn, and its beers are served within. A varying cider from the Banham range is served throughout the winter months, and various guest ciders are offered at the May beer festival. Live music weekends, no food Monday evening.

 ◖ ◗

BRENT ELEIGH

Cock ☆

Lavenham Road, OS 941478

☎ 01787 247371

12-3, 6-11; 12-3, 7-10.30 Sun

⌀Castlings Heath

An absolute gem: thatched and at peace with the world. Its unspoilt interior is on CAMRA's National Inventory.

IPSWICH

Fat Cat (Spring Tavern)

288 Spring Road

☎ 01473 726524

12(11Sat)-11; 12-10.30 Sun

⌀Banham Dry, Perry (occasional), Sweet

Suffolk CAMRA Pub of the Year 1998, serving a vast range of ever-changing real ales (16 guests).

LOWESTOFT

Oak Tavern

73 Crown Street West

☎ 01502 537246

11-11; 12-10.30 Sun

⌀Kingfisher Medium/Dry

Community pub known for its Real Ale selection. Belgian beer a speciality.

Triangle Tavern

29 St Peters Street

☎ 01502 582711

11-11; 12-10.30 Sun

⌀Cider varies

Refurbished town-centre pub owned by the Green Jack Brewery. Frequent live music in the front bar. Seasonal beer festivals. Customers are welcome to bring their own food into the pub. The cider on offer is typically from Banham or Burnards.

SURREY

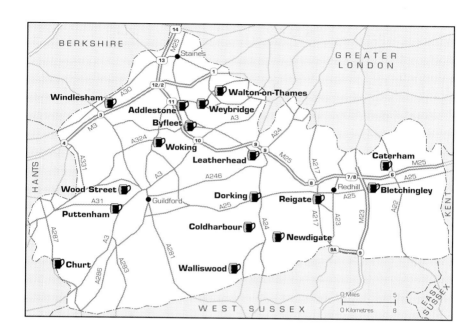

Surrey Outlets

ADDLESTONE

Safeways
179 Station Road
☎ 01932 820251

8-8; 10-4 Sun

🍂**Westons Extra Strong Scrumpy**

One of six Safeway supermarkets in Surrey.

BLETCHINGLEY

William IV
Little Common Lane
☎ 01883 743278

11-3, 6-11; 12-10.30 Sun

🍂**Chiddingstone Medium Dry**

Friendly country inn built as two cottages in the 1850s. Two bars, and a dining room serving good food. Has a secluded old English garden.

◖ ◗

BYFLEET

Tesco

Brooklands, Barns Wallace Drive

☎ 01932 747400

8am Mon-10pm Sat (24 hours); 10-4 Sun

⌂**Westons Extra Strong Scrumpy**

A very large Tesco store.

CATERHAM

Clifton Arms

110 Chaldon Road

☎ 01883 343525

11-2.30, 5.30-11; 11-3, 6-11 Sat; 12-10.30 Sun

⌂**Biddenden; guest cider or perry (summer)**

Lots of local photos on the walls of this pub, as well as collections of cameras and musical instruments. The back room is sometimes used for music and dinner dances.

◖ ◗

CHURT

Crossways

Churt Road

☎ 01428 714323

11-3.30, 5-11; 11-11 Fri/Sat; 12-4, 7-10.30 Sun

⌂**Cider range varies**

3-4 ciders sold from stillage behind the bar, in this Surrey CAMRA Pub of the Year 1999. A village local with a friendly welcome for all.

◖

COLDHARBOUR

Plough Inn

Coldharbour Lane

☎ 01306 711793

11.30-3, 6-11; 11.30-11 Sat; 12-10.30 Sun

⌂**Biddenden**

A remote country brew-pub set in the heart of the Surrey Hills. The small bar features ten hand pumps.

◖ ◗

DORKING

Surrey Yeoman (Hogshead)

220-222 High Street

☎ 01306 741492

11-11; 12-10.30 Sun

⌂**Biddenden (sometimes changes)**

An old pub converted to a Hogshead with the extension of the indoor drinking area and the addition of a garden. Up to four guest ales.

◖ ◗

Watermill

Reigate Road

☎ 01306 887831

11-3, 6-11; 11-11 Sat; 12-10.30 Sun

🍎**Rich's**

Pub/restaurant with two function rooms. Weekly folk, jazz and singles nights in the main function room. Up to three guest ales.

◖ ◗

LEATHERHEAD

Edmund Tylney

30-34 High Street

☎ 01372 362715

11-11; 12-10.30 Sun

🍎**Addlestones**

Shop conversion in the main shopping street with the usual Wetherspoon facilities. Interesting pile of books – don't try to read one!

◖ ◗

NEWDIGATE

Six Bells

Village Street

☎ 01306 631276

11-3, 6-11; 12-3, 7-10.30 Sun

🍎**Addlestones**

Attractive 16th century pub opposite the church. It has a beamed

bar with an inglenook fireplace, and a restaurant that specialises in French cuisine. No evening food Sundays or Mondays.

◖ ◗

Surrey Oaks

Parkgate Road, Parkgate

☎ 01306 631200

11.30-2.30(3 Sat), 5.30(6 Sat)-11

🍎**Thatchers Traditional Medium-Dry**

Old country inn with a very good reputation for its food. CAMRA South East Pub of the Year 1998, the guest ale changes every week. Doves, budgies and goats can be found in the attractive gardens.

◖ ◗

PUTTENHAM

Good Intent

62 The Street

☎ 01483 810387

11-2.30, 6-11; 11-11 Sat; 12-10.30 Sun

🍎**Thatchers**

Excellent free house in a pretty village. Popular with walkers. No evening food Sundays or Mondays.

◖ ◗

REIGATE

Nutley Hall

8 Nutley Lane

☎ 01737 241741

11-11; 12-3, 7-10.30 Sun

⌒Westons Old Rosie

Small drinking establishment just away from the town centre, built over a number of caves. The back bar is for diners only (lunches Tuesday to Sunday), the front bar is where all the action is – often full of enthusiastic drinkers.

◖

WALLISWOOD

Scarlett Arms

Walliswood Green Road

☎ 01306 627243

11-2.30, 5.30-11; 12-3, 7-10.30 Sun

⌒Westons Traditional Scrumpy

Classic country pub built as cottages, but converted into a pub in 1907.

◖ ▶

WALTON-ON-THAMES

Regent

19 Church Street

☎ 01932 243980

11-11; 12-10.30 Sun

⌒Addlestones

Converted cinema in an area with much film history – look at the wall displays. Usual Wetherspoons facilities.

◖ ▶

WEYBRIDGE

Oddbins

81 Queens Road

☎ 01932 841184

10-8; 12-8 Sun

⌒Westons In Bottle Conditioned Cider

Off licence with range of bottle-conditioned ales.

Waitrose

62 High Street

☎ 01932 858077

8-6(8 Thurs/Fri); 10-4 Sun

⌒Sedlescombe Organic

The UK supermarket chain with perhaps the largest cider range, although most of it is artificially carbonated. Own-label range plus other bottles from Dunkertons,

Headford Ridge, Sheppys and Westons. Various stores through-out Surrey.

WINDLESHAM

Half Moon

Church Road

☎ 01276 473329

11-3, 5.30-11; 12-4, 7-10.30 Sun; (may open all day during summer)

Westons Old Rosie

Attractive, family-run free house with a large garden. No evening food Sundays.

〇 ◗

WOKING

Wetherspoons

51-57 Chertsey Road

☎ 01483 722818

11-11; 12-10.30 Sun

Addlestones

Large, open-plan shop conversion in the town centre.

〇 ◗

WOOD STREET

Royal Oak

89 Oak Hill

☎ 01483 235137

11-3(3.30 Sat), 5-11; 12-3.30, 7-10.30 Sun

⌓Thatchers Cheddar Valley

Free house with a friendly wel-come. Constantly changing range of unusual guest beers.

〇

SUSSEX

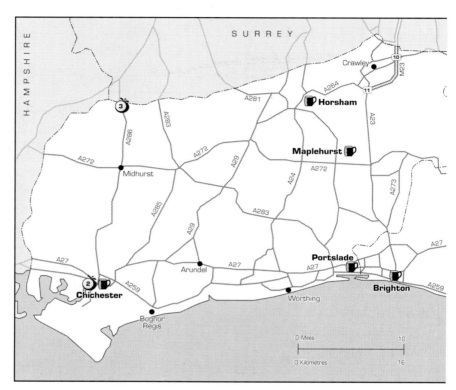

Sussex Producers

1066 CIDER

3 Bedford Road, Hastings,
E.Sussex, TN35 5JS.

☎ 01424 429588

Email info@1066cider.com

Web site www.1066cider.com

"Established in 1066 by William
the Conqueror," says proprietor
Andrew Etherton, with tongue

firmly in cheek, "and continued at
the Battle Medieval Fair from
1997 onwards." The last bit is
certainly true, and up-to-date information on other outlets, as well as
lots of cider recipes, can be found
at 1066's impressive and comprehensive web site. Andrew makes
his cider from organic apples, the
juice is fermented using natural
yeasts, and the cider is matured
for three years in old oak malt
whisky casks.

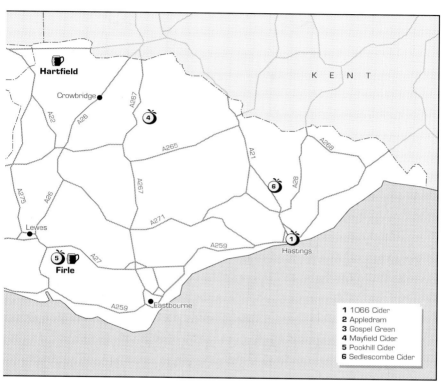

Legend:
1 1066 Cider
2 Appledram
3 Gospel Green
4 Mayfield Cider
5 Pookhill Cider
6 Sedlescombe Cider

Cider

1066 Cider, 5% abv (avalable in 50 litre kegs, 5 & 9 gallon casks, 10 & 20 litre polypins)

(The cider is available as strong, medium and light; all of which can be bought as Dry or Sweet.)

Annual Production

3000 gallons

Visitors

Welcome, by appointment only. Tours available.

Outlets

• Battle Medieval Fair (each summer).

• Fubar, Havelock Road, Hastings.

APPLEDRAM

Pump Bottom Farm, Birdham Road, Chichester, West Sussex.

☎ 01243 773828

pumpbottomfarm@argonet.co.uk

Julian Moores founded Appledram in 1983, and produces unfiltered wine-like ciders from a blend of dessert and culinary fruit. His range also includes a 'West Country Style' that uses West Country cider apples, and a perry made from Devonshire perry pears.

The 'Dram 'O Apples' is a fully licensed cider house on the farm, in which guest ciders and Appledram's own outsell ale 2:1.

Ciders

Appledram Dry, Medium, Sweet, 7% abv.

Appledram 'West Country Style', 6% abv.

Appledram Perry, 6.2% abv.

(2 and 4 pint; 1, 2 and 5 gallon containers)

Annual Production

3500 gallons

Visitors

Welcome

Directions

A27 South of Chichester. Take the A296 South for approximately 1¹/₂ miles, Pump Bottom

Farm is on the left past the Black Horse pub.

Sales

Shop open 10am to 6pm.

Also on sale: honey, jams, beers.

Wholesalers

The Beer Seller, 01703 252299. Tavern Wholesale, 0845 177177.

Awards

CAMRA National Cider and Perry Championship 1998. Dry Cider class, 2nd.

GOSPEL GREEN

Gospel Green Cottage, Haslemere, Surrey, GU27 3BH.

☎ 01428 654120

James Lane is the doyen of British bottle-fermented cider producers. His entire cider output is converted into a champagne-style product by the Traditional Method of bottle fermentation and disgorging, and he has won over initial cider-prejudice to find his Sussex Cyder being served at local weddings and other special occasions. BBC's 'Food and Drink' described it as the best of the bottle-fermented ciders, and Jancis Robinson writing in the FT said that it "Would satisfy the most wine-fixated palate."

James started commercial production in 1990, and still today uses a 70:30 blend of eaters to cookers that include varieties such as Cox, Russet and Laxton Superb. Cider apples would not be used even if available locally, since James believes that South Eastern fruit produces a cider with a more vinous character. Pressing and fermentation happens in the old Cider

House that can be found both at the rear of Gospel Green Cottage and on the cider labels. After at least a year in bottles the Sussex Cyder is ready to be drunk. Served in champagne glasses it is very pale and not too fizzy, medium-dry and has a good apple flavour. "It's an easy-drinking cyder," says James, "try it in the garden or at a dinner party."

Cider
Gospel Green Sussex Cyder, 8% abv (75cl &150cl bottles).
Annual Production
8000 bottles.
Visitors
By appointment only.
Sales
Farm gate sales by appointment only.
Outlets
• Secretts Farm Shop, Milford, Surrey.
• Durleigh Marsh Farm Shop, Rogate, W.Sussex.
• English Farm Cider Centre, Lewes, Sussex.

MAYFIELD CIDER

Pennybridge Farm, Mayfield, East Sussex, TN20 6QB.
☎ 01435 873173
Email sales@mayfieldcider.co.uk
Most of Martin Clarke's farmhouse cider is produced in a traditional manner with organic apples milled by a tractor-driven scratter, pressed hydraulically and then fermented using natural yeasts. However the way he makes his special brew is ultra-traditional – his own cider apples are crushed in his Herefordshire stone mill, and the pulp is pressed with his Somerset oak beam press.
Ciders
Pennybridge Special (cider apples only).
Donkey Kick.
(1/2 pint to 2 gallon stoneware jars, 2 and 5 gallon containers)
Annual Production
Up to 500 gallons.
Visitors
Welcome.
Directions
From Mayfield High Street take the road to Witherenden (Fletching St). Keep left at the Rose and Crown (Coggins Mill Lane), Pennybridge Lane is at the bottom of the hill on the left after the bridge.
Sales
Farm gate sales: telephone first or take pot luck!

Also on sale: stoneware jars.

Outlets
• New Orchard Farm Shop, Maidstone Rd, Horsmonden, Kent.
• Franchise Farm Shop, Spring Lane, Burwash, East Sussex.

POOKHILL CIDER

Lower Tilton Farm, West Firle, Lewes, East Sussex, BN8 6LT.

☎ 01323 811208

Email helen@roecott.demon.co.uk

Ian ('Rod') and Helen Marsh are the proprietors of the marvellous English Farm Cider Centre, so who better to start their own cider making company. They use wholly traditional methods to produce their unfiltered ciders, which include fermenting in oak and adding no chemicals whatsoever. This includes adding no sugar, so to achieve a natural sweetness they use a technique – keeving – popular amongst French cider makers. Of course their ciders and perries are readily available from the English Farm Cider Centre, and apart from the three blends outlined below, they occasionally produce a single-varietal Dabinett or Coat Jersey cider.

Ciders
Bittersweet, 6% abv.
Sussex Orchard, 6% abv. (A blend of culinary and dessert apples)
Puck's Perry, 7% abv. (75% Conference pears, 25% Bramley apples)

Annual Production
1200 gallons
Visitors
Welcome.
Directions
Lower Tilton is on the north hand side of the main A27 road midway between Lewes and
Eastbourne; the only building between Selmeston and Charleston Farmhouse lane.
OS map reference: TQ 497074.
Sales
Farm gate sales, please ring first.
Outlets
• English Farm Cider Centre, Lewes.
• Various festivals.

SEDLESCOMBE CIDER

Sedlescombe Vineyard, Cripp's Corner, Sedlescombe, Near Robertsbridge, East Sussex, TN32 5SA.

☎ 01580 830715

Email rcook91137@aol.com

Web site www.tor.co.uk/sedle-scombe/

Sedlescombe Vineyard, established in 1979, is one of Englands leading producers of organic wines. They also produce two still farmhouse-style ciders, according to Soil Association standards. The Organic Dry Cider has a yeast sediment in the bottle and is very flavoursome, with a lovely balance of fruit and sharpness.

Ciders

1066 Country Organic Dry Cider, 7.5% abv (75cl glass bottles)

1066 Country Organic Reserve Cider, 7.5% abv (75cl glass bottles)

Annual Production

7000 litres.

Visitors

Welcome. Tours available.

Directions

8 miles North of Hastings, East Sussex. On the B2244, 1¹/₂ miles North of Sedlescombe village.

Sales

Shop open: Easter to Christmas, 7 days a week, 10am to 6pm.

January to March, weekends only, midday to 5pm.

Also on sale: organic English wines, organic imported wines, organic fruit juices.

Outlets

Waitrose.

Sussex Outlets

BRIGHTON

Cobblers Thumb

10 New England Road

☎ 01273 605636

11-11; 12-10.30 Sun

⌂Westons Old Rosie

A good, old-fashioned type of pub popular with customers of all ages. Good food and free pool. Offers a food and drink takeaway from Friday evenings through to Tuesday evenings. Quiz night Tuesdays, Party night Thursdays.

◖   ▶

Evening Star

55-56 Surrey Street

☎ 01273 328931

11.30(11 Sat)-11, 12-10.30 Sun

⌂Thatchers Traditional Medium; Westons Perry (often); guest cider or perry

Busy brewpub situated close to Brighton station. Beer range varies, usually 3 from Dark Star and 4 guest ales.

◖

CHICHESTER

TRY: Dram O' Apples, Pump Bottom Farm, Birdham Road

FIRLE

English Farm Cider Centre

Middle Farm

☎ 01323 811324

10-5, 7 days a week

○Draught: **100-150 British ciders and perries.**
Bottled: About 100 British ciders and perries.

Quite simply the World's largest permanent collection of cider and perry. Housed in a traditional Sussex flint farm building at the Middle Farm Countryside Centre (open farm, farm shop, tea room, children's play area, etc), the Cider Centre off-licence is nothing short of a cider/perry Aladdin's cave. Customers can saunter along the rows of polycasks, pouring and tasting free samples, before choosing which to take away in a wide selection of containers. The exact cider selection always varies, but Pook Hill Cider, made by proprietors Rod and Helen Marsh, is always available. There's also a comprehensive selection of bottled ciders, plus some 30 meads, lots of country wines and liqueurs, local English wines, organic cordials, and fresh apple juice from Kent and Sussex. Up to 4 draught Sussex ales are available to take away, as well as a bottled range. There are books on cider and perry for sale, as well as free printed sheets on subjects such as Cider Books and Cider Equipment Suppliers. In the autumn, customers may bring their apples for pressing, and during the winter months the hot, spiced cider is well worth trying. A Mecca for all cider and perry lovers.

HARTFIELD

Kent and Sussex Apple Juice and Cider Centre

Perryhill Orchard, Edenbridge Road

☎ 01892 770595

10.30-5, Tues- Sun

○Draught: **Biddenden Dry, Sweet; Bushells; Chiddingstone; Inch's; New Forest Snake Catcher; Perryhill Scrumpy; Westons 1st Quality, Bounds Brand, Old Rosie, Perry, Special Vintage; various guest ciders**

Farm shop and PYO centre with the largest range of apple juices in the south east of England, and an ever-increasing range of ciders. Free tasting of all ciders and apple juices before buying, ciders are then poured from the cask into a container for taking away (many sizes of container available).

HORSHAM

Brewery Shop

16 Bishopric

☎ 01403 225710

11-7; 9-7 Sat; (closed Sun)

⌂**Draught: Westons 1st Quality, Old Rosie**

⌂**Bottled: Westons Old Rosie**

Retail trading division of the King & Barnes Brewery. The shop is located in the original family home of the brewery founder. King & Barnes draught beer range also available. (At the time of writing the brewery has just been bought, and there are plans to close it down).

Photographs

Gospel Green cork.

Photo: Dave Matthews

Rod Marsh at the English Farm Cider Centre.

Photo: Dave Matthews

MAPLEHURST

White Horse

Park Lane

☎ 01403 891208

12-2.30(3 Sat), 6-11; 12-3, 7-10.30 Sun

⌂**Maplehurst Scrumpy; guest cider**

Friendly country pub with good views from the garden. Very popular, with several guest beers and cider always available. The landlord is an avid classic car enthusiast.

PORTSLADE

Stanley Arms

47 Wolseley Road

☎ 01273 701590

1-11; 12-11 Fri/Sat; 12-10.30 Sun

⌂**Cider varies**

Victorian street-corner boozer, with a public bar and lounge. The cider varies, but is always a medium. The 3 ever-changing real ales are usually from micro-breweries. Live music every other weekend, bar billiards, food limited to sandwiches.

TYNE & WEAR

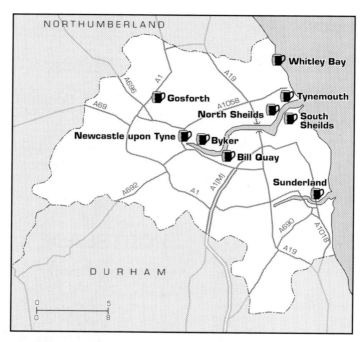

Tyne & Wear Outlets

BILL QUAY

Albion Inn

Reay Street

☎ 0191 469 2418

4-11; 11-11 Sat; 12-10.30 Sun

⌂Westons Old Rosie

Small cosy pub on the banks of the River Tyne with excellent views down river. Interesting use of an old rowing boat as the door entrance.

BYKER

Fighting Cocks

127 Albion Row

☎ 0191 265 2106

12-11; 7-10.30 Sun

⌂Bulmers Traditional

A Castle Eden inn offering the full range from this local brewery. Stands overlooking the Tyne and has spectacular views up river of the famous Tyne Bridge.

Ouseburn Tavern

33 Shields Road

☎ 0191 276 5120

11-11; 12-10.30 Sun

⌂Westons Old Rosie, Special Vintage

Former Tap & Spile on the main road near the local shops with a good choice of real ales and cider. ⌐

GOSFORTH

County

70 High Street

☎ 0191 285 6919

12-11; 11-11 Fri/Sat; 12-3, 7-10.30 Sun

⌂Bulmers Traditional

Large TJ Bernard alehouse in a local shopping area, dispensing 10 ales from an impressive bank of 21 handpulls. ⌐

Oddbins

101 High Street

☎ 0191 285 8151

10-9; 12-9 Sun

⌂Westons In Bottle Conditioned Cider

National off-licence chain selling a range of bottle-conditioned products.

NEWCASTLE UPON TYNE

Oddbins

130 Grainger Street

☎ 0191 261 7488

9-7; 9-8 Thur-Sat; (closed Sun)

⌂Westons In Bottle Conditioned Cider

National off-licence chain outlet near the Monument selling a range of bottle-conditioned products.

Tap & Spile

25 Nun Street

☎ 0191 232 0026

11-11; 12-10.30 Sun

⌂Westons Old Rosie

One of the former Tap & Spile ale-houses, now run by Castle Eden and offering a range of Castle Eden products as well as a couple of guest ales. ⌐

NORTH SHIELDS

Tap & Spile

184 Tynemouth Road

☎ 0191 257 2523

11.30-11; 12-10.30 Sun

⌂Westons Old Rosie

Popular two-roomed pub selling a variety of guest ales. ⌐ ▶

SOUTH SHIELDS

Riverside

3 Mill Dam

☎ 0191 455 2328

12-11; 12-3, 7-10.30 Sun

⏾Guest cider(s)

Former German seaman's mission, now a deservedly popular free house offering a range of ales and two ever-changing guest ales. Handy for the nearby Customs House, ferry and market place. Local CAMRA Pub of the Year 1999. Often serves perry.

SUNDERLAND

William Jameson

30-32 Fawcett Street

☎ 0191 514 5016

11-11; 12-10.30 Sun

⏾Addlestones

Large air conditioned former department store in typical Wetherspoons style offering a wide range of guest ales and value for money food. Named after a local town planner. An additional guest cider is sometimes available during beer festivals.

◖ ◗

TYNEMOUTH

Tynemouth Lodge

Tynemouth Road

☎ 0191 257 7565

11-11; 12-10.30 Sun

⏾Addlestones

Traditional free house dating from the 18th century, on the outskirts of a popular seaside village.

WHITLEY BAY

Fat Ox

278 Whitley Bay Road

☎ 0191 251 3852

11-11; 12-10.30 Sun

⏾Westons Old Rosie

Large stone-flagged roadside pub in popular seaside resort with a choice of guest ales. Busy at weekends and bank holidays.

◖

WARWICKSHIRE

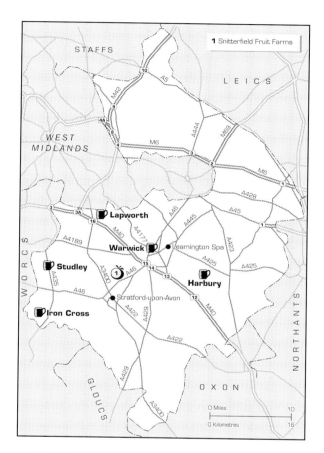

1 Snitterfield Fruit Farms

Warwickshire Producers

SNITTERFIELD FRUIT FARMS

Kings Lane, Snitterfield, Stratford-upon-Avon, CV37 0QA.

☎ 01789 731244

Email steve@snit.freeserve.co.uk

The farm has been a fruit farm since before the Second World War, and in 1999 reached the last three in the 'Top Fruit Grower of the Year' awards. As a side line, Steve Dawkes ferments some of his apple juice in oak barrels, before filtering it and selling it on draught.

Cider

Farm Cider, abv varies (4 pint keg or 40 pint cask)

Annual Production

7000 litres

Visitors

Welcome. Tours available if requested.

Directions

On the A46 between Stratford and Warwick.

Sales

Farm gate sales 8am to 6pm. Other items on sale: Apple juice, vacuum packed Bramley slices, preserves, chutney, etc.

Warwickshire Outlets

HARBURY

Crown Inn

Crown Street

☎ 01926 612283

12-3, 5.30-11; 12-11 Fri/Sat; 12-5, 7-10.30 Sun

Bulmers Traditional; Westons **Traditional Scrumpy**

Cosy, old, stone-built village pub, once a farmhouse. Pub games are well supported.

IRON CROSS

Queens Head & Fat Gods Brewery

On B4088

☎ 01386 871012

11(12 winter)-11; 12-10.30 Sun

Bulmers Traditional

Lively pub with a strong commitment to the local community and good causes. Home of Fat God's Brewery, it hosts a beer festival in June with 30 beers and a couple of guest ciders over a week.

LAPWORTH

Navigation

Old Warwick Road (B4439)
☎ 01564 783337

*11-2.30, 5.30-11; 11-11 Sat;
12-10.30 Sun*

⌁**Biddenden**

Excellent pub with many attributes: traditional atmosphere, flagged floor, canalside garden, good food, real cider and a varied selection of real ales.

⌁ ▶

STUDLEY

Needlemakers Arms

7 Watts Road
☎ 01527 852262

*11-3.30, 6-11; 11-5.30, 7-11
Sat; 12.30-3, 7-10.30 Sun*

⌁**Bulmers Traditional Medium**

The public and lounge bars share a central serving area at this friendly local. The Bulmers Traditional cider is chilled. Darts and quoits played.

WARWICK

Rose & Crown

30 Market Place
☎ 01926 492876

11-11; 12-10.30 Sun

⌁**Cider varies**

Traditional English town-centre pub, first on the map in the 1780s. Attracts customers of all ages, who can choose between a non-smoking lounge, a bar and a traditional old snug. The cider on offer is typically from Biddendens or Westons. Four real ales, folk evenings Mondays and Fridays.

⌁

WEST MIDLANDS

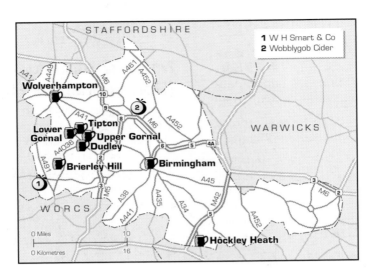

West Midlands Producers

W.H.SMART & CO. LTD

17 St Peters Road, Pedmore, Stourbridge, West Midlands, DY9 OTY.

☎ 01384 824353

Email cider@wychbury.swinter-net.co.uk

At the time of writing Charles Smart and Shaun Hodgkins make a claim to be running one of the smallest cider companies in the world, with an annual production of just 200 gallons. All this is set to change as the fame of their cider and perry increases :- their Wychbury Cider is one of the dark-est and most characterful ciders I have ever tasted. The fruit used is all genuine cider and perry fruit from the Tenbury Wells area of Worcestershire, and at the moment sales are confined to beer festivals and licensed events such as fetes.

Ciders
Wychbury Cider, 6.5%.
Perry, 6.5%.
Annual Production
200 gallons (150 cider, 50 perry).

WOBBLYGOB CIDER

Hamstead Brewing Centre, 37 Newton Road, Great Barr, Birmingham, B43 6AD.

☎ 0121 358 6800

Email wobblygob@hamstead-brewing-centre.co.uk

Chris and Robert Hogg must be two of Birmingham's greatest entrepreneurs. Not content with a simple home-brew shop, they sell over 100 bottled beers, 17 varieties of coffee bean, supply cask and keg beer, have developed a home beer-making kit with York Brewery, and, best of all, make their own cider. WobblyGob Cider is made from Midlands apples they press themselves, has no added sugar or water, is neither filtered nor pasteurised, and is matured in oak casks for at least 12 months.

Ciders WobblyGob **Dry, Medium,** both 8% abv (2¹/₂ **litre, 5 litre and 20 litre containers)**

Annual Production

5000 litres

Visitors

Welcome

Directions

Just off the M6 on the Newton Road, just down from the Scott Arms near to Pages Lane. Look out for the red sign.

Sales

Shop open Monday to Saturday 9am to 6pm.

West Midlands Outlets

BIRMINGHAM

Monkey Mix Cider Bar (Ben Johnson P.H.)

275 Corporation Street

☎ 0121 359 6298

11-11; 12-10.30 Sun

⌂Bulmers Traditional; West Croft Dry, Medium

Two-roomed city centre cider bar, popular with university students. Entertainment Thursday to Saturday evenings.

◖ ▶

BRIERLEY HILL

Old New Inn

17 High Street

☎ 01384 485493

11-3, 7-11; 11-4, 7-11 Fri/Sat; 12-3, 7-10.30 Sun

⌂Cider varies

Popular two-roomed hostelry at the Stourbridge end of the High Street.

Plough Inn

7 Church Street

☎ 01384 78692

11-3(4 Sat), 6-11; 12-4, 7-10.30 Sun

⌂Thatchers

Unspoilt two-roomed boozer just off the southern end of the High Street. Very reasonable prices. Sells as much cider as beer.

~~REAL ALE~~

DUDLEY

Bush Inn

2 Buffery Road, Dixon's Green

☎ 01384 253753

11.30-11; 12-10.30 Sun

⌂Bulmers Traditional

Sports-oriented community pub. Regular live entertainment. Food limited to bar snacks at lunchtimes.

Full Moon

58-60 High Street

☎ 01384 212294

10-11; 12-10.30 Sun

⌂Addlestones

A JD Wetherspoon free house.
◖ ◗

HOCKLEY HEATH

Blue Bell Cider House

Warings Green Road, Warings Green

☎ 01564 702328

11.30-2.30, 5.30-11; 11.30-11 Fri/Sat; 12-3, 7.30-10.30 Sun

⌂Bulmers Traditional Dry, Medium

Traditional drinking pub beside the Stratford Canal, with its own moorings. Originally a beer home-brew pub, it was bought by Bulmers in the 1950s, has been privately owned now for some 30 years, providing the inspiration for the Brandy Wharf Cider Centre in Lincolnshire. There's a traditional bar, lounge, and children are allowed either in the conservatory or in the large garden. Two guest ales, quiz night Wednesday, no food Sunday evenings.
◖ ◗

LOWER GORNAL

Fountain Inn

8 Temple Street

☎ 01384 242777

12-3, 6-11; 12-11 Sat; 12-4, 7-10.30 Sun

⌂Crossmans; guest cider

Real-deal free house serving nine real ales. Cider is poured in the cellar and fetched to the bar by the staff. Extra ciders are to be found at the twice-yearly beer festival.

(

TIPTON
Port 'N' Ale
178 Horseley Heath

☎ 0121 557 7249

12.30-3, 5-11; 12-11 Sat; 12-4.30, 7-10.30 Sun

⌣Biddenden Dry; Thatchers Cheddar Valley, Traditional Medium

A lively free house with regular live music.

(▶

Rising Sun
116 Horseley Road

☎ 0121 520 7033

12-2.30(3 Sat), 5-11; 12-3, 7-10.30 Sun

⌣Bulmers Traditional Medium; Inch's West Country

Two-roomed Victorian free house. CAMRA National Pub of the Year 1999.

(

UPPER GORNAL
Crown
16 Holloway Street

☎ 01902 665209

4-11; 1-11 Fri; 12-11 Sat; 12-10.30 Sun

⌣Thatchers Dry, Medium

Bostin' back street boozer at the top o' the bonk! Sells as much cider as beer. Accommodation available.

Shakespeare Inn
105 Kent Street

☎ 01902 885484

11.30-11; 12-3, 7-10.30 Sun

⌣Bulmers Traditional Medium; Westons Traditional Scrumpy

Genuine Black Country local on the main road.

WOLVERHAMPTON
Hogshead
186 Stafford Street

☎ 01902 717955

11-11; 12-10.30 Sun

⌣Inch's Stonehouse; Westons guest

Popular new town centre pub. No smoking areas, leaded skylight above the bar.

(▶

Newhampton
Riches Street, Whitmore

☎ 01902 745773

11-11; 12-10.30 Sun

⌣Guest cider

Surprisingly-large street corner local with cosmopolitan clientele.

(▶

WILTSHIRE

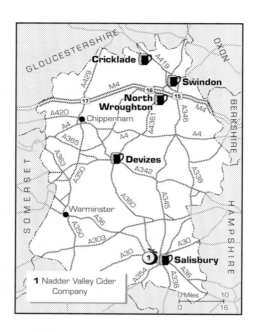

Map showing: GLOUCESTERSHIRE, OXON, BERKSHIRE, SOMERSET, HAMPSHIRE. Cricklade, Swindon, North Wroughton, Chippenham, Devizes, Warminster, Salisbury. **1** Nadder Valley Cider Company. 0 Miles 10 / 0 16.

Wiltshire Producers

BLACK RAT CIDER

Moles Brewery, 5 Merlin Way, Bowerhill, Melksham, Wiltshire, SN12 6TJ.

☎ 01225 704734

Email cascade@cableinet.co.uk

Web site www.molesbrewery.com

(See Thatchers, Somerset.)

NADDER VALLEY CIDER COMPANY

31 Wordsworth Road, Salisbury, Wiltshire, SP1 3BH.

☎ 01722 500169

In 1995 Philippa Sprott decided to produce a cider that 'was noted for a real apple taste'. A job with Hop Back Brewery provided an ideal distribution partnership, and as a result Nadder Valley's two cask and one keg ciders are available throughout Hop Back's trading area (most of the South of England). The ciders are a blend of 60% cider apple and 40% dessert apple, fermented using natural yeast with a late pitching of wine yeast.

Ciders

Ambush, 5.5% abv (medium dry)
Nadder Bite, 7.5% abv (dry)
(Both available in polypins, firkins and kilderkins)
(Also available:
Nadder Valley Keg, 5% abv, medium dry, filtered and carbonated)

Outlets

There are no regular outlets for the cask Nadder Valley ciders, but the keg can be found at:
• Wyndham Arms, Salisbury, Wilts.
• Queens Head, Broad Chalk, Wilts.
• Pear Tree, Whitley, Wilts.
• Salisbury Arms, Christchurch, Dorset.
Wholesaler: Hop Back Brewery (01725 510986)

Wiltshire Outlets

CRICKLADE

Red Lion

74 High Street
☎ 01793 750776

12(11 summer)-11; 12-10.30 Sun

⌒Westons Old Rosie, Special Vintage

17th century inn situated on the Thames Path near the famous National Trust watermeadows. Warm and friendly with a real fire, garden, skittle alley and function room. Stocks a comprehensive selection of Westons bottled ciders and perries.

DEVIZES

British Lion

9 Estcourt Street
☎ 01380 720665

11-11; 12-10.30 Sun

⌒Westons 1st Quality; guest cider

A community locals pub with 3 or 4 ever-changing real ales. The guest cider is typically, but not always, one from Black Rat, Rich's, Thatchers or Nadder Valley. Beer garden at the rear. Described as "A small pub with a big atmosphere!"

NORTH WROUGHTON

Check Inn

Woodland View

☎ 01793 845584

11.30-3.30, 6.30-11; 11.30-11 Sat; 12-10.30 Sun

⏱Nadder Valley Ambush

A totally independent free house with garden area, barbecue and traditional pub games. Six real ales on at any one time (over 500 since September 1996), and draught Leffe Blond from Belgium. Accommodation available.

◖ ◗

SALISBURY

Bird In Hand

North Street

☎ 01722 327238

10-11; 12-10.30 Sun

⏱Taunton Traditional

A locals pub, a back-street boozer. Pool, darts teams, music nights.

SWINDON

Savoy

38-40 Regent Street

10.30-11; 12-10.30 Sun

⏱Addlestones

Wetherspoons pub in a converted cinema in the centre of town. Curry Club Thursdays.

◖ ◗

WORCESTERSHIRE

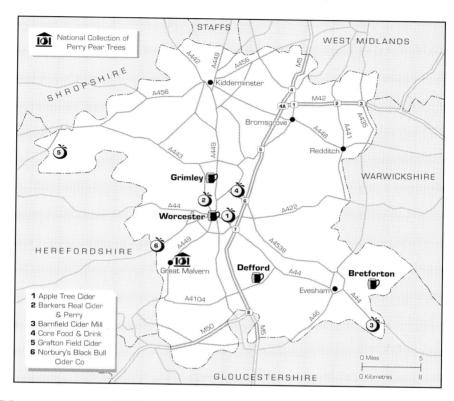

National Collection of Perry Pear Trees

STAFFS

WEST MIDLANDS

SHROPSHIRE

Kidderminster

Bromsgrove

Redditch

WARWICKSHIRE

Grimley

Worcester

HEREFORDSHIRE

Great Malvern

Defford

Bretforton

Evesham

GLOUCESTERSHIRE

1 Apple Tree Cider
2 Barkers Real Cider
   & Perry
3 Barnfield Cider Mill
4 Core Food & Drink
5 Grafton Field Cider
6 Norbury's Black Bull
   Cider Co

0 Miles 5

0 Kilometres 8

Worcestershire Producers

APPLE TREE CIDER

SINGLE VARIETY KINGSTON BLACK CIDER
Kingston Beamer
MADE BY THE APPLE TREE

Lothian Applesmith & Perry Ltd,
The Apple Tree, 54 Lowesmoor,
Worcester, WR1 2SE.

☎ 01905 613132

Email   lothian@supanet.com

The Apple Tree pub in Worcester is an outstanding city centre cider house, and the only pub in Britain to make and sell significant quantities of its own cider. As a teenager Hamish Lothian used to frequent the greatly missed Plough at Elmley Castle in Worcestershire, drinking the excellent cider home-brew. This inspired him to open the Apple Tree in 1997, and every autumn since that time he has taken cider apples to be pressed elsewhere, and then fermented the juice in the pub's cellar. The 1999 pressing was at Castle Morton with the help of Dave Weaver (who can supply you with cider apples and perry pears, tel 01684 833504). The result is some excellent ciders and perries that comfortably outsell the guest ciders in the pub.

Hamish and his wife Nancy have now successfully restored a four-screw Victorian press, and the plan for the autumn of 2000 is to press cider fruit in the pub garden with the help of the pub customers, who will have the opportunity to produce, buy and take away a barrel of juice to ferment at home. Another superb renovation has produced a scratter with stone rollers, dated 1854 and powered by a stationary steam engine, that will further add to the atmosphere and history of the pub garden cidermaking.

Ciders

Kingston Black (single varietal cider), 7% abv.

Nice Pear (blended perry), 6.5% abv.

Old Toothbrush (blended cider), 7% abv.

Somerset Redstreak (single varietal cider), 6.5% abv.

(Occasional ciders include a

Kingston Black/ Somerset Redstreak blend; and 'Pider', a blend of Kingston Black and Nice Pear.)

Annual Production

1450 gallons.

Visitors

Pub customers are always welcome!

Directions

The Apple Tree is located in Worcester City Centre, halfway between the main shopping area (High Street) and Shrub Hill station.

Sales

At the bar during the pub's opening hours (see under Worcestershire Outlets).

Awards

"Only those we give ourselves," says Hamish, "we entered one competition and they said it was too strong!"

BARKERS REAL CIDER & PERRY

Greenstreet Farm, Hallow, Worcestershire, WR2 6PY.

☎ 01905 640697

Tremendous modern interpretation of a traditional cider house that makes and sells its own cider. Usually, two of the house brews are available at any one time, and roughly equal quantities of cider and beer are sold to the many and varied customers drawn from all walks of life. There's a main bar, snug, games room, rooftop terrace and beer garden. The welcome is always warm and genuine, this is definitely *not* an off-the-shelf corporate theme pub. Live music, DJs, quizzes. Cider available to take out (in 3 pint containers) to the local Indian restaurants. An absolute must for all cider fans.

Crown Inn

66 Bransford Road
☎ 01905 421091

12-3, 5-11; 11-11 Sat; 12-10.30 Sun

⌂Bulmers Traditional

Single-roomed traditional town pub. Live music, barbecues, Sunday lunches.

Dragon Inn

51 The Tything
☎ 01905 25845

11-11; 12-10.30 Sun

⌂Cider varies

Traditional pub surrounded by Indian restaurant takeaways and antique shops. On the A38, 200 yards north of Foregate Street station. The real ale range typically includes some local brews. Live music Sunday and Tuesday evenings.

New Pope Iron Inn

Pope Iron Road, Barbourne
☎ 01905 21178

11-11; 12-10.30 Sun

⌂Bulmers Traditional, Inch's Stonehouse

Hard-to-find local between Ghevuhelt Park and the River Severn, selling perhaps as much cider as beer. Very much a local clientele, dogs welcome.

~~REAL ALE~~

Postal Order

18 Foregate Street (Right next to Foregate Street station)
☎ 01905 22373

11-11; 12-10.30 Sun

⌂Addlestones

Wetherspoons pub in a former telephone exchange and post office. Spacious, good prices and no music.

◖ ◗

Washington Inn

42 Washington Street, Arboretum
☎ 01905 24876

11-11; 12-10.30 Sun

⌂Thatchers

Locals pub in a quiet residential area near the town centre.

Other Places of Cider Interest in Worcestershire

National Collection of Perry Pear Trees

The Three Counties Agricultural Society, The Showground, Malvern, Worcs, WR13 6NW

☎ 01684 584900

Fax: 01684 584910

Since 1991, a group of dedicated people including retired scientist Ray Williams (former Pomologist at Long Ashton Research Station, one of the most respected cider people in the UK) and farmer Charles Martell (producer of some fabulous unpasteurised cheeses, notably "Stinking Bishop" – a cheese that Charles washes in perry) have scoured the country-side for the last remnants of the once great orchards of perry pear trees that stood in the 18th and 19th centuries.

As a result, the Three Counties Showground is today home to some 126 trees of 59 different varieties.

The Three Counties Agricultural Society has published an excellent leaflet, describing each variety and showing its exact location in the showground. The leaflet only costs 20p (at the time of writing), and can be obtained from the address above.

Core Food & Drink

Core Food & Drink, formerly The Hindlip Centre for the Cider Food and Drink Industries, is a Centre of Excellence for the Cider Industry.

Core Food & Drink provide specialist expertise for industry in the form of training and educational schemes, innovative research and development programmes, analytical and microbiological testing services, together with state of the art cider making, brewing and contract pressing facilities.

Formerly located at Hindlip College in Worcestershire, Core Food & Drink relocated to an expanded and purpose built centre at Pershore College in June 2000.

Web site:
www.corefoodanddrink.co.uk

Photographs

Cider handpulls in the Apple Tree.

Photo: Dave Matthews

Apple Tree.

Photo: Dave Matthews

Cider pomologist Ray Williams and James Ellis with perry pear varieties at the 1998 Malvern Autumn Show.

Photo: Three Counties Agricultural Society

Gloucestershire farmer and perry pear conservationist, Charles Martell, surveys another crop of perry pears at his orchards in Dymock.

Photo: Three Counties Agricultural Society

YORKSHIRE (EAST)

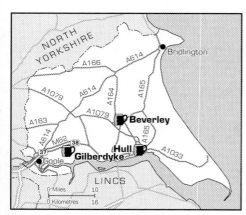

Yorkshire (East) Outlets

BEVERLEY

Tap & Spile (Sun Inn)

1 Flemingate

☎ 01482 881547

12-3, 5-11; 12-11 Fri/Sat; 12-10.30 Sun

⌂Westons Old Rosie

Medieval timber-framed building with stone flagged floors, opposite Beverley Minster. Enterprising real ale range. No lunches Wednesdays.

◖

GILBERDYKE

Cross Keys

Main Road

☎ 01430 440310

12-11; 12-10.30 Sun

⌂Inch's Stonehouse

Roadside pub at the western end of the village. Guest real ales and draught Hoegaarden wheat beer.

HULL

Olde Black Boy

150 High Street

☎ 01482 326516

11-11; 12-10.30 Sun

⌂Westons 1st Quality, Herefordshire County Perry, Old Rosie

Historical multi-roomed pub in the heart of Hull's Old Town. Five guest ales, a regular Good Beer Guide entrant.

◖ ▶

Tap & Spile

169-171 Spring Bank

☎ 01482 323518

12-11; 12-10.30 Sun

⌂Westons Old Rosie

Large corner ale house with two no smoking areas. Pleasant atmosphere, live acoustic music Mondays and Tuesdays. 8 to 12 varying real ales, occasional guest cider or perry from the Westons range. Sunday lunches.

YORKSHIRE (NORTH)

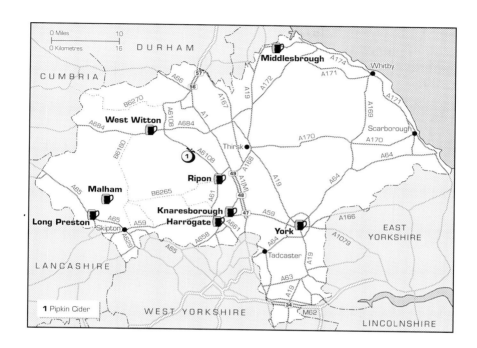

0 Miles 10
0 Kilometres 16 DURHAM

CUMBRIA

Middlesbrough A174 Whitby

A66 A171

B6270 A167 A19 A172

A169

West Witton A684 A1 Scarborough

A6108 Thirsk A170 A170

B6160 A6108 A64

Ripon A1(M) A19 A64

Malham B6265 A61

Long Preston Knaresborough A59 A166

Skipton A59 Harrogate York EAST YORKSHIRE

A65 Tadcaster A1079

LANCASHIRE A63

WEST YORKSHIRE M62

LINCOLNSHIRE

1 Pipkin Cider

Yorkshire (North) Producers

PIPKIN CIDER

1 Swinton Terrace, Masham, North Yorkshire, HG4 4HS.

☎ 01765 689102/01423 866876 (answer phone)

Set up in 1995 by two CAMRA members in an effort to try to promote cider in a non-cider drinking area. They initially went to the trouble of using Kent apples, but have since sourced supplies from North Yorkshire. One or two local outlets are supplied, but their main customers are beer festivals. A true cottage industry, production takes place in their kitchen! They hope to move to more convenient premises soon.

Ciders

Pipkin Dry, Pipkin Medium, both 5.5-6% abv (5 gallon polycasks)

An occasional strong cider is made: Hardcore, 7% abv.

Annual Production

Approx. 300 gallons

Sales

Farm gate sales in 5 gallon quantities only. Please ring first.

Outlets

• Fox & Hounds, West Witton, North Yorks.

• The Maltings, Tanners Moat, York (occasional).

Awards

Cider of the Festival at Keighley (twice). Runner-up at Leeds Festival.

Yorkshire (North) Outlets

HARROGATE

Tap & Spile

Tower Street

☎ 01423 526785

11-11; 12-10.30 Sun

⌂Westons Old Rosie

Ale range includes regulars from Roosters and up to 7 guests. No lunches Sundays.

(

KNARESBOROUGH

Beer-Ritz

17 Market Place

☎ 01423 862850

10-10; 11-10 Sun

⌂Cider varies

Enterprising off licence situated in the corner of an attractive and historic market square. The draught cider on offer is usually Biddenden or Westons; draught real ale available too.

LONG PRESTON

Maypole Inn

☎ 01729 840219

11-3, 6-11; 11-11 Sat; 12-10.30 Sun

⌁Saxon Gold Digger

Two-roomed pub facing the village green with its maypole. Separate dining room serving good food.

MALHAM

Lister Arms

Gordale Scar Road

☎ 01729 830330

12-3, 7-11; 12-3, 7-10.30 Sun; (open all day Sat/Sun in summer)

⌁Thatchers (summer only)

Popular village pub dating from 1702. Three distinct areas plus a pleasant sheltered garden at the rear. The cider on handpump is usually Thatchers, but may vary. Wide range of bottled beers and malt whiskies. Accommodation available.

MIDDLESBROUGH

Hogshead

14 Corporation Road

☎ 01642 219320

11-11; 12-10.30 Sun

⌁Westons

Modern town centre alehouse, popular with office staff and shoppers, selling a variety of ales. The cider is one from the Westons range. Numerous beer festivals held during the year.

RIPON

One Eyed Rat

51 Allhallowgate

☎ 01765 607704

12-2(3 Sat), 6(5.30 Fri)-11; 12-3, 7-10.30 Sun; (closed lunchtimes Mon-Wed)

⌁Westons Old Rosie

Old, terraced, bare-boarded ale house popular with a wide range of clientele. No music.

WEST WITTON

Fox & Hounds

Main Street

☎ 01969 623650

11-4, 7-11(11-11 summer); 12-4, 7-10.30 (12-10.30 summer) Sun

⛄Addlestones; Pipkin

Historic, friendly, 14th century village inn which was originally built as a resting house by the monks of Jervaulx Abbey. Popular with both locals and visitors. Beautiful views of Wensleydale from the garden at the rear.

◖ ◗

YORK

Maltings

Tanners Moat

☎ 01904 655387

Web site www.maltings.co.uk

11-11; 12-10.30 Sun

⛄**Cider range varies**

Famous and popular real ale pub, winner of the Licensee & Morning Advertiser's "Cask Ale Pub of Great Britain 2000" award. Four traditional ciders are offered at any one time, and although they rotate, a typical selection would be two from Saxon, one from Biddenden, plus Thatchers Cheddar Valley. The seven real ales include five guests, and there's a beer festival every September. Blues evening Mondays, folk on Tuesdays.

◖

York Beer & Wine Shop

28 Sandringham Street, Fishergate

☎ 01904 647136 (also fax)

Email
ybws@york10.freeserve.co.uk

Web site www.yorkbeerand-wineshop.co.uk

6-10, Sun/Mon; 11-10 Tues-Fri; 10-10 Sat

⛄**Draught: Thatchers Dry, Medium; guest ciders and perries**

Bottled: Burrow Hill range; Dunkertons range; Gospel Green; Minchews range

Formerly the York Beer Shop, this enterprising specialist off-licence, in a quiet street just outside the city walls and close to the River Ouse, was first established in 1985. The guest cider or perry on tap is often from a classic farmhouse producer. Draught real ale to take away includes Timothy Taylors Landlord, and there's a huge selection of bottled beers. The award-winning wine range specialises in Spanish vintages, and the ever-popular cheese counter features British classics collected directly from the farm by the shop's owner.

YORKSHIRE (SOUTH)

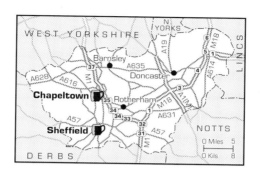

Yorkshire (South) Outlets

CHAPELTOWN

Commercial

107 Station Road

☎ 0114 246 9066

11-3, 5-11; 11-11 Sat; 12-3, 7-10.30 Sun

⏏Cider varies

An outstanding 3-roomed pub with lounge, games room and non smoking snug (with walls covered in pump clips). Lots of activities including quizzes, folk club and beer festivals. Wentworth beers plus three rotating guest ales. Good food, vegetarian menu available. The cider or perry is typically, but not always, from Westons or Saxon.

◖ ▶

SHEFFIELD

Cask & Cutler

1 Henry Street

☎ 0114 249 2295

12-2, 5.30-11; 12-11 Fri/Sat; 12-3, 7-10.30 Sun; (closed Mon lunchtime)

⏏Westons Herefordshire County Perry, Old Rosie

Cosy, two-roomed independent free house dating back to the 1840s, run by two CAMRA stalwarts. Six ever-changing guest beers, mainly from micro-breweries. Food at Friday lunchtime only.

Fat Cat

23 Alma Street

☎ 0114 249 4801

11-3, 5.30-11; 12-3, 7-10.30 Sun

Cider varies

Sheffield's famous independent free house, situated in the Kelham Island conservation area, adjacent to the Kelham Island Brewery. Two rooms (one no smoking) and a pleasant beer garden. Beer range includes offerings from Kelham Island, and seven guest ales.

◖ ▶

Hogshead

25 Orchard Street, Orchard Square

☎ 0114 272 1980

11-11; 12-10.30 Sun

Biddenden

Modernised three-level Hogshead pub.

◖ ▶

New Barrack Tavern

601 Penistone Road

☎ 0114 234 9148

12-11; 12-10.30 Sun

Cider varies

Renowned, three-roomed real ale establishment. Famed also for its good food.

◖ ▶

PUB SUPERCHEFS

Susan Nowak

Price: £7.99   Pages: 192 pages

Pub Superchefs brings together the crème de la crème of recipes from Britain's top pub kitchens. The Campaign for Real Ale features recipes from pub superchefs in its various magazines and newspapers and this is a compilation of the favourites, from traditional lamb and apple pie to Nepalese Chicken Korma; and how about a Stilton Soup recipe from the Bell Inn in Stilton?

The superchefs' recipes have been organised under the following headings:

• Soups and Starters
• Fish
• Meat, Poultry and Game
• Vegetarian
• Ethnic
• Snacks, Sauces and Pickles
• Puddings
• Recipes made with Beer
• Recipes made with Cider

The recipe measurements and methods have been standardised so that they are easy to use.

Use the following code to order this book:

ISBN 1-85249-162-0

Order direct on 01727 867201

YORKSHIRE (WEST)

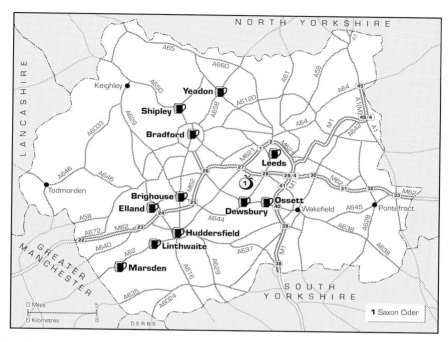

Yorkshire (West) Producers

SAXON CIDER

La Cantina, Unit 4B, Saxonmill, 218 Bradford Road, Batley Carr, West Yorkshire, WF17 6JF.

☎ 01924 457979

Since starting in 1997, La Cantina cider company has made a big impact upon the North of England cider scene. Italian owner Bartolomeo says that production of his Saxon Ciders followed on naturally from his life-long work as an oenologist (wine maker).

Ciders

Ciders: **Saxon Platinum Blonde, 6% abv.**

Saxon Ruby Tuesday, 6.2% abv.

Saxon Gold Digger, 7.4% abv.

Saxon Diamond Lil, 8.2% abv.

Saxon Silver Cloud, 5.5% abv.

Perries: Saxon Harvest Perry, 5.5% abv.

Saxon Manor Perry, 7.4% abv.

(All available in 5 or 9 gallon casks, Gold Digger and Diamond Lil also available in 500 ml and 750ml bottles)

Annual Production

Approx 4700 gallons

Visitors

Welcome

Directions

From M1 Junction 40, follow to Bradford Road, Batley, Saxonmill can be seen on the main road.

Outlets

• Brandy Wharf Cider Centre, Lincs.

• Maltings, Tanners Moat, York.

• Head of Steam, St Georges Square, Huddersfield.

Awards

Peterborough Beer Festival '99: Saxon Diamond Lil – Bronze, Saxon Harvest Perry – Silver.

Yorkshire (West) Outlets

BRADFORD

Fighting Cock

21-23 Preston Street

☎ 01274 726907

11.30-11; 12-10.30 Sun

⌒Biddenden Dry, Monks Delight; Thatchers Medium

Always at least 10 ales plus real cider. Legendary "Docker's Wedge" sandwiches served Mon-Sat until 6pm. Cider available in 4 pint take-outs.

A

New Beehive ☆

171 Westgate

☎ 01274 721784

12-11; 11.30-1am Fri/Sat; 6-10.30 Sun

⌒Inch's Stonehouse

Friendly, multi-roomed bar with a basement skittle alley. Coal fire and gas lighting. Regular live music. Accommodation available.

BRIGHOUSE

Red Rooster

123 Elland Road, Brookfoot

☎ 01484 713737

5(4 Fri)-11; 12-11 Sat; 12-10.30 Sun

⌕**Saxon**

Welcoming, independent, real ale free house, with three inter-connected drinking areas and a real fire. The nine real ales include six guests, and the Saxon cider varies between Gold Digger (usually) and Ruby Tuesday. Quiz night Wednesdays, live band every 4th Sunday. A welcome is given to both bikers and cyclists, infact "Monday night is leather and lycra night!"

DEWSBURY

West Riding Licensed Refreshment Rooms

Railway Station, Wellington Road

☎ 01924 459193

11-11; 12-10.30 Sun

⌕**Cider varies**

Part of a Grade II listed building, with access to the railway station platform. Guest ales focus on smaller breweries' products. Disabled access. No food at weekends.

ELLAND

Barge & Barrel

10-20 Park Road

☎ 01422 375039

⌕**Saxon Platinum Blonde**

Large multi-roomed pub, with the Barge & Barrel Brewery next door.

HUDDERSFIELD

Head of Steam

St Georges Square

☎ 01484 454533

11-2.30am(2am Fri/Sat); 12-10.30 Sun

⌕**Saxon Platinum Blonde**

Multi-roomed pub occupying one wing of the Grade I listed Huddersfield railway station. Its walls are adorned with railway memorabilia. Hosts regular themed beer festivals.

LEEDS

Beer-Ritz

14 Weetwood Lane, Far Headingley

☎ 0113 275 3464

10-10; 11-9.00 Sun

⌕**Draught: Biddenden**

Enterprising off-licence that sells both draught cider and beer.

Cobourg Bar

Claypit Lane

☎ 0113 244 9550

11-11; 12-10.30 Sun

⌀**Westons**

Colourful, modern, industrial and individual, the Cobourg attracts a variety of customers who come for the ale, the cider (a changing Westons product, usually Old Rosie), live music and a good atmosphere.

◖

Duck & Drake

43 Kirkgate

☎ 0113 246 5806

11-11; 12-10.30 Sun

⌀**Westons**

Basic, two-roomed wooden-floored ale house, situated beside a railway bridge. Live jazz Mondays and Thursdays. Lunches limited to Pie & Peas. Plans to extend the cider range.

◖

Scarbrough Hotel

Bishopgate Street

☎ 0113 243 4590

11-11; 12-10.30 Sun

⌀**Westons Herefordshire County Perry, Old Rosie**

City centre pub selling one of Leeds' widest choices of real ales, ciders and perries. Up to 8 guest ales, occasional guest cider or perry.

◖

LINTHWAITE

Sair

139 Lane Top

☎ 01484 842370

7(5 Fri)-11; 12-11 Sat; 12-10.30 Sun

⌀**Westons Traditional Scrumpy**

Renowned brew pub in an elevated location overlooking the Colne Valley. Its numerous awards include CAMRA National Pub of the Year 1997. Sells the Linfit Brewery's range of ales.

MARSDEN

Riverhead Brewery Tap

2 Peel Street

☎ 01484 841270

5-11; 11-11 Sat; 12-10.30 Sun

⌒Addlestones; guest cider

Village brew pub converted from a former Co-op store. The Riverhead beers are named after reservoirs on the nearby Pennine uplands.

OSSETT

Brewers Pride

Low Mill Road

☎ 01924 273865

12-3, 5.30-11; 12-11 Fri/Sat; 12-10.30 Sun

⌒Addlestones

Free house decorated with old brewery memorabilia, directly infront of the Ossett Brewery.
◖

SHIPLEY

Fanny's Ale & Cider House

63 Saltaire Road

☎ 01274 591419

11.30-3, 5.30-11; 11.30-11 Fri/Sat; 12-10.30 Sun

⌒Cider varies

Pub adjacent to the historic village of Saltaire. Cosy bar, gas-lit lounge with traditional furniture. Usually four guest beers and up to three ciders.

YEADON

Woolpack

18 New Road

☎ 0113 250 6079

11-11; 12-10.30 Sun

⌒Cider varies

Busy roadside pub, a Punch Tavern festival ale house. Up to five guest beers.
◖

GLAMORGAN

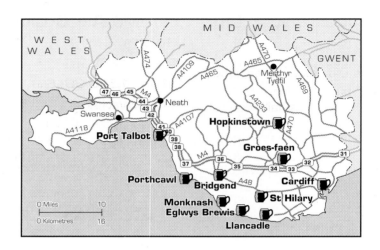

Glamorgan Outlets

BRIDGEND

Wyndham Arms

Dunraven Place

☎ 01656 663608

11-11; 12-10.30 Sun

⏦**Addlestones**

Quiet Wetherspoons pub near to the train station, a welcome drinking island in a sea of keg. Disabled toilet, no smoking area.

◖ ▶

CARDIFF

Chapter Arts Centre

Market Road, Canton

☎ 029 2031 1050

6-11(12 Fri); 6-10.30 Sun

⏦**Gwatkin (occasional)**

Bar in a cinema/arts centre, offering a vast and interesting range of Continental beers, real ales and malt whiskies. Continental beer festivals. Cardiff CAMRA Pub of the Year 2000.

◖ ▶

Y Gasgen

St Johns Square

☎ 029 2022 1980

11-11; 12-10.30 Sun

⌒Westons Old Rosie (occasional)

"Y Gasgen" is Welsh for Hogshead, and this small, wood-fitted city centre ale house is attached to the larger RSVP pub.
◖

EGLWYS BREWIS

Carpenters Arms

☎ 01446 792063

11-11; 6.30-11 Wed; 12-10.30 Sun

⌒Gwatkin cider or perry (summer)

Superbly refurbished pub with excellent family facilities. Attracts a varied clientele.
◖ ◗

GROES-FAEN

Dynevor Arms

Llantrisant Road (A4119)

☎ 029 2089 0530

11-11; 12-3, 7-10.30 Sun

⌒Addlestones

Cosy country pub. One long bar, non smoking conservatory, separate restaurant.
◖ ◗

HOPKINSTOWN

Hollybush

Ty Mawr Road

☎ 01443 402325

11-11; 12-10.30 Sun

⌒Cider varies

Mid Glamorgan Pub of the Year 1998 and 1999. Food at all times, public bar, pub games, disabled toilet, over-sized glasses.
◖ ◗

LLANCADLE

Green Dragon

☎ 01446 750913

11-3, 6-11; 12-3, 6-10.30 Sun

⌒Addlestones

Attractive free house, rebuilt after a fire a few years ago.
◖ ◗

Photographs (following page)

Plough & Harrow.

Photo: Dave Matthews

Bush Inn.

Photo: Dave Matthews

MONKNASH

Plough & Harrow

☎ 01656 890209

11-11; 12-10.30

⌢**Cider range varies**

Tremendous country pub, probably
the best in South Wales; winner of
many CAMRA awards. A 12th
century monastic grange with a
large garden, lively locals and a
very lively licensee! Home to Wick
RFC. Large and interesting real ale
range, up to three traditional
ciders. Beer festival in June.

PORTHCAWL

Lorelei Hotel

36-38 Esplanade Avenue

☎ 01656 788342

*5(4 Fri)-11; 12-11 Sat; 12-3, 7-
10.30 Sun*

⌢**Cider varies (occasional)**

Hotel with guest ales and occasional beer festivals. Campsite

nearby. Neath & Bridgend CAMRA
branch Pub of the Year 2000.

PORT TALBOT

Lord Caradoc

69-72 Station Road

☎ 01639 896007

11-11; 12-10.30 Sun

⌢**Addlestones**

Spacious, open-plan
Wetherspoons, with one large 'L'
shaped bar. No smoking area, disabled toilet.

ST HILARY

Bush Inn

☎ 01446 772745

11.30-11; 12-10.30 Sun

⌢**Westons Old Rosie**

Attractive country inn in a 16th
century village. Excellent range of
home-made meals available.

GWENT

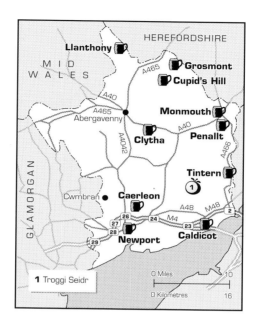

1 Troggi Seidr

Gwent Producers

TROGGI SEIDR

Lower House Cottage, Earlswood,
Monmouthshire.

☎ 01291 650653

'Seidr' is the Welsh word for cider,
and Troggi Seidr is the only cider
maker in this part of Wales – the
area of Monmouthshire around
Chepstow – once famed for its
cider. Founded in 1986 by hospital
pathologist Michael Penney, he
describes Troggi Seidr as "a small
producer of 'whole juice' cider and
perry using traditional techniques

and equipment: the press dates
from 1892." His eventual aim is to
re-establish high quality bottle-fermented produce, particularly
perry. In the meantime his outstanding draught perry won Best
Perry at the 1999 CAMRA Cardiff
Beer Festival.

Ciders
Seidr, 6.5% abv.
Perry, 7.5% abv.
**(On draught only, buyer provides
own containers)**
Annual Production
1500 litres
Visitors
By prior appointment only.

GWENT PRODUCERS

Sales

Farm gate sales, by prior appointment only.

Awards

Best Perry, 1999 CAMRA Cardiff Beer & Cider Festival.

Gwent Outlets

CAERLEON

White Hart

High Street

☎ 01633 420255

11-11; 12-10.30 Sun

🍏**Addlestones**

Popular pub in the heart of the village that can get very busy at weekends. Near to local Roman attractions and the Fwrrwm craft centre.

◖

CALDICOT

Cross Inn

Newport Road

☎ 01291 420692

11-11; 12-10.30 Sun

🍏**Cider varies (April-Oct)**

Busy, whitewashed pub at the crossroads in the centre of town. Cider in the public bar.

CLYTHA

Clytha Arms

(On the old Abergavenny/Raglan road)

☎ 01873 840206

12-3.30, 6-11; 12-3, 7-10 Sun; (closed Mon lunch)

Westons

Much-acclaimed free house set in large gardens. Separate restaurant serves award-winning food. Unusual bar snacks include dishes such as leek and laverbread rissoles. Occasional Welsh Beer & Cheese festivals. The cider on handpump alternates between one or other of the Westons range. The landlord is developing his own bottled perry.

CUPIDS HILL

 CIDER PUB

sells more cider than beer!

Cupids Hill Inn ☆

Near Grosmont

☎ 01981 240733

12-2, 6-11; 12-2, 7-10.30 Sun

Bottled: Gwatkin Cider

Tiny, basic, old-fashioned local. Make the most of it while it survives! The cider may not be visible – so ask. No draught cider or beer. The basic toilet facilities are not for the faint-hearted!

REAL ALE

GROSMONT

Angel Inn

☎ 01981 240646

12-2.30, 6-11; 12-11 Sat; 12-10.30 Sun

Bulmers Traditional (summer)

Comfortable community local at the heart of a village with former historical and strategic significance. Mid-summer beer festival features local ciders. The local church and castle are worth a visit.

LLANTHONY

Half Moon Inn

☎ 01873 890611

7-11 Fri; 12-3, 6-11 Sat; 12-3, 7-10.30 Sun; (ring for midweek times in summer)

Addlestones

Old country inn with a traditional public bar and a separate restaurant. Very close to the magnificent ruins of Llanthony Abbey. Rare outlet for Bullmastiff's fine ales. Best to ring ahead to check opening times and availability of food.

MONMOUTH

Irma Fingal-Rock

64 Monnow Street

☎ 01600 712372

9-3; 9-5.30 Thurs/Fri; 9-5 Sat; (closed Sun)

🍎Bottled: Dunkertons range

Tremendous delicatessen, offering an excellent selection of local meat, cheese, bread and eggs. Aside from Dunkertons ciders and perries, a selection of Normandy bottled ciders are also available.

Kings Head

Agincourt Square

☎ 01600 713417

11-11; 12-10.30 Sun

🍎Addlestones

Old town centre coaching inn, tastefully refurbished by Wetherspoons. Wheelchairs lifts allow the disabled access to the split-levelled interior.

NEWPORT

Godfrey Morgan

Chepstow Road, Maindee

☎ 01633 221928

11-11; 12-10.30 Sun

🍎Addlestones

Tasteful Wetherspoon's renovation of a former cinema. The multi-level interior features pictures of local stars of the silver screen and long-demolished Newport cinemas.

Hornblower

126 Commercial Street

☎ 01633 668001

11-11; 12-10.30 Sun

🍎Cider varies

Loud, lively pub with a good atmosphere. The haunt of beer lovers, bikers, rock music lovers and cider drinkers! Always sells a guest mild. The cider is usually one from Westons, Bulmers or Thatchers.

Oddfellows & Foresters Arms

39 St Mary's Street, Baneswell

☎ 01633 267570

12-11; 12-10.30 Sun

🍎Bulmers Traditional

Friendly, no-frills backstreet locals pub.

Wetherspoons

10-12 Cambrian Centre

☎ 01633 251752

11-11; 12-10.30 Sun

🍎Addlestones

Large open-plan pub, close to the railway station. Typical Wetherspoons décor and format, with a no-smoking area at the rear.

PENALLT

Boat Inn

Lone Lane

☎ 01600 712615

11-11; 12-10.30 Sun

⌂**Thatchers Traditional Dry, Medium**

Traditional, stone-built country pub, over 350 years old, on the banks of the River Wye. The car park is in England, on the A466 at Redbrook, and the pub is then approached by crossing a foot-bridge (attached to the old railway bridge) over the river. There are 6 or 7 varying real ales, and these, together with the polycasks of cider, are stillaged behind the bar. The tiered garden, with its 5 waterfalls and natural pond, offers a lovely view of the river. Live music Tuesday and Thursday nights.

◖ ◗

TINTERN

Cherry Tree

Devauden Road

☎ 0129 689292

11-2.30, 6-11; 12-3, 7-10.30 Sun; (closed Mon/Tue lunch in winter)

⌂**Bulmers Traditional Medium**

Single-roomed gem of a pub. The only Welsh pub to have been in every edition of the Good Beer Guide. A short stroll from Tintern village. Bulmers served by gravity, as is the Hancocks HB.

Photograph

The Cherry Tree sign
Photo: Dave Matthews

MID WALES

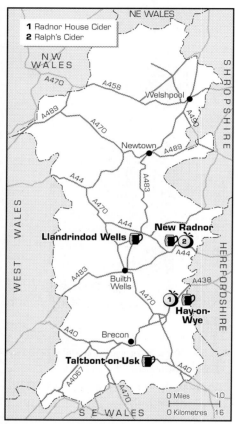

1 Radnor House Cider
2 Ralph's Cider

cider for the past ten years. With an annual output of just 20 gallons, making her possibly Britain's smallest commercial producer, her cider could prove hard to find. Keep an eye on the local pubs and fairs in and around Hay-on-Wye.

Cider

Vintage Radnor House Cider (1 gallon containers or 70cl bottles)

Annual Production

20 gallons

Sales

Farm gate sales by appointment only.

RALPH'S CIDER

Old Badland Farm, New Radnor, Radnorshire, LD8 2TG.

☎ 01544 350304

Ralph Owen first started to make cider 20 years ago, for his own consumption, when working as a farm manager (for Bertram Bulmer, coincidentally) on Anglesey in North Wales. Moving to

Mid Wales Producers

RADNOR HOUSE CIDER

Radnor House, Llowes, Hereford, HR3 5JA.

☎ 01497 847322

Margaret Morris has been making her organic, vintage, Radnorshire

Radnorshire in 1986, the orchard of White Norman cider apples at his own farm was too good an opportunity to miss, and so Ralph's Cider was born. As the fame and popularity of his cider grew, so in 1997 his ancient mobile twin-screw press made way for a hydraulic version, although the former can still be seen both at Old Badlands Farm and on Ralph's labels. Winning 'Cider of the Festival' at Cardiff CAMRA Beer and Cider Festival in 1997 gave a further boost to sales, and persuaded Ralph to apply for a full off-licence that was granted in March 1999.

Ralph's cider is a beautifully balanced, golden, traditional cider. Starting with his own White Norman apples, he blends in varieties such as Bulmers Norman, Dabinett and Foxwhelp, all sourced from other small Radnorshire orchards. At the time of writing Ralph's plans to install a bottling line at the farm, and to release a traditional filtered cider in 330ml bottles for distribution throughout Wales and beyond, have just reached fruition. "Ralph's Welsh Cider is here to stay and to be enjoyed," says Ralph, "so all you cider drinkers out there – watch this space!"

Ciders

Ralph's Traditional Dry, 6.5-7.5% abv. (Also filtered, in 330ml bottles.)
Ralph's Medium, 6.5-7.5% abv.
(1, 2, 2¹/₂ and 5 litre containers)
(Also available:
Ralph's Sparkling Welsh Cider in 750ml bottles)
Annual Production
1500 gallons
Visitors
Welcome
Directions
Between New Radnor and Kinnerton on the B4372.
Sales
Farm gate sales. Any time, but please ring ahead.

Outlets
• Radnor Arms, New Radnor.
• The Stores, New Radnor.
• The Restaurant, Brecon Beacons National Park Centre, Libanus.
• English Farm Cider Centre, Lewes, East Sussex.
• Stag Inn, Titley, Kington, Herefordshire.
• Red Lion, Llanfihangel, Nant Melan.

Awards
Cider of the Festival, Cardiff CAMRA Beer and Cider Festival 1997.

Mid Wales Outlets
HAY-ON-WYE

 CIDER PUB
sells more cider than beer!

Three Tuns ☆
Belmont Road
12-3, 6-11 (or as trade demands)
⌣**Westons range**
Don't miss this Edwardian gem! Unchanged for over 90 years and frequently used as a film set. Sells no real ale, but always offers at least three Westons ciders poured direct from polycasks on the bar, including Westons Perry in the summer. The unspoilt interior is on CAMRA's National Inventory. Small beer garden to the rear.

LLANDRINDOD WELLS
Royal British Legion
Tremont Road (A483)
☎ 01597 822558

7(12 Sat)-11; 12-10.30 Sun
⌣**Westons Old Rosie**
Friendly club with home-cooked food and lots of traditional pub games. Non-members must be signed in. South & Mid Wales CAMRA Club of the Year 1999.
▶

NEW RADNOR

Eagle Hotel

Broad Street

☎ 01544 350208

12(8am for breakfast)-11(11.30 supper licence); 12-10.30 Sun

Draught: **Westons**
Bottled: **Ralph's**

Old coaching inn with two bars, a restaurant, coffee shop and terrace. Ralph's cider is made locally. Both licensees are micro-light flying enthusiasts, with the husband a member of the UK paramotor team.

◖ ▶

TALYBONT-ON-USK

Star Inn

☎ 01874 676635

11-3, 6-11; 11-11 Sat; 12-10.30 Sun; (open 11-11 peak summer period)

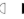**Westons Old Rosie**

Cosy, canalside pub with a large, welcoming fireplace in the main bar. Up to 12 varying real ales available, with Bullmastiff often represented. Accommodation, nice garden, camping nearby.

◖ ▶

Ralph's Premium Dry Welsh Cider (Still)

Photo: Dave Matthews

NORTH-EAST WALES

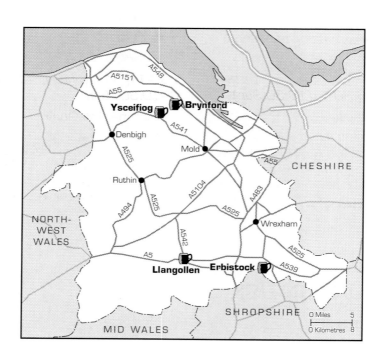

North-East Wales Outlets

BRYNFORD

Llyn-y-Mawn

Brynford Hill

☎ 01352 714367

5.30-11; 12-3, 6-11 Sat; 12-3, 7-10.30 Sun

👃Draught: Westons 1st Quality or Bounds Brand

Containers: James White Suffolk Cider Dry, Medium

Family-run old village inn. Good quality ales, often from local breweries; twice Welsh CAMRA Pub of the Year. No meals Mondays, booking advisable during the rest of the week. Annual beer festival in March. Real fire.

ERBISTOCK

Boat

South off A539 (Overton Bridge),
OS SJ357413

☎ 01978 780666

12-2.30, 6.30-11(10.30 Sun)

Addlestones

Grade I listed building in a picturesque setting on the banks of the River Dee.

LLANGOLLEN

Sun

49 Regent Street

☎ 01978 860233

12-11; 12-10.30 Sun

Westons

Friendly pub near to the steam railway and the Doctor Who exhibition. Good, keenly-priced menu, plus an interesting range of real ales and foreign beers. The cider is chosen from the Westons range. Folk night Wednesdays. Pool table.

◖ ❱

YSCEIFIOG

Fox Inn

OS 152715

☎ 01352 720241

5.30-11(7-11 winter); 11-11 Sat; 12-10.30 Sun

Westons 1st Quality

Friendly pub in a 17th century building with many small rooms, visited by customers from miles around. Not easy to find, follow the signposts off the B5121 west of Mold.

NORTH-WEST WALES

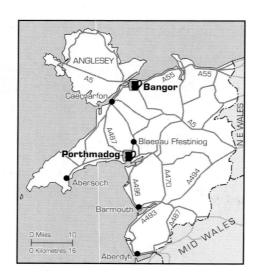

North-West Wales Outlets

BANGOR

Y Castell

Off High Street, Glanrafon

☎ 01248 355866

12-11; 12-10.30 Sun

⌂**Cider range varies**

Up to 4 cask ciders and 12 real ales in this single-roomed Hogshead opposite the cathedral. Frequented by both students and locals. No smoking area.

◖　◗

PORTHMADOC

Ship

14 Lombard Street

☎ 01766 512990

11-11; 11-10.30(6.30 winter) Sun

⌂**Addlestones**

Characterful pub near the harbour, displaying maritime memorabilia. Beer festival the first two weeks in March. 10 Irish and 88 Scotch whiskies.

◖　◗

WEST WALES

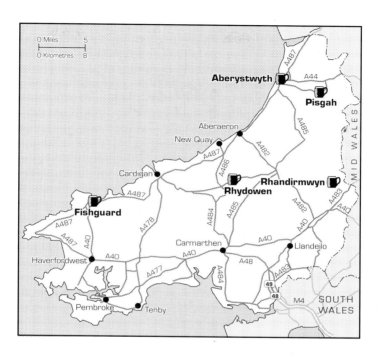

West Wales Outlets

ABERYSTWYTH

Welsh Cellar

19 Pier Street

☎ 01970 617332

9.30am-10pm, 7 days a week

⌁Bottled: Dunkertons

Delicatessen with a wide range of local foods, in particular some excellent local cheeses. Good range of bottled beers (many bottle-conditioned), and hand-pumped Flannerys real ale to take away.

FISHGUARD

Royal Oak Inn

Market Square

☎ 01348 872514

11-11; 12-10.30 Sun

⌁Bulmers Traditional Medium; Westons Old Rosie (summer & bank holidays)

A 250-300 year old free house, that was the headquarters for the British Militia when the French invaded in 1797. No juke box or piped music, just live acoustic folk on Tuesdays. Three varying real ales, and a beer festival the last weekend in May. Bar billiards, wood burning stove, beer garden. Dogs on a lead welcome.

PISGAH

Halfway Inn

(On the A4120, 7 miles east of Aberystwyth)

☎ 01970 880631

12-2.30, 6.30-11;12-2.30, 7-10.30 Sun

⌓Westons Old Rosie (June-August bank holiday)

Well-known, isolated free house in stunning countryside. Camping available in adjoining field. Closed some lunchtimes in winter.

RHANDIRMWYN

Royal Oak Inn

7 miles from Llandovery

☎ 01550 760201

11.30-3, 6-11; varies Sun (ring first)

⌓Westons Old Rosie

Excellent pub with good food, well worth finding. Popular with locals and visitors alike.

RHYDOWEN

Alltyrodyn Arms

☎ 01545 590319

12-11; 12-4 Sun

⌓Draught: Thatchers Dry or Medium
Flagons: Westons Old Rosie

Pub on the crossroads in a small village, dating back to Elizabethan times. Noted for the choice and quality of its real ales. Draught cider not always available (supply problems), but flagons of Westons Old Rosie (sold by the glass) provide an excellent alternative. Ceredigion CAMRA Pub of the Year 1997, 1998 and 2000.

DUMFRIES & GALLOWAY

GRAMPIAN

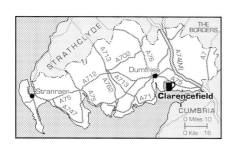

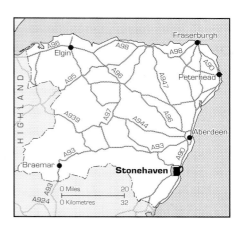

Dumfries & Galloway Outlets

CLARENCEFIELD

Farmers Arms

On B724, 7 miles from Annan
☎ 01387 870675

11.30-2.30, 6-11.30(12.30am Fri); 12-12.30am Sat; 12.30-11.30 Sun

Addlestones

Beamed, former 18th century coaching inn, with Maclays beers, brasses and antiques.

◖ ◗

Grampian Outlets

STONEHAVEN

Marine Hotel

9-10 Shorehead
☎ 01569 762155

12-midnight including Sundays

⌒**Addlestones**

Former Scottish CAMRA Pub of the Year, set in a picturesque harbour. Unusual guest ales, fish dishes a speciality.

◖ ◗

LOTHIAN

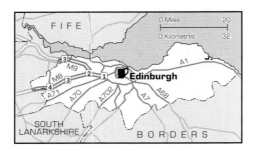

Lothian Outlets
EDINBURGH

Hogshead
30-32 Bread Street
☎ 0131 211 0575

11-1am; 12.30-1am Sun

⌣Cider varies

Former Co-op converted into a
Hogshead alehouse with a glass-
walled cellar adjacent to the bar,
offering a fine selection of guest
ales on both handpull and gravity
dispense. Annual cider festival and
numerous beer festivals.

⌣ ▶

Hogshead
133 Rose Street
☎ 0131 226 1224

11-1am; 12.30-1am Sun

⌣Cider varies

Basement alehouse on one of
Edinburgh's most famous streets,
offering an extensive choice of ales
in modern surroundings. Annual
cider festival in the summer and
numerous beer festivals throughout the year.

⌣ ▶

Malt & Hops
45 The Shore, Leith
☎ 0131 555 0083

*12-11; 12-12 Thur; 12-1am
Fri/Sat; 12.30-11 Sun*

⌣Addlestones

Small pub dating from 1749, overlooking the Water of Leith and
reputedly haunted by the ghost of
a former licensee. A choice of
guest ales is available. No lunches
Sundays.

⌣

STRATHCLYDE

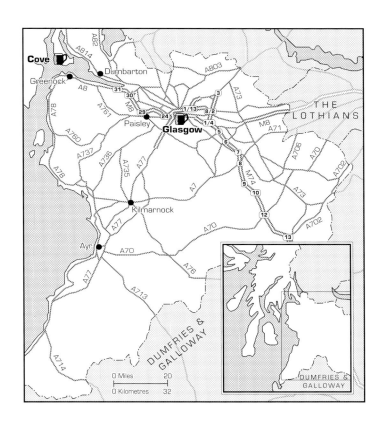

Strathclyde Outlets

COVE

Knockderry Hotel
204 Shore Road
☎ 01436 842283

11-midnight; 12.30-11 Sunday

○ **Addlestones**

Magnificent Victorian country mansion with oak panelled walls, superb ceilings, and a tree-strewn lawn that rolls down to Loch Long. Excellent, value-for-money food, three constantly changing guest beers.

◖

GLASGOW

Babbity Bowster

16-18 Blackfriars Street

☎ 0141 552 5055

11-12am; 12.30-12am Sun

🍏**Bulmer Traditional**

Beautifully restored Georgian town house converted to a small hotel/restaurant/bar. Good quality pub food available all day. Opens for breakfasts at 8am, but no alcohol can be served before 11am.

◖ ▶

Clockwork Beer Company

1153-55 Cathcart Road

☎ 0141 649 0184

11-11; 11-12am Thurs-Sat; 12.30-11 Sun

🍏**Westons**

Bright, modern brew pub whose home-brewed ales cover a range of international styles. Good selection of foreign bottled beers. All beer/cider served in oversized glasses. Handy for Hampden Park.

◖ ▶

Photograph (Tayside opposite)

Mark Waterstone checks the specific gravity at Taycider.

Photo: Taycider Co.

TAYSIDE

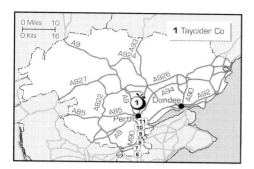

1 Taycider Co

TAYSIDE Producer

TAYCIDER CO.

A Bothy, Lynton Farm, Stanley, Perthshire, PH1 4QQ

(No telephone)

Mark Waterston describes his Taycider Company as "a tiny one-man operation". He only makes about 100 gallons a year, and attempts to secure local outlets have fallen on stony ground. "Tastes in this area are conservative," Mark says, "and cider is not traditional here." Getting dangerously close to stating the obvious,

he continues: "This is not cider country. If you want real cider, I am it in Perthshire." Long may his crusade continue.

Ciders

Cookers Cider, Eaters Cider, both 8% abv (1 and 2 litre bottles). (A perry and a cider made with honey instead of sugar have both been made in the past.)

Annual Production

100 gallons

Visitors

Welcome. Tours available.

Directions

North of Stanley on the B9099 to Murthly. Round the first bend, track on the right (before the Kin Claven turn-off) flanked by fields to a cluster of buildings. OS map reference: NO 105341 (sheet 53).

Sales

Farm gate sales. Any time, "catch me if you can, I'm usually not far away."

Also on sale: apple trees grown from pips.

CHANNEL ISLANDS

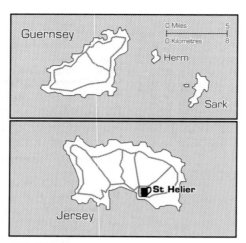

Channel Islands Outlets

Jersey

ST HELIER

Lamplighter
Mulcaster Street

☎ 01534 723119

10-11.30; 11-11.30 Sun

⌾Bulmers Traditional

The only gas-lit pub on Jersey, it serves a wide range of real ales as well as real cider. Good value, no-nonsense food.

◖

Producer Index

1066 Cider 328
Apple Tree Cider 351
Appledram 329
Avalon Vineyard 288
Badgers Hill Farm Cider 226
Banham Cider 263
Barkers Real Cider & Perry 352
Barnfield Cider Mill 353
Bennett's Cider 290
Biddenden Cider 228
Black Mac Cider 290
Black Rat Cider 348
Bland's Cider 170
Bollhayes Cider 137
Brains Cider 170
Bridge Farm Cider 291
Brimblecombe's Farmhouse Cider 138
Broadoak Cider 292
Bromells Cider 140
Brook Apple Farm Cider And Perry 171
Brooklyn Farm Cider 284
Broome Farm Cider 191
Bulmers 192
Burrow Hill Cider 293
Burscombe Farm Cider 140
Cassels Cider 114
Castle Cider Co. 229
Castles Cider 158
Castlings Heath Cottage Cider 320
Chafford Cider 229
Cheshire Cider 118
Cheyney Lodge Cider 194
Coombes Cider 294
Core Food & Drink 353
Countryman Cider 141
Cowhill Cider 172
Crippledick Cider Co. 230
Crone's Organic Cider 264
Crossmans Prime Farmhouse Cider 295
Day's Cottage Cider 172
Derricks Cider 295
Dewchurch Cider 195
Double Vision Cider Company 230
Dunkertons Cider Co. 196
Fernihough's Cider 285
Franklins Cider 197
Godshill Cider Co. 223
Gospel Green 330
Grafton Field Cider 354
Gray's Farm Cider 142

Great Oak Cider 198
Green Valley Cyder 143
Greenwood's Apple Juice & Cider 265
Gregg's Pit Cider & Perry 198
Gwatkin Cider 199
Hackney Cider 251
Hamstead Vineyard 224
Hancock's Devon Cider 144
Hartland Farmhouse Cider And Perry 173
Haye Farm Cider 123
Hecks Farmhouse Cider 296
Henry's Farmhouse Scrumpy 297
Heron Valley Cider 144
Hunt's Farm Cider 145
Inch's Cider – See Bulmers 192
James White 321
John Waltham 159
Johnsons Farmhouse Cider 231
Kennford Cider 146
Killerton Estate Cider 146
King Offa Distillery 200
Knights Cider 201
Lambourn Valley Cider Company 107
Liquid Fruits 232
Little Foxes Cider 115
Lizard Cider Barn 124
Luscombe Cider 147
Lyme Bay Cider 148
Lyne Down Cider 201
Mackay's Aylton Perry & Cider 203
Matching Cider Company 164
Matthew Clark Plc 297
Mayfield Cider 332
Minchew's Real Cyder & Perry 174
Nadder Valley Cider Company 348
Naish's Cider 299
New Forest Cider 186
Norbury's Black Bull Cider Co. 355
Norfolk Cider Company 265
Olivers Cider And Perry 203
Ostler's Cider 149
Palmerhayes Devon Scrumpy 149
Paradise Juices 322
Park Cider 165
Parsons Choice Cider 299
Pawley Farm Cider 232
Penpol Farm Cider 125
Perry's Cider 300
Pipkin Cider 361
Pippins Cider Company 233
Pookhill Cider 334
Porthallow 126

Prinknash Abbey Cider 176
Radnor House Cider 380
Ralph's Cider 380
Rathays Old Goat Cider 204
Reddaways Farm Cider 150
Rich's Farmhouse Cider 301
Riddle's Cider 177
Rosemary Vineyard 224
Sam's (See Winkleigh)
Saxon Cider 367
Sedlescombe Cider 334
Sepham Farm Cider 233
Shawsgate Vineyard 323
Sheppys Cider 302
Shortwood Farm Cider 205
Snitterfield Fruit Farms 341
Summers' Cider & Perry 178
Swamp Donkey Cider 188
Symons Farmhouse Cider 150
Taunton (See Matthew Clark)
Taycider Co. 393
Thatchers Cider 303
Three Counties Cider 251
Tilley's Cider 178
Toritona 151
Torre Cider 305
Troggi Seidr 375
Upton Cider Co. 281
Valley Vineyards 109
Veryan Cyder 127
W.H.Smart & Co. Ltd 344
West Croft Cider 306
Westons Cider 206
Whin Hill Cider Ltd 266
Wilkins Farmhouse Cider 307
Windmill Vineyard 273
Winkleigh Cider 152
Wobblygob Cider 344
Wolfeton Cider 159

A short guide to the companies that can deliver traditional cider to your pub or cider festival, compiled by Sean Kelleher and Dave Matthews.

Cider Specialists

Jon Hallam

Tel: 0117 966 0221

Based: Bristol

Ciders: Extensive list – 40 cidermakers visited regularly, another 80 occasionally.

Delivery area: Ring for details. Typically the larger the order, the further he will deliver.

Notes: Founded 20 years ago, widely credited with saving perry. Also distributes pork scratchings and other snacks.

Rob Wilson

Tel: 01805 624746

Based: North Devon

Ciders: West Country ciders from Devon to Herefordshire.

Delivery area: South of England, the Midlands, Wales.

Notes: Rob only supplies ciders and perries made from unsprayed fruit, containing no additives whatsoever. Only supplies cider festivals/outside bars, not pubs.

Inn-Cider Trading

Tel: 01782 502548 or 0973 660309

Based: Leek, Staffordshire.

Ciders: Extensive list, can get virtually anything.

Delivery area: Midlands, North West England, or festivals anywhere in the UK.

Merrylegs

Tel: 0161 432 6126 or 0777 601 3787

Based: Teignmouth, Devon and Stockport.

Ciders: Most ciders from South West England.

Delivery area: North West England, Devon, (further afield for large orders).

A selection of Beer Agents/Wholesalers that offer some cider

Beer Seller

Tel: 01963 32255

Based: Wincanton, Somerset. 19 depots throughout the UK.

Ciders: Westons, Bulmers, Matthew Clark, Thatchers.

Delivery area: The whole of the UK.

Crouch Vale Brewery

Tel: 01245 322744

Based: Essex.

Ciders: Westons, Thatchers, Chiddingstone, Biddenden, Theobolds, Crones, Lambourne Valley, Coombes, Crossman, Castlings Heath, Banham, and many more.

Delivery area: Essex, South Suffolk, East & Central London.

East-West Ales

Tel: 01892 834040

Based: Kent.

Ciders: Thatchers, Biddenden, (occasional other brand).

Delivery area: All of England, Welsh Borders.

Oliver Hare

Tel: 01799 508058

Based: Essex.

Ciders: Thatchers, Westons.

Delivery area: Nationally.

RCH Brewery

Tel: 01934 834447

Based: Somerset

Ciders: Thatchers, Coombes, Rich's, Crossman's, Wilkins, Westcroft.

Delivery area: South Devon, Somerset, Gloucestershire, West Midlands.

Ringwood Brewery

Tel: 01425 471177

Based: Hampshire

Cider: Thatchers

Delivery area: Roughly a 50 mile radius around Ringwood.

Small Beer

Tel: 01522 540431

Based: Lincoln

Ciders: Westons, Biddenden, Thatchers, Broadoak, Bulmers, Saxon, Reedcutter.

Delivery area: Mainly East Midlands and surroundings. Further afield for large orders.

Wye Valley Brewery

Tel: 01432 342546

Based: Hereford.

Cider: Gwatkins cider and perry.

Delivery area: The whole of Wales; most of England as far as Cumbria, Yorkshire, Norfolk, London, Devon. Please ring for viability of delivery.

CIDER CONSULTANTS

K.G.Consultants

Tel: 01761 490624

Email: keith@goverd.freeserve.co.uk

Based: Compton Dando, Bristol.

Notes: Keith Goverd has 20 years research experience at Long Ashton, and has been a globe-trotting cider consultant for some 12 years now. Also produces his own cider (pasteurised and sweetened – uniquely – with apple juice), perry, juice and cider vinegar.

GCW Technology

Tel & Fax: 01568 797278

Based: Bodenham, Herefordshire.

Notes: Geoff Warren was the Cider Maker at Westons, and more recently the Chairman of the Three Counties Cider & Perry Association.

BIBLIOGRAPHY

Perry Pears

L.C. Luckwill & A. Pollard (1963)

Bristol University Press (tel: Harry Anderson, 01275 392181)

£25.00

Cider & Apple Juices

Ray Williams

Bristol University Press (tel: Harry Anderson, 01275 392181)

£5.50

Real Cider Making on a Small Scale

Michael Pooley & John Lomax (1999)

Nexus Special Interests Ltd.

Cider – Making, Using & Enjoying Sweet & Hard Cider

Annie Proulx & Lew Nichols (US, 1997)

Storey Communications, Inc.

$14.95

Cider's Story – Rough and Smooth

Mark Foot (1999)

8 Kingston Drive, Nailsea, North Somerset, BS48 4RB.

£9.99

See article on page 84.

Cider Lore

Fiona Mac (due to be published Spring 2001)

Logaston Press

Stories about cider and perry in the Three Counties over the last century. See www.ciderlore.com

Instruction to your
Bank or Building Society
to pay by Direct Debit

Please fill in the whole form using a ball point pen and send it to:

Campaign for Real Ale Ltd,
230 Hatfield Road,
St. Albans,
Herts
AL1 4LW

Originator's Identification Number

| 9 | 2 | 6 | 1 | 2 | 9 |

Reference Number

| | | | | | | | | | | | | | | | | |

Name of Account Holder(s)

Bank/Building Society account number

| | | | | | | | |

Branch Sort Code

| | | | | |

Instructions to your Bank or Building Society
Please pay CAMRA Direct Debits from the account detailed on this instruction subject to the safeguards assured by the Direct Debit Guarantee. I understand that this instruction may remain with CAMRA and, if so, will be passed electronically to my Bank/Building Society

Name and full postal address of your Bank or Building Society

To The Manager   Bank/Building Society

Address

Postcode

Signature(s)

Date

Banks and Building Societies may not accept Direct Debit instructions for some types of account

- - - - - - - ✂ -

This guarantee should be detached and retained by the Payer.

The
Direct Debit
Guarantee

■ This Guarantee is offered by all Banks and Building Societies that take part in the Direct Debit Scheme. The efficiency and security of the Scheme is monited and protected by your own Bank or Building Society.

■ If the amounts to be paid or the payment dates change CAMRA will notify you 10 working days in advance of your account being debited or as otherwise agreed.

■ If an error is made by CAMRA or your Bank or Building Society, you are guaranteed a full and immediate refund from your branch of the amount paid.

■ You can cancel a Direct Debit at any time by writing to your Bank or Building Society. Please also send a copy of your letter to us.

JOIN CAMRA

If you like good beer and good pubs you could be helping to fight to preserve, protect and promote them. CAMRA was set up in the early seventies to fight against the mass destruction of a part of Britain's heritage.

The giant brewers are still pushing through takeovers, mergers and closures of their smaller regional rivals. They are still trying to impose national brands of beer and lager on their customers whether they like it or not, and they are still closing down town and village pubs or converting them into grotesque 'theme' pubs.

CAMRA wants to see genuine free competition in the brewing industry, fair prices, and, above all, a top quality product brewed by local breweries in accordance with local tastes, and served in pubs that maintain the best features of a tradition that goes back centuries.

As a CAMRA member you will be able to enjoy generous discounts on CAMRA products and receive the highly rated monthly newspaper What's Brewing. You will be given the CAMRA members' handbook and be able to join in local social events and brewery trips.

To join, complete the form below and, if you wish, arrange for direct debit payments by filling in the form overleaf and returning it to CAMRA. To pay by credit card, contact the membership secretary on (01727) 867201.

I/We wish to join the Campaign for Real Ale and agree to abide by the Rules.

Name(s) . . . .

. . . .

Address . . . .

. . . .

. . . .

Postcode . . . .

Signature . . . . .Date . . . .

I/We enclose the remittance for:

Single:	£14	Joint	£17	(at same address)
OAP Single	£8	OAP Joint	£11	(at same address)
Unemployed/Disabled £8				
Under 26	£8	date of birth:		

For Life and Overseas rates please contact CAMRA HQ (tel: 01727 867201)

Send you remittance (payable to CAMRA) to:

The Membership Secretary, CAMRA, 230 Hatfield Road, St Albans, Herts., AL1 4LW